Jean Fox O'Barr

The

University

of North

Carolina

Press

Chapel Hill

& London

OMEN'S STUDIES

Feminism
in Action

© 1994 The University of North Carolina Press
All rights reserved
Manufactured in the United States of America

Library of Congress Cataloging-in-Publication Data
O'Barr, Jean F.
   Feminism in action : building institutions and
community through women's studies / Jean Fox O'Barr.
      p. cm.
   Includes bibliographical references and index.
   ISBN 0-8078-2129-2 (cloth : alk. paper).
—ISBN 0-8078-4439-x (pbk. : alk. paper)
   1. Women's studies—United States.   I. Title.
HQ1181.U5024   1994
305.42'0973—dc20   93-33313
                                              CIP

The paper in this book meets the guidelines for
permanence and durability of the Committee on
Production Guidelines for Book Longevity of the Council
on Library Resources.

98   97   96   95   94   5   4   3   2   1

Chapter 2 was published in somewhat different form in
*Educating the Majority: Women Challenge Tradition in
Higher Education*, edited by Carol S. Pearson, Donna L.
Shavlik, and Judith G. Touchton. © 1989 by American
Council of Education and The Oryx Press, 4041 N. Central
at Indian School Rd., Phoenix, Ariz. 85012. Used by
permission.

Jean Fox O'Barr is director of the Women's Studies
Program and professor of the practice of women's studies
at Duke University. Her books include *Engaging Feminism:
Students Speak Up and Speak Out.*

To Bessie Jenkins Trice

who has inspired and

enabled my work by the

way she does her own

CONTENTS

In his charming book *Small Decencies: Reflections and Meditations on Being Human at Work*, Catholic priest-turned-management-consultant John Cowan notes the small signs that indicate the heart and soul of the organization that has called him in as a consultant. Is there a place to hang his coat? Is he welcomed by someone who tells him that he is expected and that the person he is meeting will be along shortly? Is he offered coffee?

If Cowan were lucky enough to visit the offices of the Women's Studies Program at Duke University, where Jean O'Barr is the director, he would soon realize that he was in a very unusual place indeed. Instead of the dreariness and shabbiness typical of university offices (even in fine private universities such as Duke), the Women's Studies Program offices are filled with sunlight, plants, and carefully chosen art. In the entryway, greeting the visitor is a display of ten years of T-shirts from various national women's studies conferences, all striking for their bright colors and clever puns (one reads, "desperately seeking Susan"—meaning Susan B. Anthony).

In the same waiting area, the visitor finds a comfortable couch, recent issues of the *Chronicle of Higher Education*, and the campus newspaper. While he or she waits, the smell of good coffee wafts in, and without prompting, someone walking by—faculty member, staffperson, or Jean O'Barr herself—will offer some. In the main part of the office, people go about their work with an air of happy busyness, and in another area, students and faculty consult about several ongoing research projects on women. From the conference room down the hall, the passionate sounds of the weekly meeting on "feminist pedagogy" spill out, as a dozen or so faculty members argue, laugh, and struggle to think into existence a new way of teaching that respects both the insights of feminist theory and the imperatives of the modern university.

O'Barr's particular contribution to feminist theory is in realizing that these events do not just happen spontaneously and that there is a deep (although rarely articulated) connection between the plants, coffee, and T-shirts on the one hand and new ways of teaching and of doing scholarship and the general work of the academy on the other. This book is about feminist institution building, and it is written by someone who is brilliant at it.

Two important—and related—insights structure this book, which is a must-have for anyone, scholar or administrator, who cares about what it means to be affiliated with an institution that speaks to the needs of all of its members.

First, every essay in this book draws on the insight that the towering dilemma of modern feminist thought and practice is figuring out how and why gender equity is so hard to come by. Many of the readers of this book are old enough to remember the days of formal barriers against women, in the academy as in the larger world. Merely two decades ago, for example, fine undergraduate programs like those at Princeton and Yale universities did not admit women, while others, like Harvard's, admitted them but underlined their "special" status by not permitting them to use facilities such as libraries that were open only to men. At the graduate level, virtually all elite Ph.D. and professional programs unabashedly had quotas limiting the number of women they would admit. Those were the days when Hannah Holborn Gray, then acting president of Yale, had to use the back door at a local club to go to a faculty meeting because the club did not admit women—and no one thought twice about holding faculty meetings there.

But the last twenty years have seen the rapid crumbling of these formal barriers, so much so that the incidents above seem to be from the Dark Ages rather than from the recent past. Yet what is in some ways an astonishingly rapid achievement of formal equality in the academy has not been matched by real equality. Almost thirty years after the most recent wave of the women's movement, women students are still far more likely to avoid majoring in math and science than are their male peers; women are much less visible in the ranks of full professors than they are in the ranks of assistant professors; and female administrators—especially in the higher ranks—are still a distinct minority. Thus O'Barr's first insight is that formal equality is the beginning, not the end, of the process.

O'Barr's second insight concerns how to get from here to there, how to build substantive equality into structures that at least nominally recognize formal equality. As O'Barr shares her "case studies" with us in this book, it is apparent that she is at the cutting edge of social science theory. Modern social scientists (and especially "postmodern" social scientists) are acutely aware that inequality gets built at the microlevel, that the politics of touch, of language, of how we think of things, all come to structure what we think is possible. Although Michel Foucault is generally given credit by social scientists for this insight, O'Barr's case studies remind us that feminists were there first. When feminists in this most recent wave of the women's movement insisted (long before Foucault was known on these shores) that the personal is political, they grasped that it is the patterns and practices of daily life that create "difference" even as institutions increasingly recognize sameness. It is the micropolitics of power that count.

This book is a brilliant exposition of the micropolitics of feminist power, told in concrete, real terms rather than the increasingly abstract and sometimes inaccessible terms of feminist theory. This is *lived* feminist theory. O'Barr tells us about redecorating the parlor where university events take place to include portraits of women prominent in the university's history. She tells us about raising money, in an innovative partnership with the university Development Office, to build one of the finest and liveliest women's studies programs in the United States. She tells us what real continuing education is and could be.

This book, read quickly, is about how to build a rich, welcoming, enticing structure responsive to the needs of a broad range of members of the academic community. It is about elegant ways of solving problems that bedevil women's studies programs across the United States—raising money, holding on to space, attracting busy students and overcommitted faculty, creating worthwhile programs—by someone who has a rare flair for it. As a handbook for how to run *any* innovative program (women's studies or other), this book belongs on the shelf of every administrator and would-be administrator.

But make no mistake: this is also a deeply political book. In no-nonsense, problem-solving ways, O'Barr brings to life a new vision of what it would mean to have a genuinely new university; a dream of a common language made real. Feminists from Mary Wollstonecraft to Catharine MacKinnon have worried about a profound dilemma in feminist thought: How do we build a new world that does not merely invert or re-create the male world of dominance and hierarchy? And in trying to avoid that risk, how do we keep from creating "women's spaces" that are in reality nothing more than the ghettos of the powerless? How do we engage in the real world with all of its constraints while staying true to a vision of a different kind? How do we compromise without selling out?

None of these are easy questions, and we are further hampered by having to imagine a world yet unborn. But feminists of every stripe who think this is a project worthy of the liberatory potential of feminism must study this book and read it several times. The personal *is* political, and in the pages that follow, Jean O'Barr shows us how to transform the world in which we live, one step— and one day—at a time. In so doing, she shows us our potential.

Kristin Luker
Princeton University

ACKNOWLEDGMENTS

Ideas come to each of us in context. They are elaborated in classrooms and over meal tables; they are refined as we write and speak to one another.

This manuscript, more than most, owes a profound debt to the hundreds of women and men who have joined me in generating the ideas that built Women's Studies at Duke University. I acknowledge the generous opportunities they have afforded me to explore what it means to focus a feminist lens on the contemporary academy. Among the many who have shaped my experiences, a few must be thanked by name, for my debt to them is great. Mentors Jean Campbell, Ernestine Friedl, George Maddox, Margaret Taylor Smith, and Emily Taylor recognized early efforts, opened doors, and modeled what it means to be a change agent in the academic world. The editorship of *Signs: Journal of Women in Culture and Society* showed me the importance of documenting our daily efforts to place women, gender, and feminist theories at the center of scholarship. My family, Mack, Claire, Emily, and Jimmy, provide the support that makes a sustained effort possible. Vivian Robinson and Nancy Rosebaugh are my professional partners whose perspectives and energies fuel my own. Alice Kaplan and Kristin Luker read portions of the manuscript at the level of sentences, and those details enable me to improve the rest. Ann Burlein's insightful suggestions, keen editing skills, and reliable assistance made this collection possible. Several of these chapters have been coauthored with students, and I am especially grateful to them. The Duke University community, its administrators, alumnae, faculty, and especially its students, have provided the organizational and intellectual opportunity to work out both ideas and practices as well as reflect on them; I am indebted to all of them, particularly the students, for the challenges and sustenance they offer.

FEMINISM IN ACTION

Introduction

On Parlors

and Portraits

This book is about building feminist institutions and community through women's studies. The common thread that runs through all of these diverse essays is my attempt to explore the process of institution building by focusing on the way that spaces—physical, psychological, and intellectual—enable transformations of all kinds to occur. Each part of the book emphasizes the importance of recording our experiences so that we can pass on the various processes through which feminists turn ideas into actions in the academy. My analysis moves between concrete episodes in program building and conceptualizations of feminism.

Sometimes I think, "It's all because of the parlors." The Women's Studies Program at Duke University uses two large reception rooms commonly referred to as "the parlors." The rooms are decorated in elaborate, formal styles with furniture from the Duke family homes. One is Victorian, crowded with Chinese antiques. The other is filled with delicate and original seventeenth-century French pieces. As the traditional reception areas of what was once a women's college, the parlors epitomize the spaces for gracious living that pepper campuses which separated women's education from men's. In the 1930s, again in 1968, and most recently in 1986, the parlors were refurbished by the Duke family women and by the alumnae to symbolize both their support for the university generally and their specific commitment to a place for women in it.

The parlors were once the offices of the Woman's College, a coordinate college for women that existed at Duke between 1930 and 1972. Between 1972 and 1983 the parlors were managed by an administrator in the dean's office. When the Women's Studies Program was set up in 1983 and no regular office

1

space was available, a desk for the program was placed in the corner of one parlor. As the program grew and regular offices were obtained in the building, the parlors were officially designated for Women's Studies functions as well as shared with other university units on request.

Physical space is a scarce and highly valued commodity on a university campus. Access to the parlors enabled the Women's Studies Program to conduct activities and be visible. But the space was intricately interwoven with the institution's many different stances toward women and education. The story of building connections between the parlors and feminist scholarship weaves throughout subsequent chapters. Yet long before we faced such considerations, we confronted a more immediate challenge—benefiting from the power that access to this space bestowed while making the space work for feminist goals.

Duke had never been an institution that forbade white women entry; it spent the better part of a century defining the spaces that women should occupy within its walls. The parlors demonstrated wealth, prized delicate movements, restricted interactions to stylized exchanges, displayed ornamental objects, required the labor of other women to clean and maintain them, idealized past times as essentially good times, and claimed such spaces as the embodiment of women. In the parlors we felt constrained to an idealized and abstract model of womanhood in which women were more a part of the decoration than of the action. How could Women's Studies occupy such spaces without becoming limited by the ideas about women that such settings suggest?

We relegated the more fragile furniture to the corners. We recovered the upholstered furniture with fabrics that could withstand the occasional drop of coffee and running-shoe smudge. We arranged the furniture to facilitate conversation as opposed to display. Initially these minor adjustments helped; the parlors become more livable.

Nothing, however, modified the gaze of the university's founding benefactors, Washington Duke and his sons, James B. and Benjamin N. Their large oil portraits looked down on our every discussion. Sometimes we joked with them, bringing them into the conversations. Other times we ignored them, hoping they had not heard the things we were saying. Often we wondered what we could do about them. We knew the portraits would stay. The general university community also used and admired the parlors. Many administrators and former students wanted the parlors maintained; they valued the portraits and the decor as important reminders of the university's history. Removing the portraits was not a solution.

But the portraits continued to bother us. We were bothered by the absence of female images in this space designated to talk about women's possibilities. Where were the portraits of our institutional foremothers? Had the women of the Woman's College who worked in these rooms in earlier decades reacted to these portraits as we did? We wanted to build on the work of these earlier women, but we wanted to move beyond the gaze of protective fathers. We wanted to control and create institutional spaces for all women. As feminist scholars, we were finding our own pictures and voices; this discovery depended upon learning our connectedness with others not present in those parlors. Thus, breaking the men's exclusive hold on the rooms was an important symbolic step in acquiring our own intellectual and psychological spaces. Naming the gap reinforced for us the understanding that claiming the space was not enough—we had to transform the space.

The portraits in the parlors typified the situation throughout the university. While most campus buildings boasted portraits of men prominent in the university's history, women were absent from its public symbolic display. We counted. Aside from the lecture hall in the Nursing School, the entire university had but a few minor portraits of women: two of former deans (hung in obscure places), one female donor pictured with her husband, and an occasional woman from the Duke family displayed in a building or room named after her.

As the university prepared to celebrate its sesquicentennial in 1989, an idea began to form among those of us in Women's Studies who had been talking about the absence of women on the university's walls. Could we use the occasion of the 150th anniversary to call attention to all the women—faculty, students, and staff—who had shaped the university? Knowing the program could not afford an oil portrait, we decided to figure out what we could do with photographs. Photographs, we reasoned, were a standard feature of Victorian design—why not get a series hung in one parlor?

After much discussion among students, faculty, and staff, we hit upon the idea of honoring "women firsts." With the decorator's go-ahead, we set about finding and reproducing archival photographs of women. Who was the university's first female graduate? the first African American woman to complete a Ph.D.? the first woman full professor? the first female elected student body president of the coeducational university? the first woman to be a university officer? the founding dean of the Woman's College? the first woman to teach in Women's Studies? the first woman on the Board of Trustees? the first dean of women? the first benefactor to Women's Studies? We located photographs of twelve "women firsts," then worked with the decorator on questions of style until the photographs were hung in three groupings around the room.

During the sesquicentennial weekend, a small ceremony was held to unveil the photographic portraits. The ceremony was attended by a number of the women (or their descendants) being honored in the photographs. The change in the dynamics of the parlor was immediate. No longer did the space belong only to the Duke men. While their portraits continued to hang bigger and more imposing than the photographs of the women, the women's intense and lively faces now looked back at men's from three sides. Most important, no matter where you stood or sat in the room, you felt that you were in a space that belonged to many different people.

The "women firsts" project sparked the imagination of Louise Dunlap, a 1968 graduate of the Woman's College and now the head of a Washington-based environmental consulting firm. She became determined to see that at least one formal portrait of a leading female figure join the many men commemorated in the university's main buildings. She and her sister, Constance Santareli, decided to honor their mother through a portrait of their mother's closest college friend, Mary Duke Biddle Trent Semans, the great-granddaughter of Washington Duke and a major figure on the contemporary campus. Mary Semans heads the Duke Endowment; she has been a member of the Duke Board of Trustees for over twenty years; she has been a member of the Durham City Council and its mayor pro tem; and she was the founding honorary member of the alumnae advisory Council on Women's Studies.

Dunlap's decision set in motion the long and complicated process of getting a major portrait commissioned, completed, framed, and displayed. The President's Office and the Board of Trustees had to agree on its placement. The University Archives had a say in who was hanging where, why, and in what arrangement. Mary Semans herself was consulted: where did she prefer? Those responsible for space allocation within the university also had to approve where the portrait might hang. We in Women's Studies insisted on hanging this portrait in a prominent place where it would be seen frequently by many sectors of the university. Finally, the Development Office had to coordinate the gift, the national search for an artist, the arrangements for a sitting, and the wishes of the donor. Some three years after the idea first came into being, the portrait of Mary Semans was placed in the university library's main reading room, the site of many official functions. The locations of some of the other portraits were indeed shifted. Mary Semans had joined the founders and presidents of the university.

The dedication of Mary Semans's portrait was a major official occasion. In attendance were the donor, the Duke family, university officials, and members of the Council on Women's Studies. Ann Curry, a 1965 graduate who was an active alumna as well as widely respected as a moving force in Atlanta civic affairs, was then the chairwoman of the council. She presented the portrait, saying:

It is an enormous pleasure for us to present this gift to the University in appreciation for what Duke has given us. It is important for you to understand that the Women's Studies Program—its content, its outreach, its Council, the symposium this weekend—binds us to Duke in a very special way. For me personally, it is Duke speaking to me in a voice I can hear, a voice that for almost twenty years after my graduation was silent. This gift makes that feeling of being included possible for today's women at Duke and for young women to come.

. . . Mary Semans' life is rich with accomplishments, filled with commitments, and distinguished by her caring and compassion for others. Hanging her portrait not only makes women feel included—it makes us feel inspired.

I was at the NCAA finals in Indianapolis this time last week, and I think there's a symbolic connection between the accomplishments there—the hanging of the first NCAA Championship banner in our stadium—and this portrait hanging today. Both were a long time coming. And these are only the first; more will follow.[1]

The basketball analogy was electric. The university officials attending the portrait dedication believe without question that prominence in athletics legitimizes the university in the public domain. To have an alumna, herself a Duke basketball fan, link this success they know so well with a success they were being asked to consider caused one of those moments feminists identify as "clicks." You could hear the minds whirling as those less familiar with Women's Studies pondered the assertion that the two events held equal value. And you could see in the eyes of those involved with Women's Studies the recognition that equating the hanging of the portrait of a feminist with the national basketball championship was a brilliant and a memorable move.

The portrait hangs opposite the main door to the reading room. Walking down the library's corridor, the viewer is struck by this single magnificent portrait of a woman—as he or she is meant to be. The portrait depicts Mary Semans seated but leaning forward, as if about to get involved in a conversation; there is nothing distant or retiring about her. Painted in vibrant tones by John Howard Sanden of New York, everything about the portrait stands in contrast to the dark, drab, withdrawn figures of the men who surround her. Yet its composition, quality, and magnificence make it comparable to the others.

A few weeks after the dedication, a student in my senior seminar in political science told me that a strange thing had happened to him.[2] He had been in the library, he reported, and noticed this picture of a woman. It had really struck him; it was the first portrait of a woman that he had seen on campus and he wondered whether I knew anything about it. I thought back to the many years his predecessors had spent under the gaze of Mary Semans's male ancestors. I speculated about the impact her portrait might have on this student and his successors. I thought of the many thousands of hours, dollars, and discussions it had taken to bring this one picture into being. Yes, I responded, I knew a bit about it. But first, I said, tell me what difference seeing her portrait makes. "Well," he replied, "it made me think a lot about women at Duke, what I know about the old ones and how things are for the ones here now." "Good," I said, and I thought, "Keep thinking." Only then did I retell the tale.

There is a great deal more to building women's studies, in any college or university, than hanging pictures in parlors and libraries. But this episode contains the central idea of building feminist institutions through women's studies: the need to have women and their stories at the center of education, the necessity of having appropriate resources, the importance of working within an institutional context in order to transform it, and the opportunity to reflect on the ways that thinking and doing shift when these ingredients mix. These themes run throughout the chapters that follow.

This is a book, then, about women's studies, culled from some of the talks I have given over the past decade and developed in a number of newly crafted essays. For some twenty-five years now, women's studies programs have excelled at calling attention to absences, silences, the gaps in our scholarship where women's lives and experiences should be. But naming the gaps is not enough. Without filling spaces with people and resources, we cannot come up with interventions capable of turning ideas into actions and eventually initiating transformations. Working out the process of feminist institution building is the central theme of this book; the stories and analyses in the chapters that follow suggest myriad building blocks.

The position of women in contemporary American society is a problematic issue for just about everyone. Many conservatives think that women are an important issue because they have changed too much, endangering themselves, society, and especially children. Such fears have a very long history. People of a more liberal persuasion know that women's issues are central in family, work, and public policy; yet liberals often hesitate when trying to articulate whether and in what ways further change should play itself out. An increasing number of observers know that while women are bound together by many similarities, they have many differences among them. Lots of people think that all the talk about women is enough; surely the situation of women must be changing for the better given how much it is discussed. For many women, and some men, the recognition is dawning that although so many people are talking constantly about women's issues, the situations of *some* women's lives (although improving) are by no means satisfactory while the circumstances of *many* women's lives are deteriorating in spite of their best efforts. If women as a problem, subject, or possibility have been called to the attention of contemporary society by a combination of factors outside the academy, what can women's studies as an academic discipline contribute to this discussion?

I believe women's studies is the place where these public concerns are tested in scholarship. The relationship between the two has altered over time as feminist acting and thinking have grown more sophisticated. In the beginning of the second wave of feminism in the late 1960s and early 1970s, queries about women came from outside the academy; activists who demanded answers to their more troubling questions forced the academy to refocus itself in order to provide answers. In the two decades since, feminist scholarship and women's studies have worked from within the academy to produce graduates equipped with knowledge about women and gender that can enable our society to understand social dynamics. It is sometimes said that a liberal education ensures that you can do anything you want to and women's studies explains why the "girl-yous" will have to do so in particular ways.

Naming women's issues is only the first step in a much larger process of education for social change that moves from ideas into actions. Information about women's lives comes from systematically researching those lives. Such research is now carried out in every discipline. I am interested in how that research comes together and is furthered in the space that women's studies provides. Such research offers more than a mere record of the past; it is a record that contains suggestions for the future. My experiences tell me that learners are most empowered when they have interpretive frameworks that enable them to interact with data and experiences. I want to know how words and ideas initiate a process of naming, claiming, and transforming space as well as how concrete political steps make that space an intellectual, personal, and physical reality.

From the very beginning of women's studies in the earliest mimeographed bibliographies and stories in *Female Studies*[3] that passed from hand to hand among the pioneers to current projects (such as *The Courage to Question*),[4] those in the field have claimed that the space provided by women's studies programs does make a difference. But what kind of difference? And how does it work? In the rush to create programs, the hassles to keep them (and help them flourish), and the desire to meet the real daily needs of those who come through the program office's doors, priority has never gone to researching the processes being carried out in that very space. *Feminism in Action* is one step in beginning to do so.

In writing about women's studies, I take experience as the location for the construction of theory. This understanding situates me between two current traditions in feminism. On the one hand, scholars generate knowledge that is to be taught. I am a keen reader of those diverse and sometimes conflicting ideas. On the other, I am interested in the way society works, how institutions are organized, what assumptions lie behind that organization, and what ends those assumptions serve. I work daily at the question of how to put ideas into practice and how to articulate the assumptions and limits behind current practices. In recent years I have found myself particularly interested in the gaps in our understanding that separate the development of new ideas, the process of transmitting them, the consequences of acting on them, and the interventions that can transform the gaps. It is these gaps I hope *Feminism in Action* starts to fill by recounting interventions that have made a difference in one sample university.

This collection of essays is directed toward two quite different audiences. The first audience consists of those already engaged (or in the process of becoming engaged) in women's studies—students taking courses, faculty doing research, administrators committed to furthering the enterprise, and university graduates who wish they had learned these things when they were in school. These people constitute the primary actors in women's studies. Not only do they have knowledge, experiences, and enthusiasm—they are in the business of putting these ingredients together effectively. In order to help them do so, the essays that follow encourage this audience to do two things. First, I push them to reflect on what they are doing, to explain it, to talk about it, and to record their process so that their successes can be replicated, their failures avoided. Second, I urge them to document in a way that is sufficiently free of specialized language to be capable of pulling in other audiences.

The second audience for this collection includes people who stand outside women's studies per se—students who shy away from feminist classes but get into arguments about women with their friends; parents, faculty, administrators, and former students who know that women's studies elicits enthusiastic reports but would be hard pressed to say just what women's studies is; and members of the public who want more explanation for how higher education works and have never considered gender as part of the explanation.

The two audiences need each other. Feminist scholars have information and explanatory power that clarify a wide range of issues. Members of the public need those ideas and explanations to make sense of the way in which personal and political choices are intertwined. I talk to both groups in the pages that follow, trusting that they will hear each other as I have heard them. In the process, I suggest what such a joint enterprise might look like in the future. Women's studies is a particularly apt example of how learning and doing come together for the mutual benefit of both. It is education for social change.

What do I mean? Two perspectives, elaborated through the text, may prove useful. First, I believe ideas are socially constructed entities. We can and do create new ones all the time. The ideas about women that are limiting and counterproductive can—with some work—be left behind and new ones put in place. Second, ideas interweave actions. The notion that ideas, thoughts, and theory are divorced from action in everyday activities is both erroneous and harmful. What we experience fuels our interests, and our interests direct our learning. While it is true that much academic work is not grounded in daily concerns and while it is also true that a great deal of what we encounter each day is not informed by a reflective stance, the gap between what we think and what we do can be constantly reduced rather than assumed to be inevitable. This is what it means to be an educated person.

My scholarly observations and my political goals coalesce around the belief that women and men of all ages, classes, races, abilities, and sexual orientations share a great deal with each other in their various identities. I have learned through long conversations with male colleagues, particularly my husband, who is an ethnographer of contemporary American culture, just how reciprocal gender concerns are. I also know from literally thousands of conversations and observations, as well as scholarly investigations, that men and women experience different realities in their daily lives. Those differences are daily and systematically forced into a model of "human" that glorifies the masculine and dismisses the feminine in the dominant culture. I see this model as not only increasingly outdated but outrageously destructive. As a feminist educator, I teach students to see the ways in which such gendered realities are reconstructed in their daily lives; I ask them to consider how they are going to think and live in the world consonant with their new knowledge.

As an educator, I am deeply influenced by the Society of Friends. While not a Quaker by profession of faith, I have spent many years involved in Quaker education and find myself constantly learning from their practice, as did earlier generations of feminist activists during abolition. It is difficult to summarize neatly the Quaker philosophy of education, for this philosophy resides in the process by which it is put into practice. Like any other philosophy of education, the Quaker philosophy has many variants. What I have learned from my association with the Society of Friends and their thoughts on education is twofold: (1) education is a process that engages the whole student—her emotions and her spirit as well as her mind; and (2) students mix their school learning and their out-of-school experiences in ways that we as teachers rarely capitalize on—to our mutual detriment.

My entire academic career has been spent as an administrator in a single institution, Duke University. At first, an administrative career was forced upon me. In 1969 academic women simply were not a possible addition to the faculty of a conservative southern university. So I taught on a per-course basis whenever funds were available, in addition to filling in for an administrative colleague who went on leave. When no tenure track job appeared and I was faced with the prospect of no work, I stayed with my administrative job, thinking it was "for a while." I was able to teach occasionally, and I continued to write. Over time I came to see the situation differently.

Looking back, I realize clearly that the situation created an unusually rich opportunity for what I discovered were my talents and energies. Had I waited for a departmental position to open up and had I been chosen to fill it, I think I would have been much less challenged and hence much less satisfied. By looking around me and seeing what needed doing, I have created a series of positions in which I have had the opportunity to initiate hundreds of educational projects as well as to teach both graduates and undergraduates. For more than twenty years, first as the director of a continuing education program that grew into numerous components and now as the director of a multifaceted women's studies program, I have opened up new spaces and have grown in the process. When I was considering the move from Continuing Education to Women's Studies, my husband observed that the new position was better for me. Universities, he observed, might eventually incorporate older students and the need for advocacy would diminish. But he felt quite sure the prejudice against women ran much deeper and I would experience an unfolding series of challenges that would last a lifetime. I think he was right.

I have intervened when I believed that women's situations could be altered. The gratitude that women express when engaged in feminist learning is often matched by the indifference of many men who observe and dismiss women and issues surrounding them. Increasingly some men take the time to listen, learn, and change; those men come to see things in much the same way that women do. Such reactions only further fuel my determination to bring about circumstances that enhance the ability of women to flourish in the academy. Without an administrative base, my interests would have remained ideas, without being turned into actions.

Over the last decade I have been asked to describe the programs and projects I direct. The invitations have come from nascent women's studies programs on other campuses, from community organizations, from alumni and alumnae groups, and from colleagues and professional associations. In the last five years, thanks to a stable program here at Duke with a remarkable staff, I have been able to give more systematic attention to the task of writing down what I have been saying. Writing intensifies my understanding that naming is only the first step and doing something about women's situations a necessary second. I am haunted by the idea that we have had to relearn so much of our mothers' stories. I want our daughters, and our sons, to have a head start.

Ethnography plays a key role in the writing process for me. Trained in the anthropological method in graduate school in African studies, I have always thought of myself as a participant observer. I am part of the groups for whom and with whom I plan programs and classes. Yet I also stand outside them, having entered them with prior knowledge, current questions, future agendas. I see the everyday practices and cultural models of dominant groups in a constant tug of war with women's realities. In this process I am always on an epistemological quest: what do we know? why is that what's known? what difference does it make? how can we explain it and muster the resources to alter it?

The topic of my Ph.D. dissertation in political science from Northwestern University in 1970 was the system of ten-house political party cells in rural Tanzania. I was interested in the way African socialism was being built from the ground up. It is only in the last few years that I have realized why I chose this topic. At the time, it was simply one more hurdle to clear. I now realize the topic reflects a very basic and personal political philosophy: change is sustained only when it reaches the people most affected by it, at the grassroots level. Middle-level and elite acquiescence—if not support—in any structure is always necessary. The failure of change is attributable to many causes (historical, idiosyncratic, organizational, cultural, etc.). But ultimately I am a bottom-up, rather than a top-down, thinker and activist. Top-down is, of course, a more common administrative style and one that I am still learning. The tension between these two perspectives is a creative one for me.

All of these essays draw on my twenty-five years of experience at Duke University. I do not claim that the students and the issues I have encountered are representative of all students and every issue in contemporary higher education. Nor, of course, do I claim to consider every question of import to the future of feminist scholarship. Each institution and situation creates a different context that must be approached both on its own terms and in light of feminist thought. I further understand that blending practical problem solving with theoretical analyses is a more successful strategy than pursuing either task independently. I will claim that the process of feminist institution building through women's studies; thinking about teaching and learning, listening, explaining, and acting; coming to grips with the politics of knowledge and reflecting on the relationships among women, education, and institutional power all transcend the experiences of a single university.

Readers may approach the collection in a number of different ways. They may wish to follow my own intellectual journey as I move through the years and take up the parts in turn. Others may wish to read for particular subjects, projects, or audiences that are scattered throughout the four parts.

The four essays in Part 1 were written over a fifteen-year span. They focus on listening. The Quaker and ethnographer in me was listening to what various members of the educational community and the public had to say about women. As teacher, writer, and administrator, I tried to hear their multiple messages and appreciate their positions in a way that went beyond passively receiving information. Such listening is active listening, requiring an interpretation and a response in turn. The introduction to Part 1 charts the context in which ideas became actions.

How can women's studies be explained to audiences outside it, be they within the university or beyond academic walls? How does one explain that feminist scholarship is a necessary corrective to the extant disciplines in the academy while simultaneously claiming that the transformation of knowledge set in motion by feminist scholarship challenges the very basis of those disciplines and institutions? And how do I explain the difference women's studies makes in the lives of individual students as they gain new voices both in classes where women are the subject matter and within a campus culture whose male prerogatives are beginning to be named and confronted? These questions form the basis of Part 2, which focuses on explanations. What I explain and how I explain it depends on the audience that I am addressing; at this stage I become increasingly interested in matching my frameworks with those of my hearers. Wanting to draw them into the conversation about women's studies, I find that the space to do so is rarely available. The introduction to Part 2 gives additional background for reading these essays, which were originally public lectures.

The third part of the book records classroom investigations: what is involved in actually taking students seriously and designing classes that build on the differences they bring to the inquiry. Setting up courses and structures within courses enables students both to learn about self, community, and society as well as to give voice to that knowledge. Two of these essays are coauthored with students; another includes a graduate student's internal dialogue as she records how what she is reading changes her outlook.

The book's final part takes up a number of initiatives that further the process of naming, intervening, acting, and recording. I explore editing a scholarly journal and the vantage point on the academy it provides; fundraising for women's studies; making students allies in the political process of transforming campuses; rethinking teaching through curriculum transformation; and reflecting on women's studies as a discipline, particularly in conversation with ethnic studies. These projects explore some possible horizons for women's studies in the next century.

Listening

One of the first public lectures I ever gave was in 1976. The lecture was for the monthly colloquium sponsored by the Center for the Study of Aging and Human Development, a joint Medical Center and university program at Duke. At that time I was the director of the Continuing Education Program at the university, an office with four distinct facets. It assisted adult students in entering university courses, sponsored noncredit classes for both personal enhancement and professional development, offered a counseling program for reentry women, and recently had set up a program for retired people.

I was asked to describe the beginnings of the Institute for Learning in Retirement, an innovative educational project that had been jointly founded by the center and Continuing Education, by placing the project within the broader context of adult education. The director of the center, sociologist George Maddox, was one of the pioneers in the field of gerontology, and the center he headed was one of the first and foremost in the country to address the issues of aging. Maddox believed that the social components of aging were neglected in the study of physical aging and that the study of aging was isolated, rarely tied to the more general process of human development. This was especially the case during the mid-1970s when the relationship between geriatrics and gerontology was much less developed than it is today. Maddox's collaboration with the institute and his invitation to me were part of his efforts to bring sociological perspectives into medical research.

I knew the audience at the colloquium would consist of the faculty and postdoctoral students in geriatrics and gerontology, with a sprinkling of social scientists. Given the medical emphasis of the listeners, I suspected that the information on adult learning would strike them as new and interesting but hardly central to their day-to-day work of documenting the physical aging process. In my lecture I tried to give them a feel for both the contours and the centrality of the emerging field of continuing education by getting them to listen to the voices of returning students. These adults struggle to fashion an education that responds in an ongoing way both to their own changing needs as well as to the complex changes that occur in contemporary postindustrial societies.

At the time I gave the lecture, the university's Continuing Education Program was barely ten years old. It had begun as a reentry and counseling program for women and soon expanded to enroll men as well. Students paid on a per-course basis and did not receive any form of tuition break, as was later done at other schools. The numbers remained small, rarely reaching a hundred in any given year, largely because of the tuition costs. This credit part of the Continuing Education Program was important for two reasons. First, although the numbers were small, the impact was large, forcing the institution to confront a changing landscape in higher education and to consider its practices that restricted adult enrollment. While Duke itself did not choose to go in the direction of welcoming large numbers of adult learners to its credit programs, a point I discuss elsewhere in these essays, it did modify its admissions policies, its continuation requirements, and its general stance toward adults who did register. Second, the push from adults for access to the university led to the development of a now-vast set of course offerings that are credit free, an extensive career counseling program, and the establishment of this particular retirement institute.

The lecture records my first analytical attempt to make a series of observations on the basis of my experiences and then identify patterns in what I had observed. I thought a great deal about the audience I was addressing, constructing the patterns I was finding to be effective for that particular audience. I found myself here, as in many future situations, bringing information about one group to another. Experience taught me that groups have very different traditions of explanation. One of my tasks was to bridge the explanatory gap, finding ways to create awareness and dialogue around common issues.

I would never have undertaken such a task without George Maddox's acting as a mentor for me. One of his most important contributions to my thinking was his insistence that my daily experiences as the head of Continuing Education constituted valuable "data" for understanding social process and institutional change. Trained as I was in the behavioral sciences, I thought only aggregate data, generated by others, constituted real information. As a response to Maddox's invitation to share what I was learning, the talk reproduced in Chapter 1 documents the first time I dimly understood that my own observations constituted a form of research.

The Institute for Learning in Retirement continues fifteen years later to be one of the most vigorous programs at the university. It annually enrolls about five hundred retired people, supports its own staff and programs, and constantly overflows the space allocated to it. At a fifteenth-anniversary celebration in 1992, the officers showcased not only the institute's accomplishments but the way in which it has served as a model for similar programs and become an object of study itself.

The roots of my interest in education as a process are laid out in this first chapter. It is my attempt to describe the ways in which classroom content and personal experience shuttle back and forth for each learner. I also emphasize students' need for institutional spaces that allow the diverse needs of different groups to be heard. I am beginning to recognize that when older students are left out, our understanding of education, of what constitutes a "good" student, is limited. Through the process of naming an absence (in this case, older students) I learned to see other absences. Later I would come to see the absence of attention to gender, race, class, and sexual orientation as fundamentally damaging to our understanding of education as well. But then I did not make the link between the fact that the majority of these returning adults were women and the fact that the institution did not listen to them.

Returning after fifteen years to this lecture, which appears here as Chapter 1, I am struck with the ways in which the tenets of my work in Women's Studies lie in Continuing Education experiences. It seems important to begin this book where I began some twenty years ago, by listening and by fashioning responses to what I was hearing. I heard women wanting more out of their educations but lacking the vision, vocabulary, or voice to know how to get it. I suffered from the same lacks. But because I sat on the other side of the desk, I found myself searching for ways to respond to their needs, listening hard, and determined to respond; it seemed to me that something larger was at stake, although in the mid-1970s I could not have told you what that something might be.

I had the opportunity to explore the links between continuing education and women's studies for the first time almost ten years later when the editors of a volume on women in higher education asked me to write about reentry women because I had administered a continuing education program from 1970 through 1982. By the time I was writing and revising this piece in the mid-1980s, I had become the director of Women's Studies. From this standpoint, looking back at the relationship between reentry women and women's studies was intriguing.

As I began to reflect on the ways women make a place for themselves in the academy, I was struck with how often women believed that the burden of adjustment was on them to fit in rather than on institutions to listen to women and modify their practices accordingly. This was (and still is!) a perspective that many women bring from their personal lives to their emergent political and professional ones. It certainly worked this way for me.

Yet through the process of writing the essay that appears here as Chapter 2, I came to quite a different conclusion. So did the other authors in the volume. As a result, the editors framed their introduction to emphasize this new conclusion: women have been changing for over two decades to fit into the system of North American higher education; it is now the responsibility of educational institutions to make the changes necessary to ensure the future success of both women and higher education.

This was the conclusion we came to; it was not the position from which I began. I began with a question that I was frequently asked, usually in tones of despair: how can we possibly go about changing ideas about women as well as women themselves? In endless conversations with reentry women students and with my peers, I came to see that the process involved three basic parts. It was never clear to me whether a particular step had to come first. I knew only that all three must be engaged before change, individually or institutionally, could come about. One has to ask, first, what is said about women? What does received knowledge, folk wisdom, and your boss say about women? Second, based on your own experiences, are these accounts true? Here it is important to keep in mind that what these accounts leave unsaid is often a more telling sign of what is important and powerful than what they actually say. And, finally, what does this received wisdom mean? Why this particular emphasis, and what does it mean for what we can and cannot see?

As I moved through the process of counseling women and living my own life, I found that I often did not see how differences between men and women got played out, much less how those differences contributed to the construction of what was male and female, valued and devalued, powerful and powerless. I needed to learn to see and think in new ways. As these pages proceed, the stories of how ideas change and results follow emerge. Here I introduce the process by a confession that now seems absurd but then seemed ordinary. It is the L. L. Bean click.

In the 1970s, like millions of other dual-career couples, my husband and I discovered mail order catalogs. And, of course, they discovered us, bombarding the house. We found them a wonderful way to acquire the basics at ten o'clock at night, long after the mall had closed and without any of the hassle associated with taking the children shopping. We would both order cotton, button-down shirts—often from the same page of the catalog; one size for women, the other for men, but identical in color and style. The shirts came by UPS. We wore them. And then they had to be cared for.

My husband had always taken his shirts to a commercial laundry before we were married. Except for a few years when money was especially tight, I would take his shirts to the laundry each Monday, picking them up at the end of the day. Each Saturday I did the family laundry, setting aside my shirts, the ones identical to his, spending an hour or more ironing them. One day, in the midst of thinking I would never be done, I asked myself a fundamental question. Since we both had the same jobs as professors at the same university and both wore the same shirts, basic L. L. Bean, why did his go to the laundry while mine were washed and ironed by me at home? Why had we both agreed that his professional look was important, and why had we never discussed mine? Why was it acceptable to allocate *my* time to ironing my shirts but to spend *our* money laundering his? I turned the iron off, tossed my newly washed shirts into the basket for Monday's trip, and never looked back.

But I never forgot the lesson I learned that day, a lesson about double standards, automatically and willing applied, that went unquestioned until I arrived at a new perspective with which to think through what I was doing and why. I had to think about what was said—commercially done shirts contribute to a professional look. I had to think about what we did not say—anything about my professional appearance. And I had to think about what it all meant—money was allocated to his career while my career was fit into ongoing family tasks that I performed. The click over shirts was a valuable lesson in understanding and implementing a feminist perspective to change social practices as well as to free me from a task I never really enjoyed.

Feminist scholarship gave me the information and permission necessary to engage in asking questions. Starting with shirts, I extended these questions over the years to broader issues associated with privilege. Putting a mirror up to my own experiences taught me how to construct windows onto the experiences of others whose backgrounds and needs differed from my own.

In a similar way, by incorporating returning women students, educational institutions have had to confront the limitations of their traditional understanding of education. The record of the continuing education movement precedes and then overlaps the growth of feminist scholarship. I argue in Chapter 2 that their relationship probably could not have been reversed. The lessons I learned observing reentry women struggling with institutions and figuring out how to get room in them became the basis of my perspectives in women's studies. And my own struggles to live what I was learning to think made additional contributions to the process!

Talking about women, education, and feminist scholarship involves listening to audiences beyond the ivy walls. In Chapter 3 I offer one analysis that I gave to an audience of business professionals who had few routine university contacts with liberal arts scholars. In 1990, a group of faculty from Women's Studies was invited by the Executive Training Center of the Ford Motor Company to conduct a one-day program on the new scholarship on women and its relevance for company policy. The link between Duke and Ford had come about through an alumna who was active in Women's Studies and knew Ford's director of training. The alumna had talked with the director about the importance of employing feminist perspectives if the company's executives were to deal successfully with the changing (read increasingly female) work force.

Executive education programs occur frequently at both business schools and large corporations. Yet this invitation by a car company to a women's studies program was unusual; everyone involved spent many hours planning the kinds of presentations that would successfully introduce executives to the new scholarship on women. Having offered similar day-long sessions during the late 1980s for alumni and alumnae as well as for Saatchi and Saatchi (at the invitation of the Advertising Educational Foundation), we relied on those previous experiences to suggest topics and formats.

The program began with a lecture on women's autobiography, a way to bring each person and their story into the discussion. Afterward I presented a discussion of feminism as both a social movement and an academic subject. I concluded by showing how women's studies today teaches students to think about these topics. Later in the day we listened to a history lecture on violence against women that illustrated continuing legacies in women's lives. We concluded with a practical discussion of the gendered nature of benefits packages, demonstrating how even contemporary innovations are shaped by assumptions about gender.

Certain patterns emerge in listening to groups of professional women and men outside the academy talk about "women." These men and women are experiencing changes in their own lives, personally and professionally. They read about women's liberation, the women's movement, women's studies, and feminism as well as teenage pregnancy, rape, child care, abortion, gender-neutral language, single-parent families, and sexual harassment. Some read only short news accounts and opinion pieces; others follow the news media and the talk show circuit. Some have picked up the occasional book. Most have participated in training programs about the "changing work force." Yet while all have voiced opinions in conversations and exercised power though the policy decisions they make in their professional positions, they have never studied women and gender issues systematically in a formal setting. Nor have they had the opportunity to place their lived experiences within explanatory frameworks. Without the opportunity to probe many of the assumptions about women put forward in popular discourse, individuals tend to generalize their own experiences without realizing the dangers of ignoring differences.

Hoping to address this lack of reflection upon their own experiences, I keyed my overview of the relation between the women's movement and women's studies as it has emerged during the last twenty years according to my understanding of the ways in which working professionals often define "women's issues." Having listened to many of the same questions from different people, I tried to construct my remarks around the queries that they themselves had yet to bring together. I did not tie my observations to the specifics of the Duke curriculum, for this audience had no particular links with the university. Rather, I grounded my observations in topics frequently discussed in conversations among educated professionals and mapped out relationships among contemporary topics, the contours of feminist scholarship, and the reactions of current students.

Along with the difference in audience for this lecture there corresponds an important shift in the nature of the observations I am making. As the lectures in the first two chapters show, when speaking to academic audiences I often used narratives about students to make a point. In the Ford presentation I used the students' own words as a way to get others to join me in listening. The student comments came from a variety of sources: observations students had made in their papers, journals, or exams; letters written to me about a particular issue; remarks taped from discussion groups. In every case, the students' voices constituted a compelling way to explain issues to working professionals. The power struggle between me-as-professor and them-as-managers evaporates when we both listen to someone else's firsthand experience and discuss what we are hearing. This particular talk ends with a student query about the ways in which professionalization isolates women; it literally echoed through the conference room as I read it.

As I continued in Women's Studies, I found myself engaged in yet another exercise in listening. Those doing feminist scholarship were increasingly the object of attack by those outside the field as well as those outside the academy. How might I hear what those critics were saying and respond? The lecture in Chapter 4 was my attempt to put some sense into a debate that I thought had become senseless. The debate about classical education kept moving farther and farther away from thinking about students. I wanted to reintroduce students as learners and as teachers into the conversation.

The talk was not uniformly well received. The audience, consisting mostly of older men, all white and all unfamiliar with women's studies, wanted another level of escalation in the shouting match about what constitutes the best education, and I disappointed them by focusing on student needs rather than faculty positions. In the question period that followed, most of the men appeared confused and asked me to tell them what I thought the curriculum should include. Initially I felt a sense of failure, worrying that I had not clearly explained that curriculum transformation requires us to ask fundamental questions about the process of knowing. Yet as the questions wore on, I realized that we conceptualized education in fundamentally different ways. They used a "banking" model, assuming that the task of education is to give students capital on which they will draw for the rest of their lives. I had a process model in mind, in which education teaches critical skills of analysis through listening, in which the content to be learned must resonate with students' lives.

No women asked any questions. They sat together in the back of the room, concentrating with an intensity that was intriguing to me. At the end of the session, I saw that some of the women, many of them younger and some of them African American, were in tears. They later told me that their tears had come both from their frustrations with the reactions I was receiving and from the way the material resonated with them. They shared my desire to redefine this debate, a debate they found frustrating in its insistence on reinforcing the status quo. We concluded our informal conversations after the talk with a yearning to understand the conditions under which people listen. The pain in this particular session was intense because we were not dealing with some early period of history in which women's perspectives had not been researched and acknowledged, nor were we dealing with a set of people who were unfamiliar with developments in scholarship. We were in fact dealing with our colleagues, who should have heard the same things we did. They did not, and we struggled to understand why.

Lifelong

Learning

The Duke

Experience

On my first day as director of Continuing Education seven years ago this fall, I went confidently to my office, prepared to help the adult students admitted by the Woman's College sign up for classes. I thought I understood the job I had just taken. As academic dean for special students, I was to help them plan their courses. I had done that for undergraduates for two years at the University of North Carolina at Chapel Hill as a faculty adviser, so I faced the new position with confidence. The other Woman's College deans had conveyed the impression that adult students were somewhat different, but they did not specify *how* nor did they suggest it would involve much new. I saw four people in the first two hours; by then I was quite sure this was a whole new ball game for which neither Duke nor I was fully prepared!

My first appointment was with a woman who had become intrigued by changes in her hair color during her second pregnancy and was determined to do research into its causes. Her master's degree in music, obtained some twenty years earlier, was not much preparation. She had already gone back to Chapel Hill High School after her first child and taken a chemistry course. On this particular day she wanted to know where she could take precalculus math prior to doing university chemistry and college math or whether she could enroll simultaneously in all three. My second appointment was with a registered nurse who had just moved to the area and found she had to have a B.S.N. degree to get a meaningful job; she needed to know how many of her diploma credits would transfer into Duke's program and whether there was a limit on challenged upper-division courses. My third appointment was with a quiet

A version of this chapter was presented on October 5, 1976, to the monthly seminar of the Duke University Center for the Study of Aging and Human Development and was first published in *Proceedings of Seminars, 1976–1980*, edited by George Maddox and Elizabeth Auld (Durham, N.C.: Council on Aging and Human Development, Duke University, 1980).

woman who had just packed her last child off to first grade. She had long been fascinated by international relations and had majored in political science at Radcliffe before dropping out to marry. She wanted to know whether I thought she should take a course; whether I thought she would succeed; whether she could ever really get her B.A. degree; and if she did, whether I thought she should go to graduate school in political science or in international relations. The fourth was an older faculty spouse who firmly announced she had more degrees than she needed and was here to learn something. Who did I think gave a good course? Those four women and the people who have followed them since the Continuing Education Program began in 1968 represented a new range of challenges and needs for which we in higher education have few guidelines.

The growth of Duke's program parallels the phenomenal growth of continuing education nationally and internationally. At Duke we began with a narrow vision: to help women, one segment of what Patricia Cross termed the new learners, reenter traditional programs. Through the years we broadened our programs to offerings for both career preparation and personal enrichment. Now we are deeply involved in all aspects of lifelong learning, especially a new endeavor with retired people.

I would like to discuss how higher education is responding to the diverse needs of people at all points along the life cycle and to introduce you to some of the exciting developments we are pursuing here at Duke. I think it would be helpful to mention briefly the factors that have given birth to the boom in lifelong learning. Then I will outline who is in the business of providing continuing education and what kinds of education are becoming available. I want to end by pinpointing some of the tensions in switching from traditional lockstep education to new forms. My argument is that the university's claim to universality is indeed limited. While it conducts teaching, research, and service on a broad front of subjects, it still does so for a restricted clientele—and thereby undermines its own ability to understand and explore the human experience to its fullest.

Definition of Terms

I use the *life-cycle* notion as it is used in the social sciences because it seems to me to be a more accurate reflection of people's minds and bodies than chronological age or measures of educational levels. This notion also allows us to distinguish individual patterns of development, especially the quite different patterns for men and women. Men typically move through childhood and adolescence to early career commitment, not letting marriage and children seriously deter their professional focus. Only in their forties do men question where they are going and why. Women evidence another pattern. Their early career commitment is frequently more tentative, the salience of marriage and children to their professional plans more profound, their sense of resurgence and rededication at thirty-five stronger. The developmental needs of adults past twenty-one and before sixty-five have finally attracted popular attention, popularly focused for us by the compelling work of Gail Sheehy in *Passages*.[1]

In *Passages* the author talks about the predictable crises of adult life: (1) the search for self-identity in late adolescence; (2) the twenties, when one self-righteously pursues the "shoulds" of one's peer culture; (3) "catch 30," with its spurt of vitality; (4) the period of rooting and extending that follows; (5) the "deadline decade," with its full-blown authenticity crisis; and (6) the period of renewal or resignation in the fifties, when equilibrium is regained and the motto is "no more bullshit." At each passage four perceptual issues are at play, and it is these interrelationships which define how each individual develops: (1) the interior sense of self in relation to others; (2) the proportion of safeness to danger that people feel in their lives; (3) the perception of time—whether it is available or running out; and (4) finally, a gut-level sense of aliveness or stagnation.

The confines of a short paper do not allow me to relate each step of Sheehy's scheme to the educational process. I can, however, argue that the diversity which has come to characterize continuing education is a direct result of the multifaceted needs of adult learners, who are responding to their inner selves and external settings as they move through the life cycle.

Other authors remind us of the fact that the life cycle does not stop at sixty-five either. Demko, for example, delineates stages in the lives of older individuals and argues strongly that educational programs must be closely tied to the needs expressed by people over sixty-five.[2]

We need to define one more term before we begin our discussion, and that, of course, is *continuing education*. I have a hard time defining the term because it covers such a broad range of programs—from anything outside the lockstep residential degree programs (which have been the mainstay of higher education) to the noncredit and nondegree courses, conferences, and workshops on one thousand and one topics offered by associations, communities, and businesses. I prefer to define continuing education in terms of the orientations of its practitioners, most of whom would agree that continuing education starts with the belief that education is not a vaccine to prevent ignorance later in life. The belief that people of any age have a legitimate need for and right to all kinds of educational experiences is fundamental to continuing education programs and the moving force behind them.

Continuing education program directors play a key role in creating the means whereby people can achieve their varied educational aspirations. The role of these directors in aiding women is clearly borne out in *Some Action of Her Own: The Adult Woman in Education*.[3] In an in-depth survey of the clients, directors, and former students of fifteen centers, Cless found that continuing education programs, more than other programs in higher education, were characterized by strong-willed, creative directors who translated adult needs into an astonishing array of programs within universities—practically before the universities knew what hit them.

There are two aspects of continuing education that distinguish it from other streams in education. Continuing education programs differ from those whose primary focus is *adult education*. Adult education programs stress curricula that provide basic literacy up to a median level. Many adult education programs simply extend traditional programs and offer them to an older group of people. Continuing education, in contrast, often has a corrective function. Its goal is not merely to provide remedial work or traditional work to new groups, but to actively alter aspects of the existing educational system. Continuing education programs espouse the belief that learning is a continuous process that ought to respond both to external changes in society and to an individual's internal quest for meaning. There are certain affinities between Dewey's theory of progressive education and continuing education. Rather than approaching life as an "unfolding of latent possibilities," Dewey and continuing educators take a life-cycle approach. They see life as a process of development. The role of education is to provide "conditions in which reconstruction is facilitated."[4]

A second characteristic distinguishes continuing education programs from traditional programs. A traditional college education rests on a *banking and storage model* of education. This model has at least two meanings. It can denote a traditional view of the life span that divides a person's life into two main stages: first, the years of schooling that prepare for life, years in which one accumulates deposits that will later be cashed in; second, the working years or the years of life itself when one draws interest on an earlier educational investment. This view of education as capital is incongruous with the basic philosophy of continuing education. Another meaning given to the banking-and-storage model refers specifically to the method of teaching in which the student is treated as a depository or receptacle.[5] Continuing educators hope to discover a way of "integrating the rich life experiences of older people in the classroom, of tying the lessons of experience to the conceptual structure of subject matter instead of sacrificing one to the other."[6] Continuing education programs are based on an *exchange model* of learning, which sees the process of education as fundamentally a method of exchanging experiences under tutelage in order to reach new levels of understanding for both leader and participants.

What Caused the Boom?

We have come to understand fairly clearly the demographic, sociological, and technological changes that have made education in later life an attractive possibility. These changes can be summarized as follows:

1. The college-age population (the cohort group of eighteen- to twenty-one-year-olds) is stabilizing. The expansion that characterized higher education in the 1950s and 1960s is holding steady, if not declining. Thus colleges seek new students.
2. As a population we are living longer, having more leisure time both during and at the end of our working lives. Thus people seek education both as a new leisure activity and as a means to learn more skills to make leisure time more productive.[7]
3. For many, technology has meant alienation from work and dissatisfaction both with what one does to earn money and with doing it for a very long time. Career dissatisfaction has emerged as an important issue for individuals in their forties and fifties. That dissatisfaction pushes some people back to school.
4. The knowledge explosion every few years also propels people back to school—both those who are happy doing what they are doing as well as those who would like to try new career ventures.
5. Women, minorities, and the academically disadvantaged who did not receive the benefits of higher education in earlier decades are demanding entrance. These new learners often require different kinds of assistance in succeeding as students; their demands have created the support services characteristic of continuing education programs.
6. Youth themselves seem attracted to travel and cooperative education programs, suggesting that there may be a place for "real world" experiences intermingled with "education." The reverse of that proposition suggests itself—adults who live and work in the so-called real world might also be able to absorb education meaningfully. Both the creation of the College Level Entrance Program (CLEP) and the development of competency-based evaluative mechanisms for adults all point to the attempt to translate life experiences into academic credit.
7. Research has demonstrated that the ability to learn is correlated with

interest levels and relevance of topic more than the aging process, making fallacious the facile assumption that you must have acne in order to learn. The spread of the Elderhostel program is ample evidence of the eager demand for education by older people.

For these and a host of other reasons created by our postindustrial society, the idea that people can and should learn throughout their lives has gained acceptance. According to the Carnegie Commission on Nontraditional Study, one in three adults enrolls in some kind of learning activity each year. Adults demand greater convenience in setting and format; they seek institutions where the emphasis is on serving students rather than granting degrees.

Who Has Been Providing Education for the Adult?

The list of agencies that provide some sort of education to adults is long: colleges and universities, libraries, agricultural extension bureaus, professional societies, some public school systems, the extension services of universities, the Red Cross, training and development offices in business and industry, city recreation departments, community colleges, YMCAs and YWCAs, the mass media, counseling centers for women, and many more. Their educational efforts were characterized by the fact that these groups each worked with a specific population that had expressed some immediate educational objective. Only in the last decade have agencies begun to find out about each other, share techniques and programs across domains, and plan cooperatively for community needs on a long-range basis. The assumption underlying cooperation (prodded, one might add, by federal funding guidelines that mandate an awareness of other programs) is that, with so much continuing education going on, there is probably less need to create a new program than there is to identify existing programs and then refer people to the most appropriate program.

What Do Adults Want When They Come to Continuing Education?

Perhaps the best scheme of conceptualizing adult educational needs was put forth by A. A. Liveright, former secretary of the International Congress of University Adult Education, in Alvin Eurich's *Campus 1980*, a collection of papers about "the shape of the future in American higher education."[8] The key principles in this plan were, first, that continuing education could become the instrument by which professional, academic, and business enclaves become accessible to each other and to "outsiders" as learning resources; and, second, that the most significant overall goal for continuing education is the extension of a broad-gauged civic literacy and sense of empowerment throughout the population.

Liveright's plan called for a college of continuing education, working cooperatively with the media, urban governments, community agencies, and arts and sciences institutions, through the following four "institutes": (1) the Institute for Occupational and Professional Development, which would answer the needs of the adult as worker; (2) the Institute for Personal and Family Development, which would help the adult achieve maximum effectiveness in family and personal relations; (3) the Institute for Civic and Social Development, which would prepare the adult for participation in community, national, and world affairs; and (4) the Institute for Humanities and Liberal Development, which would encourage self-realization and personal fulfillment.

Adjunct faculty were to be drawn from corporations and professions; students were to participate in determining curricula; centers with a special contemporary focus (such as metropolitan studies and problem solving) were to be created in accordance with social need. Liveright acknowledged that his plan had a utopian tone, but he provided an appendix giving details of programs at a number of U.S. universities and colleges that were already engaged in carrying out components of his scheme. Since he wrote, more and more programs have been created around these four dimensions.

Will Universities Become Centers of Lifelong Learning?

If I have painted a picture of the great ease with which all this is happening, I have painted a false picture. There are still a large number of tension points and unanswered questions in what I think is clearly a transition from the university as we have known it in the United States for the last one hundred years to the university as a lifelong learning resource. What are some of these tension points?

The first question that always emerges when older students are discussed is, yes, but are they good students? The only reasonable response to this perennial question has to be, well, it depends on what you mean by "good." Measured only by grades, they certainly are competitive. A large-scale research project on returning students at the University of Michigan is showing that returning students have better-than-average grades. But to look at grade point averages alone is to ignore what continuing educators have been advocating, namely, that older students will force a reevaluation of what and how we teach. In

Individualizing the System,[9] a number of authors argue that, with the completion of the equality revolution (that is, opening admissions to diverse groups in
society), the quality revolution must begin (that is, the challenge to reconstruct
the curriculum to teach the new learners).

Adults are demanding consumers in higher education, as two anecdotes will
illustrate. In a recent guest editorial in the *Washington Post*, English professor
Burlington Lowery said his greatest complaint was that adult students were
overzealous and overconscientious; he was simply not accustomed to such
seriousness of purpose.[10] Nathan Teitel, a playwright who teaches at New York
University, is worth quoting at length on the subject:

> On that memorable Monday, precisely at 6:10 P.M., I began my non-
> credit lecture on *Hamlet* with a hollow heartiness. But in the front row
> Miss Steigmuller was unwrapping a tuna fish sandwich, and next to her
> Mr. Elias was munching on a Hershey bar. I was forced to look up. Forty-
> three tired, hungry faces, ranging in age from eighteen to a stray seventy.
> My first class at New York University's School of Continuing Education,
> the largest adult school in the country. Most of my students had come
> directly from work: scrubbed nurses—still in uniform, chic secretaries,
> ravaged fashion models, engineers, computer operators, college drop-
> outs, wan elementary school teachers, bookkeepers, and fugitive house-
> wives. "Sorry if I disturbed you," said Miss Steigmuller apologetically as
> she carefully wrapped up the remainder of her sandwich. I stared at her
> for a long moment. In preparation for my trial by fire, I had wolfed a
> T-bone steak. "You can eat," I suddenly exclaimed. "You can all eat—if
> you want to. Hamlet won't mind." Silence. Not even a titter. (But did a
> fleeting smile caress Miss Steigmuller's pinched face?) I shoved my cards
> away and began again: "*Hamlet* is a play about a mixed-up human be-
> ing—like all of us . . ." The radiator in the corner stopped hissing.
>
> The years ran. I taught courses in drama, poetry, the short story, and
> the novel. The faces were different, but the primary need was the same.
> What they invariably sought in literature was something more than either
> mere entertainment or cultural adornment; literature was always a means
> to an end, a tool to use in their unending search for self-realization. The
> classroom was their oasis: a place where they could feel free enough to
> give vent to their buried emotions and ideas. Everything had to be related
> to their lives, their experiences, their problems. Thus, in considering any
> work, background, biographical material, and specific content always
> came first. Form, technique, concepts of aesthetics—these had to be in-

troduced obliquely. "Dreiser lays the truth on the line," pronounced Mr. Timothy Walsh, embryonic stockbroker. "You bet he does!" Miss Krabowski's sputtering, angry voice plunged on: "Not like Hemingway—that male chauvinist! He cares more about those dopey bulls than he does about women." Slightly irrelevant. But the free-for-all was on. At a judicious moment—or so I hoped—I raised my hand. They were ready now, eager, waiting for the revelation. I tried not to disappoint them.

Particularly for those students who never went to college, the man at the head of the class is the final authority—the highest court of appeal. I wore my robe diffidently. I couldn't do otherwise, since I learned as much from them as they did from me. Their insights and fresh perceptions never failed to amaze me. Always they insisted on getting down to the bedrock of human relationships: "Did Cordelia have to tell the absolute truth to her senile, old father?"[11]

Let me conclude by illustrating how we at Duke are responding to the challenges and tensions I have discussed. My thesis is that we must design diverse educational programs which speak to the evolving needs of adult members in a complex society. By doing so, the whole educational endeavor will be greatly improved.

The uniqueness of our Institute for Learning in Retirement is an excellent case in point. We know from the swelling enrollments in our noncredit programs that this community is rich in especially talented and able retired people. We know that efforts to involve retired persons in the community are usually on a voluntary basis and require the individual to give of himself or herself to serve others while not dealing directly with his or her own evolving needs. We know that feelings of belonging to and being comfortable with a like-minded group are critical to adult learning experiences. By applying this understanding in a unique format, we believe we can offer a teaching and learning program that serves both retiree and community.

The Institute for Learning in Retirement is a self-governing group of older persons who design their own curriculum and teach their own classes, drawing on the resources of the university when they feel the need to do so. The classes in the first semester spanned the range from coping skills to enrichment learning. Out of their learning comes a desire to eliminate the stereotypes under which they, as older people, live. Frequently in committee meetings members can be heard laying plans to teach undergraduates, to develop a peer-run preretirement program, to be trained to lead discussion groups for older persons who are not as well adjusted to later years as themselves. All of these activities attest to the desire of older persons to integrate learning with life, to draw on their rich and unique body of experiences to aid others. Learning in the institute is an integral part of living.

How will this program turn out? I cannot say. Very talented people are involved in its creation; many equally able individuals are among the first members. We have every reason to think that the model we have created meets both the internal and external needs of the participants and their community. The parent programs on which the institute is based certainly did.

And what about the four people I described in my introductory comments? The first one graduated last year from the Physicians Associate Program and is now engaged in full-time research. The second one got a bachelor's degree in nursing and moved to Texas, where she works as head nurse in a small hospital. The third person is still taking courses. She just hasn't decided which she likes best. The fourth person found several very good courses, decided she could do with another degree, and is now in graduate school.

Reentry Women in the Academy

The Contributions of a Feminist Perspective

From 1970 until 1982, I served as director of Continuing Education at Duke University. After a year's leave of absence, I returned to the same institution to create its Women's Studies Program. Twelve years of working with reentry women combine with my present involvement in Women's Studies for college-age students to provide a particular perspective on continuing education that forms the basis of this discussion.

I often muse on whether it might have been done "the other way around"— what it would have been like to work with women returning to higher education in the 1970s if Women's Studies had been more fully in place and the curriculum transformed to reflect women's experiences, expressions, and expectations. I submit that, without the knowledge gained by hammering away at institutions to accept and assist nontraditional students, we would not have had the angle of vision required to see how limited the educational enterprise is on gender-based questions. But I know that the obstacles returning women students faced would have been minimal if feminist scholarship had been integrated into the curriculum they received when they arrived on campus.

This chapter begins with a brief overview of the recent literature on returning women students that illustrates what has been learned in two decades of incorporating older women on the campuses through continuing education programs. It then goes on to describe the process by which one administrator, myself, came to see the contradictions between the contributions older women

This essay was first published in somewhat different form in *Educating the Majority: Women Challenge Tradition in Higher Education*, edited by Carol S. Pearson, Donna L. Shavlik, and Judith G. Touchton (New York: Collier Macmillan, 1989), pp. 90–101.

were making in the academy and the nature of the institutions they were entering. Finally, this chapter analyzes how the questions posed by returning women students illustrate the "problems" of higher education with reference to gender as much as the "problems" of a group of learners.

Returning Women Students:
Numbers, Needs, Concerns

The fact that large numbers of older women students return to U.S. campuses is an increasingly familiar theme in our society. And not only those of us directly involved in reentry programs know this. College administrators note the changing age and gender composition of their applicant pools in every school and division. Households and families adjust their lifestyles as the women in them reenter training and education at all levels to better their economic prospects as well as to enlarge their personal horizons. Schools, churches, and communities acknowledge that the stay-at-home mother is now going back to school and is no longer automatically available to form the core of their volunteer work force. Employers depend increasingly on women's recent course work and degrees to maintain the skill level of the labor force and to guarantee a competitive advantage in changing labor markets.

Who are these returning women? While no technical definition is widely used, returning women are generally thought of as over twenty-five years of age and with a history of delay or interruption in their educations. They are drawn from every racial, ethnic, and regional group. Age and educational history combine in a variety of ways to create "returning women."

When continuing education programs for women first began in the 1960s at schools, colleges, and universities of all kinds, the most frequent client was likely to be a woman in her late thirties or forties who was married, who had children now in school full time, and who was either completing an associate or baccalaureate degree or going for an advanced degree. With each decade of continuing education the woman got younger and had greater variation in her personal and educational background. By the 1980s, the category also included single women in their twenties who were dissatisfied with the direction of their first college work as well as relatively well-educated women, often with young children, who were switching fields for employment purposes.

In the beginning of the continuing education movement, returning women often evidenced doubt about the legitimacy of undertaking their plans. Women raised in the 1930s and 1940s felt doubtful about putting their own aspirations up front, accustomed as they were to putting the needs of others ahead of their own and failing to see the interrelationship between their welfare and the family's well-being. Three decades later, reflecting changing cultural norms about women, returning women were living more diverse lifestyles and were more willing to see that without their own development the happiness and well-being of those around them were stymied.

Divorce played an important part in encouraging some women to return to education. When marriages break up, one strategy women frequently follow is to seek the education necessary for employment or better employment. Many continuing education counselors, working with returning women, report that educational counseling sessions often seem more like marriage counseling sessions as returning women struggle to develop their own identities through education in the process of redefining their marital status.

The evolution and diversification of continuing education programs, running the gambit from liberal education programs for masters' degrees in elite institutions to in-house half-day training programs at places of employment, meant that returning women came to understand education more as a process than as a one-time acquisition. The earlier idea that women return to the campus to "prepare for life" gave way to the contemporary approach that learning opportunities are ongoing and that women will enter and reenter for a long time period in response to their evolving personal and professional needs. Thus, in the 1980s women of many backgrounds gained access to a wide variety of educational programs and often did so more than once, viewing it as an ongoing process of self-development.

The figures on returning women students are impressive and growing:[1]

- Women were the majority of students in higher education in the 1980s.
- By 1986 women over twenty-five constituted 24 percent of all post-secondary students.
- Returning women students are found in every type of institution, pursuing every kind of degree, while continuing to confront patterns of discrimination in some areas of study and in classroom expectations generally.
- Part-time study and enrollment in community colleges are particularly strong, both because they are more accessible to large numbers of women and because of the hesitancy on the part of the more traditional and prestigious institutions to fully welcome and integrate returning women students.
- Programs of continuing education for women vary considerably in their focus, scope, and energy; yet almost every institution of higher

learning makes some accommodations for older students, and many have been highly successful in recruiting and educating large numbers of women.

- Women who have been reentry students and are now in the work force are enthusiastic advocates in their positions as co-workers, employers, and college personnel.

In short, women return to education because they want to for personal reasons and because they have to for economic reasons, as we shall see below. What are the needs and concerns of the students, on the one hand, and of the institutions in which they matriculate, on the other, as the two meet?

The research literature on reentry women has grown so that we now have a base from which to study returning women students and on which to design and implement the programs that will meet the needs they have identified. Two recent publications review the previous research literature and demonstrate what twenty years of service and research have established. Ekstrom and Marvel describe several educational barriers facing adult women: *institutional*, the formal parts of the college process that begin with admissions credentials and run to financial aid limitations, course regulations, and lack of women-centered counseling; *situational* factors, such as class and ethnic background, family responsibilities, time conflicts, and lack of mobility; and *personal* or *psychological* concerns stemming from weak self-concepts, derived in turn from the position of women in American culture and society generally.[2] The authors go on to describe in some detail the many programs for reentry women that work. The programs "work," in the authors' view, because they start with women's strengths as students (while acknowledging their relative lack of resources and skills in certain areas) and readjust the institutional policies to make them flexible enough to give reentry women a chance to succeed.

Holliday describes the specific policies of institutions of higher learning that demand alteration if reentry women are to be welcomed, citing the research literature supporting various recommendations.[3] She highlights changes in recruitment policy, admissions procedures, orientation programs, financial aid restrictions, staff attitudes, child care availability, and counseling to facilitate women's successful reentry.

The voices of reentry women themselves have begun to be heard. The Modern Language Association compiled a rich collection of women's experience in *The Road Retaken*.[4] Twenty-five women, writing from diverse perspectives, describe their eventual successes in resuming their education. A second portion of the book documents the place of women as employees of higher education, all written by women who took less than a direct path to their present positions. The final section puts forth the view of women who struggle on the perimeters of the academy and the ways in which the academy's mores resist change. Taken together, the essays give a clear portrait of the women served by reentry programs and their reactions to the processes they have undergone. While no single pattern can summarize the reentry process, all twenty-five women exhibit courage in the face of obstacles, asking of the academy that it focus on their potential and not be bound by an evaluation of their particular current characteristics or discriminatory attitudes toward women's achievement in general.

The title of McLaren's discussion of working-class women in adult education in Britain, *Ambition and Realization,* speaks directly to the need to conceptualize broadly when describing as well as planning for reentry women.[5] McLaren surveys the growth of adult education and then explores in depth a group of students from working-class backgrounds. The women she interviews see reentry programs as enabling them to change their social position, to provide them with improved job qualifications, and to assist them in finding more rewarding work. While ever cognizant of the obstacles in realizing their ambitions, she suggests that with a solid matching of individual learners and institutional needs, the goals of both can be and have been met.

The Personal as Political: Excerpts from an Administrator's Journal

The demographic trend is clear: reentry women are an important constituency in higher education. The experiences of continuing education personnel who serve adult women are equally clear: adult women students possess characteristics that are both strengths and liabilities in the reentry process. Generally, they do very well as students if their liabilities can be addressed and their strengths allowed to flourish. The lessons of twenty-five years of program development substantiate these claims; with requisite leadership and support, the academy can and does modify itself and exhibit the flexibility needed to incorporate older women as students. And the academy is rewarded; reentry students tend to do well and to show appreciation to the institutions that welcome them. And yet, after two decades of working with reentry women, a piece of the puzzle has been missing.

Clues about the characteristics of the missing piece are found in these episodes drawn from my administrative memory.

Episode 1

A biochemist by doctoral training, this reentry woman came to me through a continuing education course on life planning, explaining that the research laboratory was too demanding now and that she had come to feel she had made a career mistake. Her interest in human interaction, fostered by her work as a mother and as a civic leader, was now more decisive; she wanted to do postdoctoral courses in child development. Arrangements were made, and some faculty in the psychology department were eager to utilize her talents and interests. After several courses, the enthusiasm on the department's side slackened. She was too persistent in her questioning, I was told. She doubted the assumptions and methods behind much of the research she was being asked to replicate. Based on her experiences as a mother and as a female leader, she asked for a fundamental rethinking of what was being studied; her new colleagues resisted.

Episode 2

I discouraged another reentry woman from taking a course in American politics from an instructor who happened to be her neighbor. I felt that, for the woman's first course, she ought to try something with no previous history that might entangle things. No, she insisted, if she was going to go back for her B.A., she might as well start with her friend and neighbor; he had promised to look out for her and set her straight on political science. She took the course, and the problem that arose was not the one I had anticipated. She handled the friendship and personal relationship with maturity. What she could not handle was the subject matter. American politics as she understood it dealt with people, including women, and issues; she had, after all, been a League of Women Voters chapter president. But the course as presented to eighteen-year-olds never mentioned women, the issues she thought were on the political agenda, or the relationship between the women's movement and the changing face of politics. Not only could she never get an answer for why the material she valued was absent, she could not get the faculty member to value the question itself. Women, according to the party line, were not active in politics, and little more needed to be said.

Episode 3

Another reentry woman's love of literature was staggering. Mention a character, a plot, a poem, and she could tell you something about it, how she had reacted when she read it, and what the critics said about it. I thought she would sail through her English literature courses and was already making mental plans for encouraging her to go on to graduate school. As she resumed her college work, reading more and being required to read it from a more structured perspective increasingly frustrated her. One day, after a long talk, she said things were a bit better. She was reading Virginia Woolf and Simone de Beauvoir and Doris Lessing regularly now on the side—they were making the reading of *real* literature possible. By *real* literature, of course, she was referring to the *canon*, the writing of white males and an occasional female that constitutes the literature major. Confronted with the question of why what spoke to her was not considered literature, she explained that she would think about that problem when she finished—when, indeed, I feared she would be finished as the predetermined product of a process that denied the legitimacy of her own voice, a female voice, imposing another in its place.

Thinking back to these three students and many others like them, I realize that, as director of Continuing Education during the 1970s, I sensed something was wrong, although I lacked a coherent explanation at the time. I urged older women students to speak up, to refuse accommodation in the classroom as their political mode, to believe in and pursue the values of rationale disclosure, the very values espoused by the settings in which they found themselves.

Occasionally, confrontation between reentry women and faculty led to understanding, and understanding led to modification in what was taught. But more often, questioning led to silence. The older students made do with two worlds, the world of the classroom and the world of their experiences. The faculty and staff claimed that as soon as older women got accustomed to the campus, they would settle in, questions would disappear, and acceptance of "the way we do things" would emerge. The silence persisted through the granting of degrees, for power lay on one side, confusion on the other, and no explanatory system was readily available to say, "Now, look here . . ."

It is at this point in my experience as a program director that the new scholarship on women pointed to the missing piece of the puzzle. The early discussion of Title IX, first brought up by the American Council on Education's Commission on Women, linked the question of *who* was studying *what*. As I became more familiar with the feminist scholarship in my own field (African politics and development studies) and the interdisciplinary discourse that was sweeping the social sciences and humanities, I came to see that many of the obstacles to reentry were as rooted in the curriculum as in policies of the academy and that changes were needed to address both content and structure. Continuing education and women's studies are often linked, spoken of as parallel movements in higher education, but the way one informs the other is rarely examined in detail.[6] This is what I propose to do in the final section of this chapter.

The research literature on reentry women, the experiences of program administrators, and the testimonies of older students themselves agree with each other about what the obstacles are and the successful strategies for overcoming them. Prescriptions urge institutions out of their inertia and individuals out of their hesitancies, asking each to assume a risk-taking stance. Success stories for programs and people underscore the appropriateness of such advice.

What would this process of matching nontraditional students with traditional colleges and universities have been like if feminist scholarship had been a central force in the day-to-day workings of the schools? If the understandings derived from a study of gender systems had informed our thinking about causes and consequences? Quite different, I would argue. Consider the following examples.

A primary institutional obstacle to reentry women has been their lack of preparation and their lack of comparability to the younger students who form the majority of their class cohort. Through two decades of continuing education, programs have helped these older women get up to speed through courses, individual counseling, and general support. The women's studies perspective on this problem of the lack of fit between person and place gives us another angle of vision. It suggests that there may be less wrong with the *person* than the *place* and that the problem in making a match between the two should be conceptualized as a problem of "What constitutes a student?" rather than as "We know a student when we see one, now let's work on making this person more studentlike."

Developments in women's history spring to mind to illustrate how the issue might be recast. As social historians began to investigate women's lives—What did they do on the western frontier? How did they experience industrialization? What did they think about the moral climate of their communities? and so forth—social historians began to argue that American history as it was conceptualized was only a partial history of the American people's experience. They pointed out that understanding any of the standard topics would be both improved and corrected by an expanded definition of the topic, expansion that focused on what was happening to women and how men's and women's experiences came together to form the whole historical picture. In the process of incorporating women, historians are redefining what constitutes the study of history. Similarly, by incorporating older women students, colleges and universities have had to confront questions about what constitutes a student.

In fact, of course, both the development of women's history and the evolution of incorporating nontraditional students were going on simultaneously in higher education during the 1970s. But as reform movements they only rarely informed one another. Hindsight allows us to see how much easier it would have been to conduct the continuing education debate if the historical debate had been more fully developed and more widely disseminated outside the profession. Older women students would have been seen as new students more frequently than as deficient students, just as women's history is coming to be seen as a new perspective on all history as opposed to a specialized development in a corner of the discipline. Having argued the case for older students, those students and their mentors were among the first advocates of giving women's history a central place in the curriculum. Sensitive to what exclusion meant in a personal domain, they welcomed inclusion in the political domain of the profession.

Another obstacle for women returning to college has been articulated as the tension between their present and anticipated situations. How can a mother take courses as opposed to helping her kids with their homework? How can a wife put priority on her goals and yet keep a marriage and her husband's career in central focus? How can women of diverse backgrounds utilize institutions designed for elite white men? Situational factors, said to prevent women's reentry and to limit their educational success, take on a different cast if seen from the perspective of feminist scholarship.

Feminist scholarship in the social sciences, particularly sociology and anthropology, has argued that women's private lives as mothers, wives, workers, and carriers of culture are not only a matter of personal choices and circumstances but the result of societal arrangements created by social and historical forces and reinforced by the expectations and the training that accompany such arrangements. Feminist sociologists and anthropologists have been looking closely at the way in which economic, political, and social relationships shape the options open to individuals and showing that individual women are the recipients of a cultural system that defines and shapes women's expectations of themselves as well as the culture's view of their place. Seen from the perspective of feminist scholarship, the situational obstacles that women face in returning to college are as much social as personal. Addressing those obstacles takes on a more informed and effective cast when the woman ceases to blame circumstances and begins to address policies. While a feminist analysis of the situational obstacles by no means eliminates them, it does provide the framework of redress that is lacking when an individual reentry woman flounders over the reasons for her difficulties. Having seen how linked the personal and professional lives of reentry women were, advocates of continuing education found in the scholarly debates about private-public linkages in women's lives a powerful analytic tool for addressing individual needs and institutional policies.

A third example, drawn from the final set of reasons said to prohibit older women's easy reentry, again illustrates the contribution of a feminist analysis. Conventional wisdom has it that older women students lack confidence, rely on others for validation, and have relatively weak self-concepts. While the literature and the experiences of those returning through continuing education are replete with instances of women who grow into their own as a result of returning to school, there is consensus on the fact that many women began with few psychological resources. Why? Again the new scholarship on women suggests answers to that question.

In eliminating errors of fact about women, of adding knowledge about them, and of creating new theories about the way gender systems work, the new scholarship on women directly attacked the foundation on which women's views of themselves as inferior beings rests. Feminist literary criticism tells us women did write, even if their writing is not anthologized. It goes on to analyze women's writing on the basis of what was said, how it was said, and to whom, rather than holding it up against male-defined standards of excellence. Art history and music composition, slow to include and value the works of women, are beginning to study pre-twentieth-century painters and the musical compositions of women over the centuries. Philosophers have started to deal with feminist questions such as rape and abortion, to explore gender perspectives on moral reasoning, and to critique the ancient thinkers for their gender-based constructions of the world. All of these endeavors mean that women's experiences, expressions, and expectations are becoming part of transmitted knowledge. Through exposure to that knowledge, women, especially older returning women, validate their own sense of self and are empowered to see that women's contributions have a place in systems of meaning. Once women's creative activities are in focus, teachers, researchers, and students can explore the question of why they have not been spotlighted, what it means to women and men to keep them invisible, and how making them visible alters peoples' perceptions of men's and women's capabilities. Having worked so very hard for twenty years to get returning students recognized as visible citizens of the campus community, continuing educators readily appreciate the personal and psychological contributions that studying women makes to the individual women doing the studying.

The results of the continuing education movement, modified policies, and admitting more older students have contributed, albeit indirectly, to the development of women's studies. And the new scholarship on women has grown and been appreciated in part as a result of people having worked on parallel questions for nontraditional students. I have not argued that the two efforts were informed by one another, except indirectly. Nonetheless, both seek a similar campus climate, one that values diversity over homogeneity, applauds a larger picture instead of a narrower one, and affirms the contributions of all learners to the collective enterprise. Just as it would have been easier for continuing education if a feminist curriculum were in place, the curriculum transformation sought by women's studies will be made somewhat easier by the presence of reentry women on both sides of the lectern. And reentry women themselves, having borne the brunt of much of the experimentation in continuing education and the absence of the records of their lives in classroom textbooks, will benefit by the success of both developments. Access to education for women is the first goal and access to the curriculum is the second— without which the first will be a hollow victory.

Women and
the Politics
of Knowledge

In March of 1970 my husband and I were painting the bedroom of our newly purchased home. We had been in Durham, North Carolina, for six months; he had a job as an assistant professor of anthropology; I had been teaching one course on a part-time basis; and we had a seven-month-old daughter. He asked me what I was going to do next. I answered by saying that I was thinking about doing the hallway next. No, he responded, he meant what was I going to do now that I had finished teaching a temporary course and had set the date for my dissertation defense. I had no idea—no one had ever asked me to think in long-range terms, beyond the next immediate deadline of a course, a writing assignment, a degree. He persisted. What did I plan to do now that we had the house, a baby, and our Ph.D.'s? I became angrier and angrier. At the time I thought I was angry with him—so angry, in fact, I threw the paintbrush at him. Later I came to understand that I was angry with myself and my situation. I had to face the fact that I had no plan. I had grown up not being expected to have a plan. Now there was an expectation around, which he had voiced, that someone like me was supposed to have a plan.

In that episode, I see the shift that was occurring in social expectations about women and the fact that I was caught in the middle of the shift. Whenever the discussion turns to women's issues, people's underlying assumptions about how things got to be this way influence what they think about those issues. Exploring those assumptions is the necessary groundwork for acquiring new information and new understanding. Feminists have a slogan for this: "You can't just add women and stir."

I gave different versions of this paper to different audiences. This version was presented on September 14, 1990, at a seminar at the Executive Training Center of Ford Motor Company, Detroit. Presenting with me were Alice Kaplan, associate professor of French and French literature; Cynthia Herrup, associate professor of history and law; and Angela O'Rand, associate professor of sociology.

Therefore, I've organized my overview into the following three parts: an analysis of the women's movement and feminism over a twenty-year period; an examination of women's studies as a body of thought evolving with them; and a look at feminism today, especially on campus.

Feminism as a Social Movement

Sociologists, historians, and political activists understand some things about social movements. They know that in order for social change to occur, at least three sets of ingredients are necessary. First, there have to be individuals and groups who are dissatisfied with what they have relative to what others have. Second, those individuals and groups need to have leaders who can articulate their grievances; an organizational network of some kind that brings them together; an ideology that explains to them and to others why things are the way they are and what might be done differently; and resources to sustain their goals. But individuals and ideas can mix over long periods of time without becoming an active social movement. A third ingredient is needed: a set of precipitating events that focuses energies.

In the United States during the 1960s the ingredients existed for feminism to emerge as a social movement. The basic conditions of contemporary life were shifting. More and more women, at all points in the life cycle, were spending more and more time in wage-earning jobs. The birth control pill meant that for the first time in history pregnancies could be planned by large numbers of women with relative autonomy and predictability. Ideological certainty was challenged on all fronts: Freud might not have the last word on sexuality, powerful nation-states did not always win, people did not always act according to conventional expectations, the presence of peoples from around the globe challenged traditional "melting pot" interpretations of Anglo-American history, and so on.

Within this shifting cultural milieu, two groups of women formed that provided the precipitating events needed by a social movement. First, women on the left of the political spectrum began analyzing their own situations. They found themselves outside decision-making positions in their own organizations, assumed to be sexual partners rather than intellectual or professional colleagues. These women were operating outside society's mainstream social institutions. Their forum for generating ideas was the consciousness-raising group, small clusters of women who met in each other's homes to discuss the nature of their lives. They wrote widely of their experiences. A prime example of this process is Kate Millett's *Sexual Politics*, a book celebrating its twentieth anniversary this year.[1]

A second source of ideas and information that fueled the women's movement came from within America's major social institutions. In 1960, largely in an attempt to quiet feminists within Washington's political circles, President Kennedy appointed a national commission on the status of women, chaired by Eleanor Roosevelt. On its heels there followed state-level commissions; reports from other women's organizations, such as the American Association of University Women, Business and Professional Women, the League of Women Voters, and African American women's sororities; and congressional inquiry. These groups began documenting the realities of women's lives. They found women underpaid, legally disenfranchised, educationally discriminated against; above all, they documented the vast differences among women on the basis of race. What women were feeling, this process was documenting. Thus the situation of women came to national attention in a variety of ways. Not everyone agreed with each analysis nor were all women always included. It was a beginning.

Leaders, organizations, and ideologies developed in rapid order. We cannot detail those here. I can say that in ten short years, from the Equal Pay Act of 1963 and the Civil Rights Act of 1964 until the Supreme Court decision in *Roe v. Wade* in 1973, there was enacted a vast amount of legislation aimed at changing the resources and opportunities open to all women. These changes generated an enormous amount of thinking. In North American politics specific actions generally come before general visions. We are the heirs of this process.

Public recognition of these developments was swift. The protests at the Miss America Pageant in 1968 and the first mass rally in New York City in 1970 are but two of the well-documented instances of popular support. It is crucial to remember that while official bodies were deliberating these issues and passing laws "at the top," people, individually and in groups, in areas from TV production to Sunday school classes, were discussing changing roles for women and acting out many of those changes "from the bottom up."

And just as quickly, reactions followed. Activists quickly discovered they were not the first feminists. Women learned they had an extensive history of debating their circumstances and attempting to change them. What was initially called by the press "the women's liberation movement" came to be seen as a social movement similar to the nineteenth-century women's rights movement as well as the African American women's club movement; both were understood as part of a feminist tradition going back at least five hundred years. The idea that being female meant being different and that being different is being inferior was explored in literature and philosophy as well as in politics. Simone de Beauvoir's *The Second Sex*, published in the United States in 1953, raised the issues; Betty Friedan's *The Feminine Mystique*, published in 1963, located them in America's suburbs.[2] In politics women began to press for change. Shirley Chisholm ran for president in 1972 and Edith Green spearheaded legislative equity in Congress.

The following anecdote illustrates this process. The dictionary my mother took to college in 1933 had one entry for the word *feminism*: "a belief that men and women should have equality and a willingness to work to bring such conditions about." The dictionary my high school English teacher gave me in 1960, the year I went to college, does not have an entry for the term. My daughter, who began college in 1986, has a college dictionary with several entries. Dictionaries are records of ideas that in turn re-create those ideas. In the late 1920s, with the suffrage amendment still on the public agenda, feminism was a recognized social movement. In the 1940s, 1950s, and early 1960s, feminism vanished from popular consciousness, surviving only in specialized places. By the early 1970s, feminism was again—albeit with new characteristics—a recognized part of our political and intellectual landscape.

Feminist activity generated indifference, consolidation, and opposition. During the 1970s and 1980s, many women who were not particularly politicized experienced profound and positive benefits from the women's movement. Poll data throughout the decade show an increasing awareness of the issues put on the national agenda by the movement. Women tend to be more knowledgeable about these issues than men. And young women, born long after the pill, Title IX, and women in medical school, grew up taking equality for granted.

While feminism as a social movement disappeared from the front pages of the papers and many people voiced the opinion that things had changed about as much for women as was necessary—and articles about its death could be found—feminism was consolidating in hundreds of ways throughout society: the creation of centers for battered women in almost every community, the recognition of rape as an act of violence instead of sex, the accommodation by the military to the presence of women, the entrance of women into the first ranks of the professions and sports, the recognition of lesbians and the questions they raise for a contemporary understanding of womanhood, and the increasing leadership role of women in public life.

Opposition too is part of the picture of a social movement. Opposition first developed in the mid-1970s when the Equal Rights Amendment (ERA) failed to be added to the Constitution. Unlike the legislation and court interpretations that preceded it, the amendment asked for the establishment of a principle—fifteen words that say men and women are to be treated the same. North American culture is very pragmatic, and there is a history of accepting incremental changes rather than philosophical principles. People sensed that the idea behind the ERA was of a different order; in the absence of female decision makers in the state legislatures, the amendment failed.

Opposition to feminism developed further during the 1980s, a conservative decade in which gender consciousness and feminism both grew in strength as ideas. By gender consciousness, I mean the idea on the part of the New Right that differences between men and women are fixed in particular ways and should remain that way. Women are assigned the roles of wife and mother, nurturers of families and society. Government reinforces these roles through policies that support them. The difficulties of restoring the Civil Rights Act, the abortion debates, the gender gap in electoral politics, the divide over whether violence against women in public speech is a first amendment issue or a question of civil rights, the growing controversy over the Family Leave Act— all are evidence of the fact that the issues brought to public consciousness by the women's movement are successful enough to encounter strong resistance.

Throughout these twenty years, women's visions have not been homogeneous. Some women see themselves as free individuals and seek personal solutions to women's issues through careers that parallel those of men. Others base their feminism on a belief in individual effort but are much more concerned that that effort be directed toward social change for all men and women. Still others value their role in communities and family, seeking to work within these places as the basis for change. To cite just one example, African American women tend to see the family as a source of support for themselves and their goals, whereas white women often view families as restraints if not barriers.[3]

The Contribution of Women's Studies

I want to leave our account of the women's movement now and take up, albeit more briefly, a second and intertwined story, the story of women's studies. The story I have been telling is one of women largely outside the academy, working on a variety of personal and political issues designed to gain for women the same rights as men. They simultaneously advocate recognition of the particular responsibilities assigned to them by North American society and encourage debate about why these are the arrangements in the first place. The political dimensions of this story are clear: posing questions about women and gender poses questions about a vast array of our cultural and social arrangements. Those questions are unsettling to some, invigorating to others.

The story of women's studies is also a story about politics, but it is about the politics of knowledge. What is at stake here is not a piece of legislation but the more fundamental ideas and information people have, how they get them, and what use they make of them. Let me explain.

Women have been pressing for entrance into schools and colleges for hundreds of years, with African American and white women pursuing separate paths. By the mid-1800s in North America, they were either building their own seminaries or getting into the newly built academies. They were successful in getting into the classroom. They did not succeed in being part of the curriculum. It took the women's movement of the 1960s to make women the subjects and not just the objects of study.

The women's movement grew at the same time that higher education was expanding in the 1960s, responding to many of the same cultural and demographic shifts. For the first time since the turn of the century, the proportion of women going for advanced degrees was increasing; their talents and energies were valued in the post-Sputnik climate of the early 1960s. By and large those women, like the four of us here, and I suspect like many of you, participated in a male academy. We had few if any female teachers. We did not study anything about women. And we certainly did not understand our own lives and circumstances as examples of the very trends furthered by feminism. Like me, reacting to queries about plans by throwing paintbrushes, we did not know how our personal pursuit of advanced degrees and research on questions of women and gender would come together.

But as women entered higher education and as feminism grew, the very social process that created both developments became the object of study. Sometimes we as scholars were asked by activists to answer some specific question: Did women have a history of striving for civic rights? Did they join in coalitions with other disenfranchised groups? Had women written novels in the past? How were we to understand women's distinctive mental health needs? Sometimes faculty and students themselves were active in the movement and brought their concerns back to their studies. If women were claiming that inclusive language was imperative, what did we know about how women's speech compared with men's? If women were seeking ordination, was there any precedent? If women were being recruited into science and engineering, what did the earlier recruitment waves of the 1880s and 1920s tell us about the chances of success or failure? How did the history of ideas about women square with the reality of women's lives and their own ideas about their circumstances?

It is difficult to understand just how absent women are from the knowledge systems that Anglo-American education has put in place. Men write extensively about women, and this literature gives us the impression that we have knowledge about women. But if we closely examine what is taught, we can identify critical gaps that throw into question many of the generalizations we think are universal.

We know the names of only a few great women and hundreds of great men. Why are countless books in this country adorned with a quote of Alexis de Tocqueville and never Harriet Martineau? We think of women as exceptions and anomalies, not as ordinary and human. While we've heard of Sojourner Truth and Harriet Tubman, most of us know little about the daily struggles by which African American women nurtured families under slavery. Why is it that lists of characteristics associated with a healthy personality (confident, for example) all come from the list of male traits, while items from the female list (such as supportive) never appear? We have almost no record of women's lives in their own words and from their own point of view. Thus we have known little about how girls become women, although we have thousands of social science studies and just as many novels about how boys become men. We have little understanding of how cultural ideas about femininity and masculinity are socially constructed—that is, determined more by the values and beliefs of people than by the inherent characteristics of women or even by the material conditions of the society in which they live. Thus we attribute female attention to detail or concern with relationships to some unspecified aspect of femaleness rather than to strict cultural expectations that put women in the role of maintaining domestic order and family relationships.[4] And we have paid almost no attention to how the power in gender relations reflects social arrangements. We now understand that the story of Eve and the subsequent interpretation of man as ruling over woman are artifacts of the subsequent translator's work and not the way things were in biblical times.[5] Yet the Eve myth is all-pervasive in our culture and gives us a basic definition of who women are and what we can expect of them.

Using feminist scholarship, we can now study the social construction of Eve. Can we unlearn the ideas and policies built upon that construction? Can we reconceptualize women, emphasizing characteristics other than sexuality as their primary essence? And if we do discuss women with greater complexity and more accuracy, can we imagine women who are not white and middle class? Differences among women, the ways in which race, class, age, and sexual identity intersect with gender to create many women, are rarely mentioned.[6] Think of the number of times we hear generalizations about women that begin with, "Well, women usually . . ."

It should be clear at this point that the claims of feminist scholars have not gone down easily in the academy. To say that what we have known is incomplete, even inaccurate, is to challenge the people who create and teach the knowledge we critique. Many scholars are deeply threatened by the new approaches and have become defensive. Many are intrigued by what feminist scholars are doing and have begun to borrow some of their findings and approaches. A few have become actively engaged in researching and teaching the questions.

Let's relink the story of women's studies to the story of feminism by pointing out that both looked at the status quo and found it lacking. Both insist on a women-centered perspective and encourage concomitant changes. And they are clearly in conversation with one another. The ideas of feminist scholars and authors are read and debated by women and men in the movement. The changes in everyday life won by the movement become the conditions of life for professors and the material for scholarly analysis. While maintaining distinct priorities, both groups seek continuing conversation, for both subscribe to the central idea that the personal is political and both now have the data to prove what was once just a belief.

What Difference Does Women's Studies Make?

The argument so far has been that feminism as a social movement and that women's studies as an intellectual challenge to what we have thought and known are joined in an understanding that women's and men's lives are the result of social arrangements and cultural practices, not idiosyncratic personal cases. They see these arrangements as having deep economic, political, religious, and cultural roots that are not easily changed. Yet they join in a commitment to confronting and changing such conditions. I want to conclude my discussion with a look at the ways in which both of these developments appear to be influencing young women and men. This too is the kind of topic that requires a doctoral dissertation rather than five minutes. Nonetheless, I think we can get some strong indications about what is happening if we listen to the students themselves describe their learning.

Up to this point I have been stressing content. I have been talking about issues and ideas. But when I turn to what students are learning, the discussion must switch to process and how students link learning and living. Their approach can be summed up in the title of a new research project on women's studies being conducted by the National Women's Studies Association called *The Courage to Question*.[7] Students in women's studies question, and it takes courage to do so. They are learning about the women's movement in many of their classes. They are surrounded by information about gender and engage in many conversations about it. Many of them seek postgraduate work that integrates their concern about women's issues with their particular skills and interests. They know that social arrangements are both liberating and constraining conditions for women and men, and they know a bit about why.

Listen to the ways that they are combining what public figures and their teachers say and developing a critical perspective of their own.

Students talk a great deal about the contradiction they see between one statement—you can be anything you want to be—and another—women are this or that. The tension comes up most acutely when students listen seriously to career advice from their mentors and then hear the popular culture's messages about brutal treatment of women. Here is how one young woman, a junior in the introductory Women's Studies course, described the contradictions:

My friend says "Sexism just doesn't really exist any more. Modern women can do whatever they want to. Discrimination against women doesn't happen any longer."

If I can do whatever I want, then why am I terrified to walk to the Bio-Sci building every Sunday evening for my sorority meeting? How many men wander up and down their halls, looking for someone to walk them to their cars after dark? And how many men would be blamed or called "stupid" or "asking for it" if they couldn't find someone to walk with and were attacked on the way to the parking lot?

If sexism doesn't really exist any more, then why can I not watch a Duke basketball game on TV without seeing barely clad bimbos in every beer commercial? Why are cars and alcohol marketed as tickets to fulfilling men's fantasies: acquiring numerous, young, buxom women (girls) to decorate their automobiles or serve them beer?

If discrimination against women just doesn't happen anymore, then why are only 2 percent of people in Congress female? And why am I, by virtue of my anatomy, denied freedoms which every day men take for granted—going to the record library on East Campus any time it's open, and not only before dark; selecting my clothing by what *I feel like* wearing, and not what may be interpreted as provocative; inviting an acquaintance (Duke student or not!) into my room to talk; the unquestioned ability to control my own body.

If sexism really doesn't exist any longer, then how come, when I go to the movies, the "ideal" couple is portrayed by Richard Gere, who is probably forty-five years old, and Julia Roberts, who is probably twenty-two? If men become distinguished as they age (Robert Redford, Sean Connery . . .) but women are desirable only if they are young, is this double standard not sexist? And if sexism doesn't exist, then why am I told I am overreacting or being silly if I point this double standard out to my friends as we leave the theater?

If economic discrimination against women doesn't happen any longer, then how do you account for the study which has proven that women with generous financial resources are less likely to marry? And that the best chance a poor, divorced mother has of improving her economic status is through remarriage?

If women can do whatever they want to, then why is "women's work," housework and child-rearing, still done by women—maids and day-care workers—when upper-class women have careers? And why is this work still devalued, seen as "acts of love," not as work? And when these services are paid for—why are zoo attendants paid more than child care workers?

If sexism doesn't exist anymore, then why am I so angry?[8]

Seeing such contradictions, students question the idea that women can or should become just like men. A senior woman, writing about abortion in a course on reproductive technologies, describes how she has given up the idea that she should deny the issues about herself that are peculiar to being female:

I've struggled a lot with the place of sexuality in my life. I guess I would rather not have to deal with my sexuality—I want to be judged by my intellectual merits, and things like sex differences "get in the way." According to that reason, abortion is important because it allows a woman to lead a "normal" life—sexuality can be hidden, taken for granted, and taken care of with abortion—and decide for herself when she is ready to disrupt her life and bear a child. Of course, though, we cannot ignore our sexuality as many of us try to do. Maybe if we were more comfortable with our sexuality women would be freer in that we would openly practice whatever orientation we wanted with as many people as we wanted (taking into account disease prevention). If contraception and education were not hindered, and abortion freely obtainable, women would be unburdened of the many risks that just being a woman entails. Imagine such a world. Women would have more chance for success in business, in planning a two-career life, or simply being independent and single, and would not be as dependent on men. In many ways, restrictions on abortion only keep women in the cycle of dependency, whether it be dependency on the back-alley doctor, on a father or boyfriend, or even on the welfare system of our patriarchy. . . . I think the pure empowerment that abortion's legality offers will help many women feel more in control of their lives and this will run over into other areas of their lives. . . . I know, however, that we cannot redress all of women's problems today with the right to abortion. But at least freedom of choice is a start, hopefully with many repercussions. (Maybe that's what all those pro-lifers are worried about).[9]

These questions lead to a third question, which has to do with how to value that which is female and to reassess that which is valorized because it is male. In this first reflection, a female graduate student in religion thinks about the ways in which what men do is okay whereas the same practice is devalued when women do it:

Funny how we in women's studies are so concerned with the issue of the relationship between emotional/personal and the scholarly. Yet one of my male professors thinks nothing of spending ten or fifteen minutes each class telling personal anecdotes, or of writing his personal piques (even using first-person language!) in articles which he publishes in "respectable" journals. In his case, the connection seems charming, affording a more intimate view of a formidable scholar. Yet I wonder if my reaction would differ if a female professor would act similarly. The case of females being "personal" in the classroom brings an entirely different set of reactions for me. So this one action, done by professors of different sexes, produces different reactions.[10]

The fourth selection is from a young man, a first-year student in a course on men's relations to feminism. He is rethinking the values he sees his father having lived. Through the study of women he has come to a reexamination of men:

I am a very closed person by nature and for a long period of time I have closed my emotions and my feelings off to the outside world. When you fail to think about or talk about emotions for a long period of time, their importance is greatly diminished. I remember myself as a very emotional person up until about high school. Over the years since then, I have pretty much detached myself completely from my emotions. This detachment was reinforced by my father. While my mother is a very emotional person, my father has always been an even-tempered man, his only outlet for feeling being an occasional outburst of anger, usually justifiable. He deeply loves, cares for, and most of all respects my mother, but I believe that he views her as being of a very different species than he is, one with inherent flaws.

I am not going to criticize my father—he is a remarkable man who most likely would have been among the "enlightened" himself had he been born forty years later. I am going to criticize myself. I believe myself to be a very emotional person. Unfortunately, I have no idea as to the nature of these emotions. I have subconsciously modelled myself in my perceived image of my father—an honorable and hardworking man capable of withholding a great deal of feeling from the outside world. I have denied myself some of life's greatest sufferings and joys because of the path I have taken. There are few things in life that make me very sad. I have been able to detach myself from most death and suffering. However, I rarely go through the ecstatic periods of joy or love that I seem to remember being capable of at some point.

It is very difficult for me to deal with people on a very intimate basis. In the past, I felt as if it was because my feelings and thoughts were very different from everyone else, and to open up to someone would not only seem to present me as being weak, but also as a bit of a bore. So I remained close-lipped about my feelings and avoided intimacy.

I no longer buy that argument. I have reached a point where I would like to open my life to another person. However, I have forgotten how. I am not capable of discerning my own emotions. Last week, I was forced to call an old girlfriend to ask her how I should deal with a new one. In a matter of minutes, she was able to tell me what I was feeling inside. I was not so much shocked by the fact that she knew—she knows me better than most. What surprised me is that I did not know.[11]

This kind of unlearning and relearning leads students to a new synthesis in both their personal and professional lives. Here is a beginning male graduate student reassessing gender balance as he has seen it through his parents:

My parents separated three years ago. It was an amicable separation—they simply no longer (if they ever actually did) loved one another enough to overcome the lack of intimacy and spiritual emptiness. Two years ago, my parents began drawing up the lines of settlement. Remarkably, even this went rather smoothly—money can't buy happiness, but it sure helps one escape from unhappiness. Anyway, the point I'm trying to illuminate revolves around my mother's demand (too strong) for 60 or 70 percent of their combined assets. She showed me the divorce counselor's memo with my mom's figures juxtaposed with my dad's. My emotional reaction was that my mom was being greedy. At the time, 50 percent even seemed a little unfair to my father, who, after all, had worked hard for thirty years to achieve his high salary. What had my mom done but raise three kids? Now don't get me wrong, I appreciate the amount of physical and psychic energy involved in child-rearing, but [Charlotte Perkins] Gilman's point was that the quality and quantity of my mother's care did not increase when my father started bringing home the big bucks and we had a big house and Volvos.

That was precisely my line of thinking two years ago. My mother argued that in 1962, women gave up their jobs at Time, Inc., and their half of the partnership became housekeeping and child-rearing. She felt that she had done her part commendably (who am I to argue?) and so, with the bargain (contract) being terminated, her investment in time and energy had come due.

Retrospectively, the terms of the contract were mutually unfair. My mother was not rewarded for her good work and my father was punished for his. Under the circumstances, it was resolved in the fairest way; my mom got most of the liquid assets and my dad took his six-figure salary to San Francisco and the incipient stock-market crash.

My mother now has "a room of her own" (an eight-room house, actually), financial independence, and relative security. She is also getting a master's in journalism at age fifty-one. It would have all been much simpler and more equal had she pursued her career from the get-go.[12]

And, finally, this young woman, earning her Ph.D. in biomedical engineering, connects what she is learning in women's studies with her life as an engineer by linking the isolation she feels with her privileged status:

I had convinced myself, or had been convinced, that I was special because of what I was doing, and that other women who *weren't* striving to be engineers or "hard" scientists were just wimps who weren't trying and weren't as good as me. (Part of this is the "exceptional woman" syndrome, part is the general prejudice of "science" against the "liberal arts.") But you spend time trying to neutralize your ability, to soothe the egos of male classmates; yet you know that you are still excluded and so you tend this little secret anger inside of yourself. And . . . because there are more women in, for example, engineering than there were twenty-five years ago, your status as "exceptional" is distorted. Yes, it's normal for women to do this, we encourage them to (or at least don't discourage them), but, no, we're not going to treat you "just like one of the boys." You're not equal, your classmates resent you, female friends find you a mystery, males in social situations are intimidated by you. So you get lonely, and then you take comfort in the idea you're "special." Society creates a category, you move into it, then you have certain experiences that end up making you reinforce and perpetuate the category. You really begin to believe you're different and superior, at the same time you feel different and inferior. This effectively blocks you from uniting with other women, having any sense of solidarity, and from doing anything to change society.[13]

What Does It Mean to Be an Educated Person?

Voices from the Duke Experience

Thirty minutes is a very short time to discuss a complex issue. Indeed, most of us spend at least thirty minutes reading what the *Chronicle of Higher Education* has to say on curricular issues in each edition!

Nonetheless, I will try to live up to my charge and address three points: What are the core issues in the current debate about higher education?[1] What has the Duke experience been? What might the future hold? Rather than take up each point in turn, I will weave them together in my analysis and in some stories I have to tell.

I begin with three preliminary remarks. First, the current discussion about the future of higher education moves between "the humanities" and "the liberal arts." When a headline screams "BATTLE OF THE BOOKS STIRS CAMPUS," the discussion usually focuses on literature and the value of the humanities per se. When the panel discussion topic is "the liberal arts today," talk broadens to include the subjects we cluster together in opposition to applied, career, or professional subjects (such as business administration, nursing, engineering, etc.).

In these remarks I am thinking in terms of the liberal arts and I am assuming that the liberal arts include all those subjects of the humanities, the social sciences, the natural sciences, and the arts that teach us a process of critical thinking. I find Florence Howe's definition of the liberal arts and what they do

This paper was presented at the North Carolina annual state meeting of the American Association of University Professors, held at Davidson College on October 30, 1988.

particularly helpful: they are interdisciplinary and unifying; they teach skills in critical analysis; they clarify issues of value judgment in education; they assume a problem-solving stance; and they promote socially useful ends.[2]

Second, a largely ignored dimension of the current debate is why it is occurring now—in 1988. Yes, the popularity of specific disciplines leads to enrollment shifts. Yes, the students we produce and the society we create never reflect our highest aspirations. But all of those conditions have held in the past and Anglo-American society has not necessarily debated higher education. It is, of course, true that we have debated the role and contribution of higher education at other times in history and with just as much vehemence. But there is something different about what is happening today. The current debate reflects neither the failure of curricular programs in particular nor the liberal arts in general, but the success of particular changes on campuses. New ways of approaching questions about the formation of knowledge on the human condition have fundamentally challenged old approaches and gained credence in the academy. The debate, then, is not about which authors belong in the academic canon but rather who the authority figures in academe are.

This brings me to my third preliminary remark. I will be using women's studies as my point of reference because it is the subject I now know best. Some would agree that it is one of the most successful examples of curriculum change. Others see it as the symbol of all that is wrong. The current debate is about what it means to be an educated person and has been sparked, at least in part, by developments that are particularly beneficial to women.

The Argument

How would I characterize the debate and what do I think is happening? To quote Edward Fiske in the *New York Times*, "Curricula are public statements of a college's values. They constitute each faculty's answer to the question: 'What does it mean to be an educated person?'"[3]

The present elevated decibel level surrounding the character of the liberal arts and higher education, their value, purpose, methods, and outcomes as witnessed in the curriculum is not about *what we teach*. Rather, it is about *how we know*, about *who knows*, about *what constitutes the process of knowing*, and about *what we do with the knowledge we generate*. I think that Bloom, Bennett, Hirsch, and others have ignored the basic issues in the discussion by turning backward rather than looking forward. In doing so, they miss at least two key aspects of the contemporary scene.

The liberal arts are not a set of facts but a process for approaching information and ideas. We all recognize that our memories—whether we mean our minds or our word processors—cannot hold all the information we collect. What we are about is finding the critical stance that allows us to process the information and arrive at values and actions consonant with carefully formulated goals.

The past is a most unreliable guide unless we are conscious of how we are constantly reinterpreting and remaking it. The past of today is not the past of yesterday or of tomorrow. We reinterpret information in light of current questions, making the past serve us. The past is more than simply a set of facts or texts and authors to be called up at will. To illustrate with a single example from my own field of political science: during the struggle for suffrage, white women frequently argued that women were men's moral superiors and that bringing them into politics through the vote would change politics dramatically, resulting in world peace. In the late twentieth century we know women's political participation is much more complex than a uniform stand on a single issue. Far from being always for peace, we know that women perpetuate violence—often against other women. We also know that times of war can be advantageous to women's activities by expanding the scope of culturally sanctioned options for women. Such reinterpretations of the relationship between governments and women grow out of the new feminist scholarship and its concern with interpreting events in light of questions appropriate to different times.

Texts as Guides

Having laid out some of my assumptions, let me now weave questions about the debate, Duke, and the future into a series of stories. I would not like to repeat the conventional abstractions and universal claims that are characteristic of this debate. Instead, I want to investigate what is happening to actual students in everyday classrooms and campus situations.

I begin with a work-study student in my office—a sophomore, African American female from the Midwest, without a major. She worked with me to revise the introductory Women's Studies course for the spring semester. She annotated a revised reading list; previewed several films; investigated colleagues' syllabi and suggested guest speakers; compiled last semester's evaluations and made appropriate suggestions for changes; and worked with the theoretical and practical questions debated in the course material. She looked at me the other day and burst out, "Does anybody else do this?" "What?" I queried, not knowing what she was asking. "Make such a big deal out of designing a course—don't they usually just do what they did the year before?" We spent the next hour talking about the teaching-learning process, the way knowledge comes into being, how ideas are modified with new ones, how critical thinking proceeds. I had a clear sense, as did she, that she understood what it means to be an educated person for the first time.

Driving home that afternoon, I reflected on how this student, serious and responsible to her family and to her race, had been gathering bits of information from disciplinary offerings and was now ready to cross boundaries and unify ideas, taking another step in the process of liberal education. Before she had started the project, she had thought of herself as a consumer of knowledge. After she had experienced participating in the process of curricular design, she became an active learner in the construction of knowledge.

I teach a graduate seminar in the history of feminist thought—fifteen first- to fifth-year students from ten departments. Here is what a third-year philosophy student wrote in her journal last week:

> After reading Harriet Martineau's *Society in America*, I went back to Tocqueville's *Democracy in America*, mostly out of curiosity, in order to compare his assessment of the position of women in American society with that of Martineau. I had read *Democracy in America* as part of a course entitled "Values and Institutions in American Society," a required course at Colgate. Being the kind of student who always read everything required, but not usually any more than that, my first observation was that although I had underlined large parts of the work I had not underlined the sections on the status of women. They, presumably, were unread. I can be fairly certain that this indicates that these parts were not assigned or considered part of the required reading for the course, which was a universitywide syllabus. So anyway, my first observation on the teaching of Tocqueville as part of the canon was that only some of his observations are considered of importance to the issue of "values and institutions in America."
>
> One finds a very different characterization of American women in Tocqueville than in Martineau's writings, but it is not so much due to the "facts" of the matter as to their interpretations of those facts. I don't mean to suggest that "facts" and "values" are distinct, but only that, although their descriptions of the material conditions are consistent, one senses a great difference in their approaches to their subject and consequently a great difference in the kinds of conclusions they reach. In short, Tocqueville, playing the role of "objective observer," is primarily interested in the condition of women in relation to his theory about the effects of equality of condition on society in general. Martineau, on the other hand, treats

women as "ends-in-themselves" rather than as one case study within the framework of some larger theory. I think that this difference of approach to the condition of women also accounts for the divergence in their assessment of the "morals" of Americans. . . .

From a comparison of Martineau's and Tocqueville's works, I think we learn as much about observer as about observed. Or, at any rate, we learn that the questions asked—or not asked—will have a great effect upon the conclusions an observer is able to draw.

Critical analysis? I suggest that the student's ability to take texts, familiar and unfamiliar, and work with them at this level of understanding is the essence of what we seek in an educated person, particularly one bound for the classroom to teach the next generation.

Students concentrating in women's studies at Duke receive recognition for their work in the form of a certificate, at both the graduate and undergraduate levels. They receive both pieces of parchment that mark their progress and titles that appear on their official transcripts. Occasionally someone in Placement Services warns them to remove the title, lest they alienate prospective employers. One Sunday in September, eleven students, male and female, from seven professional schools and departments, received certificates from the dean of the Graduate School in a ceremony before family and friends. A few days later this letter arrived:

Dear Jean,

It's the middle of the night. It is only nine hours and a dinner out since you handed out your first graduate certificates in Women's Studies.

I got out of bed at this obscene hour to share a surprise with you. I truly had no idea how much it meant to me to receive this graduate acknowledgment—and to be among the first group of people to do so—and how delightful to have a man in the first class. As I looked around that room, seeing some people I didn't know but most of whom I did—not only knew, but deeply cared for—it began to dawn on me that this was in some ways an incredible event. Here were all these men and women making *women their life's work*!

It is somehow significant that my father chose not to come yesterday (which means, in our family, he and my mother) because he had a golf event with his buddies three days later. It is significant because he has driven twice as far—committing himself to twice the time on several occasions—for events involving my next sibling—male—with a father-decipherable Ph.D. in laser engineering. My brother's contribution is clear, somehow. And he has done it by the books. My parents sent him to graduate school. He is still with him at thirty-six—flying to international conferences and patenting away. He is a father's dream son.

What is his dream daughter?

What I am realizing as I digest the award, the certificate, is that it marks literally years of struggle, perhaps a lifetime, to say that women are *first-class* citizens; that women are fully contributing members of our community. It is amazing to me, in some ways—that it has been an internal commitment of surprising strength that resulted in the events yesterday.

I am *basking* in the knowledge and the growing understanding that that room and many other rooms are filled with women and men with similar commitments. As I continue to study and to work, my relationship to that work will solidify. Right now, it feels newly coalesced, newly formed. I feel sobered, settled into that work. I have a new realization of the depth and importance and perhaps even the radical nature of what we are doing. The point of this midnight rambling is to thank you and honor a program that changes lives, that allows—encourages—such moments as I experienced.

P.S. I am going to the feminist ethics conference in Minnesota. My mother sprang for the ticket as an early Christmas. How appropriate somehow.

There is little I can add to this eloquent assessment of how empowering it is to know, to know who knows and how, to know what to do with that knowledge. This young woman's reflections clarify issues of value judgment in her education in a way that no abstract exercise can. Clearly she has been informed by previous analyses, but she is integrating them with present experiences to become an educated person.

Who is teaching these students? Faculty members, who are themselves active learners, engaged in changing their minds. This is from the report of a history professor who received summer support to revise his survey courses so that they include new scholarship on women.

Dear Jean,

I have enclosed for you copies of the new syllabi I prepared this summer to show you how I will go about "mainstreaming" women's studies in my two courses. A syllabus tells you something about a course and the mind of the instructor, of course, but in this case I do not feel that it says enough about the boost this program has given to my scholarly work as a whole.

I found that the Organization of American Historians' guidebook for mainstreaming women's history was indispensable and eminently practical. A number of their suggestions have made their way into the syllabus: the stress on Christian morality and views of gender in late antiquity, more focus on the medieval family and household, the divergent experience of women and men in the spiritual life of the Middle Ages, a more social approach to the Renaissance, and a closer look at the "crisis of the seventeenth century." I have deemphasized the "great man" approach, but designed several readings and class exercises around individuals (still the first point of reference for freshmen when they first take history). The readings about the "great man" Gregory VII, however, are balanced with the voices of historical women—Julian of Norwich and English Quaker women, for example.

While the Europe to the Eighteenth Century course went smoothly, the revision of Renaissance and Reformation Germany proved to be quite a challenge. I abandoned the former approach of beginning with religious reform and now begin the course with an examination of the primary determinants of the social experience in Central Europe: life and death, disease, family, household and gender, the material culture. When I do get to the Reformation, I deemphasize Luther and focus much more on the roles of different groups—townsmen, peasants, women—in the slow process of creating confessional cultures.

This reading and research program, aided by the grant from the Women's Studies Program, has therefore helped open up perspectives which few in my field (Reformation studies and early modern Germany) are now working on. I feel very much like a pioneer, even though I can see that the vision has only begun to unfold. My research and teaching would surely not have taken the turns that it has had I been at another institution. When I wrote to a colleague in my field, one of two women who opened up the field to questions about gender in German Reformation history, asking her for advice in revising the syllabus, she said that nothing like the course that I was developing yet existed. That is an exciting yet daunting realization.

Not all students and faculty are happy. One young man, a junior who writes a regular column in the student paper, complained that women's studies was ruining his sleep. He had deliberately taken modern European history because he already knew some French history and thought he would not have to work too hard. Then along comes a professor who lectures on women's contributions to the French Revolution, a topic he had never heard of, and he had to stay awake and take notes. I enjoy his discomfort. I suspect those who worry about college students and their lack of energy would applaud his anguish along with me.

I am optimistic, perhaps too much so. I certainly work in an institution that supports these efforts. But I see daily examples of the liberal arts flourishing, and I think those examples are what we have to evaluate and to emulate. Certainly, decrying the circumstances and retreating into romanticized pasts are not the answers. We have to search for what's working and work with it.

Educational Architecture and Change

What does this all add up to? I ponder this question each day as I roam the East Duke Building. The East Duke Building was built in 1912. Downstairs are the art historians. They never appear to mention women, except in jokes, usually while discussing the nude (at least as I overhear their lectures and pause to look at their slides as I pass by). Upstairs are some of the historians; we exchange news of students, projects, research ideas, campus gossip. Russian history, Native American studies, and colonial Spain are the stuff of our daily discourse. From them I overhear thoughtful remarks about new questions being pursued. At each end of the building are large assembly rooms, one now converted to a theater, the other to a chamber music hall. But that's recent.

In the 1920s those two halls were inhabited by the rival literary societies of Trinity College. Several times each week, students and community gathered for debates and lectures, heckling each other and working hard at the arts of argumentation and procedure to win supporters. The subjects of their debates were the issues of the day not allowed into the then-classical curriculum. The university recognized that the curriculum did not encompass the issues of greatest concern to students and faculty and constructed their physical building around the division between those things deemed appropriate for study and those not.

Women's Studies lives among these colleagues with our offices, classrooms, and bulletin boards presenting contrasts. Students, faculty, and visitors to the building enter, browse, engage.

I think about the architecture of the building where I work, about the forebears who built a structure that formalized the division between curriculum and controversy. I think about some current occupants of the same building, a hundred years later, who ignore controversy in their curricula. I think as well about other occupants who are attempting to work through the fit between the two.

I think we need a building where teachers and learners together struggle with the knowledge we inherit and our needs for new knowledge. I do not want to ignore either past constructions or future possibilities, but there is no merit in two antagonistic assembly halls at opposite ends of a building with classrooms in between. We must use our critical faculties to think through the complicated issues of our day. Education is not about retrieving a falsely simple past or proceeding without effort into some technological future. Being educated means assuming a critical stance and looking for connections across subjects in order to solve problems, pursue goals, and provide meaningful ways of thinking about our lives. It means all of us being knowers, involved in the process of knowing, and constantly challenging ourselves and others to build new knowledge.

PART TWO

Explaining

As the Women's Studies Program at Duke grew, I was often invited to talk about what we were doing. The chapters in Part 2 record my attempts at explaining women's studies. The audiences for each talk varied. Sometimes I talked with various student groups located on our own campus: a dormitory; the scholarship banquet of a Greek organization; a symposium on education; or an annual retreat for merit scholars. I was also asked to other campuses to share my ideas about women's studies and higher education with broader audiences. On still other occasions I talked with fellow administrators about the challenges we face in placing women's studies within the liberal arts.

Chapter 5 records one of my early attempts to tell students about women's studies. It was 1985. The students then in college had received their formal schooling after the political ferment of the late 1960s and early 1970s but before the reawakening of political concerns in the early 1990s that I recorded in Chapter 3. I had been invited by their faculty sponsor to the annual retreat of students who have received A. B. Duke merit scholarships. The retreat introduces first-year recipients to the university in general, to their responsibilities as merit scholars, and to the second-, third-, and fourth-year students who are also A. B. Duke scholars.

I talked to this student audience about the ideas they might—or might not— meet in their classes, how those ideas might challenge many of the things they had studied earlier, and why friends and family might counter their developing perspectives with resistance. I did not focus on particular courses or in changes over time in courses as the result of feminist scholarship. The student guests that evening were new to the university and unfamiliar with its particulars. I wanted to provide a framework for their upcoming encounters rather than a critique of what they might find.

After my comments and the question-and-answer session, the staff assistant responsible for the retreat concluded her announcements for the remainder of the day's activities by saying, "And now the boys, who are stronger, should set up the tables for dinner while the girls can come into the kitchen and get the things to set the table." A shout of laughter went up and a buzz of conversation started that never ceased all evening. It seemed as if she had been set up to role play for us the very issues we had been discussing. For the students it was a wonderful click. For the staff assistant, it was an event that first provoked confusion and then an adamant defense of her position. "Boys really are better at moving tables," she insisted. The students were sensitive about how far to push the issue with her and found ways to continue debating while not offending her personally. As they struggled to get her to understand, they replicated what I had been talking about getting them to understand. It was like practice for all that would happen to them in Women's Studies classrooms and what they were going to have to deal with once they were out in the hallways. One of the those students, who went on for a Ph.D. in women's history elsewhere, has reminded me many times since of that episode and what she learned from it.

Five years into the directorship of Women's Studies, I found myself being asked by other colleges and universities to talk with them about establishing women's studies programs. In almost every case, the faculty-student committee seeking to set up a formal program would plan a Women's History Week event during March and ask me to be the keynote speaker.

In such a general audience, alongside the students and faculty who had taken leadership roles in establishing a women's studies program, there would sit members of the faculty and administration who were reserving judgment about the merits of the development. Many different students would attend: some enthusiastic as a result of having had a few classes, others hesitant about what all this meant, and many more who had never heard of women's studies. Sprinkled throughout every audience would be some locally prominent women who wanted to support a women-centered effort but had not yet met women's studies in any academic setting. Trying to explain women's studies in a way that would work for such diverse groups simultaneously, I would emphasize the multiple ways in which women's studies fits a university's liberal arts mission and generates benefits for everyone involved.

The version of the talk printed in Chapter 6 was given at Davidson College in March 1989. I gave a similar talk at the University of Virginia the same month. At Davidson, I had dinner beforehand with the committee in the president's house but hosted by the president's wife. No one ever explained just where the president himself was. At the University of Virginia the president, Robert O'Neill, introduced me and chatted afterward. I had taught his daughter in my introductory Women's Studies class at Duke, although I had not realized the connection until he brought it to my attention. Within six months the University of Virginia created a position for a director of Women's Studies. In addition to a long history of building its initiative for Women's Studies, the university had the commitment and personal interest of high-level administrators, which can tip the balance at later stages in the process.

Momentum for women's studies on any campus builds in many ways, and T-shirts often appear to make a contribution. The Davidson group had made up T-shirts for Women's History Month, and my concluding remarks fell on receptive ears. Later that year, my husband was wearing my Davidson Women's Studies T-shirt at the airport in South Bend, Indiana. At baggage claim, a young man introduced himself as a Davidson student and asked whether my husband was affiliated with the college. No, he explained, his wife had been given the T-shirt when she spoke there in March. The student reported that he had not gone to the lecture but knew all about it and about Women's Studies and that things were happening in Women's Studies, even at a formerly all-male school like Davidson. Initiatives work their way through institutions in multiple ways, and these cases are but two examples.

By the 1980s women's studies programs offered a wonderful collage of activity. Some campuses, like Duke, were just getting started. Others, like the College of Wooster, were celebrating their tenth anniversary. I was asked to the Wooster celebration to characterize the origins of women's studies and suggest its future contours. Their celebration was a particularly moving one because that weekend the college gave Adrienne Rich an honorary degree. The entire campus and town packed the chapel to hear the president honor Rich for contributing to our understanding of diversity. While not yet courageous enough to actually use the word *lesbian*, he made it clear that Rich was being praised for her many contributions, including the passion and honesty that animated her efforts to get feminist scholarship to encompass multiple perspectives.

Four years later, in 1992, I was asked to the campus of California Polytechnic University, where a women's studies initiative was just beginning under the leadership of Carolyn Stefanco, one of my former students. As late as 1991 Cal Poly was the only university in the California state system without a women's studies program. My colleague thought they needed a history lesson in women's studies and asked me to give a public lecture as well as meet with deans and administrators. I used my Wooster talk, printed here as Chapter 7, to bring Cal Poly into the conversation.

For those who are unfamiliar with the development of women's studies over the past two decades, it is necessary to place this new endeavor within general university life. For those already familiar with women's studies, recounting its history (rather than reciting merits and internal characteristics) can emphasize the importance of listening to one another as we struggle to welcome diversity. Above all, I wanted to convey my sense of how important it is, for both those new to the endeavor and those familiar with it, that we continue to document our stories, so that initiatives like women's studies programs can create spaces that further the process of transforming institutions.

The general impact of talks like these is impossible to determine. In the Cal Poly case, the results are clear. Within the year, Stefanco, then a junior member of the History Department, began as the university's first director of Women's Studies—ten years to the month since, as a graduate student at Duke, she had staffed the faculty committee that was considering the establishment of a women's studies program.

Explaining women's studies is by no means restricted to student and faculty audiences. Fellow administrators play a key role in fostering women's studies; Chapter 8 is addressed to them, based on a speech I gave to a state forum with the Office of Women in Higher Education (OWHE) at the American Council on Education (ACE) in 1990. My association with this project goes back a long way. In 1975 I headed a group called the National Coalition for Research on Women's Education and Development. The coalition consisted of those representing women's colleges in the late 1960s as well as a small group of scholars who were beginning to investigate the stages in women's lives. Their particular interest was in women's educational opportunities and career advancement. The group had published *Some Action of Her Own: The Adult Woman and Higher Education* (Lexington, Mass.: Lexington Books, 1976), the first major research account of returning women. Over time the coalition came to see that other groups, now emerging as part of other professional associations, could more appropriately undertake our charges. I went to Washington to meet with Emily Taylor at ACE to discuss this process with her. That meeting, on a hot summer afternoon, stands out vividly in my mind.

I was seven months pregnant at the time. Emily and Donna Shavlik, her associate, were the first people I had met in a professional setting who did not stare continuously at my enlarged abdomen while we were talking. I found being a pregnant female in higher education in the early 1970s to be an experience of talking to people without eye contact. You looked at their eyes. They looked at your navel. Communication was strained. Emily looked me in the eye and our discussions were successfully concluded.

It wasn't just how Emily treated me that impressed me. It was what she said.

She explained that while ACE had formed an office on women in the 1920s, this office had been closed for decades. The head of the association assumed that women could and should be treated just like men and believed that women were achieving professional status in accordance with their educations. This was one of the first specific instances I recall of learning about how the cycle of thought about women has changed over time. It shook my naive idea of women's cumulative progress in the social world.

She also outlined the basic idea behind the National Identification Program (NIP), explaining that addressing women's concerns was not a simple process that called for a single focused approach. There were many issues, many strategies, and she was developing the one most appropriate to her organization. That there were multiple strategies to changing women's situations, that some fit certain sponsors better than others, and that they could be systematically investigated was a new idea at that time. I am forever grateful to Emily for helping me think about how to effectively take on one piece of a larger issue.

In the next five years, I worked closely with the OWHE, chairing the National Commission on Women and participating in NIP forums. I was active in Women Administrators in North Carolina Higher Education, one part of the national effort. I worked with all three projects out of OWHE as the number of women in decision-making positions in higher education grew. The OWHE worked diligently to include women from the historically black colleges as well as the Asian and Hispanic women emerging in leadership roles. The meetings sponsored by the OWHE were the most diverse of my administrative experience and provided a welcome base to explore issues of race, ethnicity, and gender.

Educating the Majority: Women Challenge Tradition in Higher Education (New York: Collier Macmillan, 1989), the text for this forum, was part of what was set in motion then. Its message grew out of some fifteen years of experience with women and higher education. Women have demonstrated their abilities in every facet of higher education. Higher education now has the primary responsibility to modify itself to accommodate women with all their talents and in all their diversity. And it is administrators and faculty leaders who are primarily responsible for seeing these changes come into being.

The talk reprinted in Chapter 8 contains my observations about the importance of differences among women to those educators whose institutional positions enable them to see the campus mosaics before them and whose broad authority can chart directions for institutions. Personnel in Student Affairs, Academic Support, Business Auxiliaries, and the Physical Plant are all in positions to consider how their activities affect students and the campus climate that faculty and academic leaders endeavor to create. All too infrequently do academic and nonacademic people come together over student needs. Yet both academic and nonacademic officers know that the campus experience is not contained solely within the classroom; opportunities on the sports field, in dorms and dining halls, and in the student union all contribute directly to how students learn to deal with the multifaceted communities in which they live on campus.

CHAPTER 5

Why Do We Need Women's Studies?

Questions from Students in the 1980s

Your faculty sponsor suggested that I address, head on, the why-have-women's-studies question. The question itself contains many other, unexpressed questions. Sometimes it means *why does an excellent, nationally ranked school like Duke need women's studies?* Doesn't it admit exceptional students, half of whom are women? Don't they get the same education there as men do?

Other times the question has a critical tone: *why should we emphasize any one thing in courses, women or any other special-interest group?* Such a question is always followed by some form of the comment that next we'll be studying every obscure minority and not have time for what's really important. I'll return to this point later.

Why don't we have men's studies? is another favorite version of the question I hear often. Sometimes said with a laugh, the challenge is expressed with a seriousness that suggests how little we know about the accuracy and breadth of the information that we have. After all, this line of reasoning goes, if you want to be fair about this, we ought to have classes on men.

Finally, some people say to me that *even if women need women's studies to learn about themselves, why do men need it?* I often want to retort, well, fine, we can just forget about men. But I believe that men and women live together in this world, if not necessarily in any particular couple, and that the social construction of women is as important to men as it is to women, albeit in different ways.

Just when I think I have all the questions in hand, someone will pop up with

This talk was given at Quaker Lake in August 1985 at the annual retreat for students who have received A. B. Duke merit scholarships.

the generational challenge: *women's studies is passé—women's issues were a problem for an earlier generation. Women's studies might have been alright then. But things are different now and we don't need it.* We will return to this too.

The why-have-women's-studies question rests on three assumptions that are neither articulated in its various versions nor supported by historical and experiential evidence. One assumption is that if women and men have equal access to education, there will be no future problems to prevent women from realizing their full potential in society, now or later. While education is critical, education alone cannot remove the social inequalities that prevent many women, particularly poor women or women of color, from realizing their full potential.

A second assumption is that women and men experience society and culture in such similar ways that to isolate women's experiences for analysis is to overemphasize their importance and in turn to neglect men's. After all, if women were important, we would already be concerned with them, according to this view.

The third and perhaps most deeply held assumption underlying questions about women's studies is that knowledge is fully objective and true; whatever we study treats men and women as they ought to be treated. The "ought" in this formulation is not considered problematic.

I want to argue against all these statements by describing how feminist scholars deal with these questions and address these assumptions. Feminist scholars, male and female, argue that gender is an essential and important category of analysis in all areas of academic thought and practice, as well as in the "real world" where what we have learned in school is put into practice, modified, or indeed ignored. While feminist scholars do not maintain that every intellectual question and practical problem of interest has only gender dimensions, they argue that gender frequently informs other social dimensions. Their work demonstrates that by analyzing ideas and experiences from the point of view of women as well as men, one gains a more accurate and more explanatory account of the phenomena under observation.

Let me suggest a metaphor to use in listening to the following comments. Think about spotlights. Imagine you are watching a dancer doing a solo at the National Theatre. There is only one spot in the house. You, as a member of the audience, have a quite limited ability to see the dance in this light. You might see the torso well enough if that is where the spot is directed. But with only one spot you would miss the intricate muscle movements of the extremities, and the expressions of the face, as well as more complex silhouettes. If more spotlights are added, you would see the dancer in greater complexity. Only with a more complete system of lights would you be able both to see fully and to enjoy the more elaborate interpretations of movement and mood being presented. The dancer is analogous to understanding women in society. By turning on another switch, women's studies enables you to see more fully what has been happening all along. Light metaphors are common in women's studies. We acknowledge that we are investigating what has been and is. The difference made by women's studies is the use of more powerful tools by which to make the previously invisible visible.

The Historical Context of Ideas about Women

Before I develop my argument about contemporary scholarship more fully, let me review briefly the history of ideas about women. I am arguing that ideas about women and men and the gender systems in which we think and act are linked in close and powerful ways to general social change. By understanding the historical context in which discussions about women are occurring, you are better able to understand how your education serves the goals of culture and society as well as your own goals.

Feminist scholars have identified at least four periods in history when scholars and ordinary people alike debated women's place in society.[1] In the ancient and early medieval world, long before large-scale economic and political organizations emerged to replace the Roman Empire, women, especially elite women, occupied numerous leadership roles. Ideas about gender were much less fixed; the idea that women as a group were prohibited from doing or unable to do any particular thing was much less widespread. In later feudal times a more elaborate gender system developed. Ideas about women and women's nature as well as the social conventions that shaped women's nature came into being as a part of a more complex ideological system based on the introduction of science—itself a highly gendered enterprise.

In Elizabethan England, when feudalism was waning and commercial enterprises were arising in new urban centers, we again have a record of debate about women. Clergy, poets, royalty, and commoners debated woman's nature and how she was to fit into the new order. With scientific discoveries, religious upheavals, and the expansion of the world as Europeans knew it, gender emerged once more as an important dimension by which to order social relations.

From the 1800s on, as commercial capitalism gave way to industrial capitalism, as Western imperialism bound the globe more tightly together, and as the ideals of the French and North American revolutions began to be practiced, a social movement to alter the nature of women's participation in life outside the immediate dwelling place began. Many women were increasingly exposed to education and employment. The home itself was being transformed from a unit of production, linked in multiple ways to the community around it, into a unit of consumption, defined in opposition to the larger society around it. The home's older functions of socialization were transferred to public agencies while new responsibilities centering on consumerism and psychological nurturance were being added.

In the 1960s, feminism as a social movement reemerged to question the relevance of sex-role stereotypes in a postindustrial age. The technological base of society was transformed, with far-reaching consequences in reproductive control and ecological harm. From the civil rights movement the women's movement learned new rhetoric, new strategies, and new goals. Debates about women's position in society raged. This time they were aided by the media's power to reinforce and question simultaneously. While the debate clearly created opportunities for some (mostly middle-class white women), it narrowed them for others (most frequently poor women and women of color). We are still very much in the throes of this stage.

We know very little about how women from the tenth through the nineteenth centuries thought about their circumstances. We do know a bit about the issues that link the nineteenth- and twentieth-century debates about women and gender. One way to conceptualize the links across these past two hundred years is to review what feminist thinkers and activists have sought as their goals over time. My examples here derive mainly from North America.

At the time of the North American Revolution, many intellectuals questioned its meaning for women. Fanny Wright, the famous intellectual and lecturer who had been trained in Scotland by the heirs of the Enlightenment, publicly and relentlessly attacked Jefferson for his failure to incorporate women into the revolution. Through her experiments in residential communities as well as public calls to action, Fanny Wright provides one example of the women who articulated the missing pieces in this revolutionary experiment.

Ordinary women debated the meaning of their lives in letters and diaries. Annette Kolodny has reconstructed their ideas in *The Land Before Her*, demonstrating that women's view of the frontier emphasized the conservation and care of nature over the need to control and dominate it.[2] Slave narratives tell us of the care African American women exercised in protecting their children and maintaining their integrity in a system of oppression.[3]

Building a new society on a continent new to them, many women, African American and white, made education a high priority. By the 1820s women attempted to build schools, believing that by educating themselves they would be prepared for their part in the future. Women saw that education was a key to economic and cultural access for themselves and their children. Teaching women to read, particularly African American women, was throughout much of our history an act of rebellion. Women's academies came to be part of many communities; the push for coeducation occurred almost simultaneously; and the young women who finished academies sought higher education in newly created colleges and abroad as postgraduate work developed.

Women took their education seriously and used it for social reform. Abolition, temperance, cultural institutions, and the social inequalities experienced by both the poor and immigrants were women's avenues for participation in social life during the middle of the nineteenth century. As women experienced increasing frustration due to their inability to implement their agendas, many began to focus their energy on legal reform and, later in the century, on the vote. In the aftermath of suffrage, energy that had been primarily directed toward political reform became increasingly directed toward the need of all women for full economic determination. In the late 1960s many feminists began to emphasize ideas and attitudes, to explore relationships between women and men as well as among women, and above all to question why in the face of so many social changes women were still treated unfairly.

This is the time at which women's studies becomes a part of the story of feminism as a social movement. These debates about women's place in the nineteenth century and the first half of the twentieth took place outside colleges and universities; they were led by activists working for concrete ends. In the 1960s, as feminists contemplated continued discrimination against women in spite of sociolegal changes, they turned to colleagues in the academy and said, how come? Explain this to us: *why does this pattern of marginalization occur over and over again?* It is here that women's studies begins as the attempt to find out what the experiences, expressions, and expectations of women are and to ask how these match with what we have studied—that is, largely the experiences, expressions, and expectations of men and how they have thought about women.

Feminist Perspectives and the Study of Women

I am going to illustrate the difference that a feminist perspective makes in what we study and how we study it by using four questions that are currently being researched. To explore each one in any depth would require four separate talks. Now I only want to raise the questions with you, to engage your curiosity, and to suggest that you participate in these investigations as you take courses.

The four questions are these:

- What constitutes greatness in literature?
- Are women and men different?
- What do we mean when we say "that's public," "that's private"?
- Is science an objective endeavor?

Let's look briefly at the questions, using each to illustrate how women's studies is fundamentally altering basic perspectives in liberal arts education.

Women's studies has enabled us to understand that our definitions of greatness in literature vary with time and are linked to how we value male-female differences. Take the case of Hawthorne and Warner. You all know of Nathaniel Hawthorne. His works were on all standardized tests. He holds a place near sainthood in high school literature classes. How many of you have heard of Susan Warner and her novel *The Wide, Wide World*? How many of you know that Warner outsold Hawthorne in their time?

Jane Tompkins, a member of the Duke English Department, addresses the what-makes-a-classic question in her work *Sensational Designs*.[4] She demonstrates that it is not the intrinsic merit of a text but rather the circumstances that made both texts visible in the first place and then maintained them in preeminent positions over time. She attacks the modernist belief that art, in order to be art, must be free from propaganda. She shows that for many authors of the nineteenth century, especially women, this distinction between art and politics was meaningless. Tompkins documents how authors like Warner meant to make readers think, feel, and act in particular ways so that they would alter their social worlds.

Thus she argues that the value and significance of these novels in their time depended on precisely those characteristics that formalist criticism has taught us to deplore. These authors wanted to reach a wide audience and move the United States closer to an ideal republic, and used their writing as a vehicle of political and cultural change. Tompkins's research opens up the debate about what constitutes a literary classic in new and exciting ways. By including authors not previously included, particularly female authors, we can achieve new insights that were impossible even to name in the absence of those authors.

Let's turn from literature to psychology, linguistics, and anthropology. What do we mean when we claim that women and men are different from each other? This is a very complicated question. On the one hand, feminist scholars argue that the differences between women and men are relatively small in absolute terms and of little consequence in terms of their abilities to be social beings. According to this view, it is only the evaluation that is given to difference that is problematic. On the other hand, feminist scholars also argue that as a result of the social value given to these constructed differences, men and women do in fact exhibit differences that must be taken into account. They point out that most social arrangements are male oriented and do not take women's needs into consideration when their needs are different from those of men.

One of the most well-known illustrations of how we can understand difference is found in the work of Carol Gilligan and her colleagues in education at Harvard.[5] Gilligan, through intensive interviews with women as well as extensive observation of women's behavior, argues that women will frequently consider how decisions affect others in their reasoning processes. By contrast, previous research literature had claimed that people make decisions by applying abstract principles. Based only on observations of men, this earlier work did not allow us to see the various decision-making processes people actually use.

The public-private debate is a third area where feminist perspectives have changed much of our thinking. Conventional wisdom, as expressed in philosophy, history, politics, and economics, holds that separate spheres exist for women and men—men take care of public affairs (economics, government, the abstract) while women tend the home (children, cooking, interpersonal relationships). The two are viewed as quite separate.

Thus if you go, as I recently did, to the North Carolina Museum of History, you will see two exhibits side by side. One is about war, the other about fashion. As a feminist scholar, standing there with my family in the exhibit hall, I had to ask myself immediately, do women not have any relationship to war? have men no concern with what they wear? It is not just that men participate in domestic culture and women in public affairs. It is more. Women's reproductive roles enable men to do what we think of as "productive" roles. Without bearing and rearing children, washing the clothes and cooking the food, organizing the family activities and contributing to community endeavors—all things considered in the private realm—life in the public realm simply could not exist. And men's control of public space defines the parameters of what happens in private space. The abortion debate has been our most vivid illustration over the past decade of how public discussion and private decisions are intricately linked.

An emergent question in women's studies concerns the extent to which science is gendered. This is perhaps the most complicated, the most exciting, and the most emotionally charged query. The question can be asked on many levels. How and why have women been excluded from the practice of science? Does science undertake to research questions of greater relevance to men than to women? Are the consequences of science equally applicable to men and to women? Does the pursuit of science, which insists on objectivity, distort the process of knowing? What is the role of emotion, passion, or belief in arriving at understandings? Does feeling interact with the scientific process to influence it? How do cultural assumptions influence receptivity to scientific results?

Turning the Lights On

I have been arguing that women's studies is necessary to the full education of both women and men. Women will gain power, the ability to use resources for themselves and for society's good, only when they have knowledge of themselves. Self-knowledge begins with information. We need to know as much about Elizabeth Cady Stanton as Abraham Lincoln, as much about Charlotte Hawkins Brown as Frederick Douglass. We need to read Chopin's *The Awakening* as often as Joyce's *Portrait of the Artist as a Young Man*. We need to know that women often reason on the basis of relationships, not exclusively on the basis of rules, and that, having figured that out, we can reexamine how the "male" ability to ground decisions in abstract rules can work to obscure the power relations that are sustained by those rules. Thus men gain in this learning process just as fully, although in different ways. Their understanding of themselves, their relations with other men, and their ability to have mutually productive relationships with women increase immeasurably.

In closing, let me return to my metaphor about lights. It is not always easy to turn on more lights. It takes more skill, it requires more time, it demands more resources. But the end product, our view of human nature, is worth it. Turning the lights on is necessary. A feminist perspective is necessary for both more complete knowledge and a more useful education for each of you. To quote Rebecca West in *The Clarion* of 1913: "I myself have never been able to find out precisely what feminism is: I only know that people call me a feminist whenever I express sentiments that differentiate me from a doormat."[6]

The Necessity of Women's Studies in a Liberal Arts Education

I begin with a story about bulletin boards. As we all know, bulletin boards are the stuff of academic life. Students have small ones on their dormitory doors to let friends know of their comings and goings. Faculty members and departments rely on bulletin boards to announce events and information. Administrators use bulletin boards to comply with the requirements of the law and to advertise their activities. I'd venture to say that there is hardly an academic building on a U.S. college campus that does not have a bulletin board.

When Duke University built a new student center in the early 1980s, a series of bulletin boards was installed on the main walkway. These fancy bulletin boards—with lights, glass doors, and locks—were offered for sale to campus groups. Although I considered the price outrageous—$450—in my capacity as director of Women's Studies I immediately sent in the form and enclosed the paperwork for payment. Several weeks later, I received the paperwork back, along with a note from a student union committee saying that my request had been turned down. No reason was given. Knowing how to network, I called a friend on the student union staff to ask what was up. My friend reported that they were having trouble selling the bulletin boards, but a student committee had to approve each request. He advised me to appeal the decision. I contacted the student in charge of the committee and arranged to come to the next meeting.

I took along a senior Women's Studies student known for her keen sense of humor as well as her leadership in student politics. The chair opened the

This paper was presented at Davidson College on March 14, 1989.

meeting by saying that Dr. O'Barr and her student Colleen wanted to discuss the Women's Studies bulletin board request. He reminded the committee that the request had been turned down at the last meeting because the committee had never heard of Women's Studies. Before I could recover enough to say a word, Colleen spoke up: "Well, in that case, we are just the program that needs a bulletin board—to educate *you* as well as visitors to the student union." Silence, shock, and laughter followed in that order. I never did have to give my reasoned arguments. The committee simply agreed that the function of bulletin boards was to convey information about new ventures and we were on our way.

Getting the bulletin board was only the first step. I then had to decide how to use it, what to say—in short, to answer the question "What is Women's Studies?"

I would like now to talk with you about what I understand the women's studies enterprise to be. This is a necessary prelude to describing the contributions of women's studies to the liberal arts curriculum.

We usually date the offering of the first courses in women's studies from the late 1960s. Researchers now know that there were many courses on women and their social positions in colleges and universities from the early 1900s. Other investigators are documenting the history of women's writing about women's positions across centuries and continents. But that is another subject.

What Is Women's Studies?

In the late 1960s most of the professional positions in U.S. higher education were, of course, held by men. But beginning in the mid-1960s larger numbers of women were earning Ph.D.'s and joining faculties. While women tended to be more interested than their male colleagues in researching questions relating to women, it is important to stress that very few people could answer the questions being asked. The few feminists already in the academy, spurred by their involvement with the nascent women's movement, began to ask new questions of their own data.

I think of myself as typical. I entered graduate school in 1964 as a Woodrow Wilson fellow, bound for college teaching. I completed course work in three years and headed out for fieldwork in northeast Tanzania in the shadow of Mt. Kilimanjaro. My husband, an anthropologist, and I planned to stay for two years and study local communities. I was interested in how the then-new countries of Africa were becoming modern nation-states through setting up democratic political structures. I talked to local leaders. I hired men to help me interview people, and I went to every meeting of every local party and government unit and hung out with the male political leaders at party headquarters.

It never once occurred to me to talk to women as women. Nor were there any women in decision-making positions. I never even noticed their absence, much less stopped to consider whether women's absence was important.

At one point in my investigations, I realized that in one of the two villages I was researching, 25 percent of the lowest-level party volunteers were female. Locals explained this by the "vacuum theory" of female political participation—this was an area of high male labor migration, and women had to fill in when men were absent. But it wasn't normal (read good), they said. I also learned that the women of this same area had led tax riots in the late 1940s that succeeded in pressuring the British colonial government to reverse its policies. But people assured me this wasn't usual either. I wrote up both these bits of information in my dissertation without making anything of them.

Some five years later, Ph.D. completed, first job landed, initial courses taught, I began to read the first few collections in women's studies. I read Millett's *Sexual Politics*; I raced through Robin Morgan's collections.[1] I began to see that the small kernels of information I had observed could have led to a great deal more if I had asked some other questions. Had African women participated in politics before colonialism? Under what conditions did they become active politically? Was the political structure I studied the one that was determining outcomes, or had I failed to see other, equally influential processes at work? Why did people say having women in political decision-making roles wasn't normal?

I relay my own story, not because it is exceptional, but because I think it is typical. Literally hundreds of scholars were beginning to rethink what they did and taught once they had been confronted with a new set of questions, questions generated outside the academy.

How Did the Women's Studies Movement Get Started?

Those who were beginning to research new questions, write about new issues, and teach new topics quickly began to engage in a series of common activities. There are now more than 525 programs in women's studies across this county, offering some 30,000 courses to well over one million students. Although they began in different contexts, at different times, and with different resources, they have common characteristics:

- Programs sponsor a core course, Introduction to Women's Studies, that surveys the field. Sometimes there is a senior seminar as well.
- Faculty members in departments from art to zoology teach courses on

women in such fields as art, literature, history, religion, science, and many more.

- Course offerings are coordinated by a director who also sponsors public lectures and seminars, gives career advice to students concentrating in the field, works with the library and related student services to bring women-centered perspectives to campus, encourages faculty in the women's studies program to do ever more, and urges faculty that look askance at women's studies to consider the possibilities.

In short, women's studies programs have been created in most major colleges and universities and are flourishing after two decades of operation. They simultaneously pursue two goals. One goal relates to the generation of new knowledge through research and teaching. Programs support individual *and* collective research. They pioneer the teaching of courses. They present new knowledge in whatever forums are available. They investigate alternate pedagogies.

The other goal relates to the incorporation of new knowledge. Program personnel try to get other parts of the university to incorporate the information being generated by feminist inquiry. They are interested in curriculum transformation, integration, mainstreaming, and gender-balancing. Sometimes this is done by giving stipends to faculty so that they can rework their courses, either by participating in a seminar or individually. Sometimes curriculum transformation occurs through the adoption of new standards, the requirement that all new courses contain the appropriate amount of the new scholarship on women. Sometimes it occurs through osmosis: through simply being there, women's studies stimulates people to become curious and change their perspectives.

Every women's studies program realizes that it must pursue both goals simultaneously—both create new information and see to its widespread use. A successful women's studies program will not wither or die in five years—as critics often hope—because all the new ideas and information have been figured out. A successful one will not go off in the corner by itself rather than work with the rest of the college—hard as it may be—to accomplish change across the institution.

What Is Involved in Developing a Women's Studies Perspective?

Understanding the critical perspective that characterizes women's studies is a necessary piece in the story linking women's studies to the liberal arts curriculum. Those of us involved in setting up programs, teaching courses, and working with our colleagues often speak of a three-step process. We used to call it Correct, Add, Revise. If we are trying to be trendy these days, we say Deconstruct, Construct, Reconstruct.

Let me use three brief examples. Consider Betsy Ross. Let us pretend that we are playing Pictionary and we are to draw her. Close your eyes and imagine. Is she sitting or standing? Is she alone or with others? How is she dressed? Is there a cat and a geranium nearby? Most of us see Betsy Ross as a well-dressed, older, solitary figure, forever sewing a flag. Is our understanding of her historically accurate or does it require deconstruction? Betsy Ross was in fact an upholsterer, a Philadelphia businesswoman who won the flag contract on a competitive bid, working out of a home-based commercial enterprise. She certainly was not alone, neat, or at leisure. How did the Betsy Ross we know come to differ so markedly from her reality? Would it make a difference to you, to your understanding of women's economic roles in society, and to your belief in received wisdom if you knew the real Betsy Ross? Women's studies pushes us to correct old ideas and ask much more about what we think we know. Yes, male figures are also distorted by historical interpretation, but we have many of them; comparing their stories gives us varied ideas about male possibilities. In many cases Betsy Ross is our sole role model, our first foremother.

Consider a second case—quilts. Why are quilts not conventionally thought of as an art form? We in North Carolina have seen a great deal of recent attention given to quilts. But put that recent activity aside and ask yourself why Jansen, the most widespread art history textbook for decades, does not contain quilts. How would our understanding of what constitutes art be altered if quilts were included? What would we learn about the subject matter, the producers, the funders, and the consumers of art if we added quilts to portraits, landscapes, and still lifes? What would we learn if we insisted on considering multipatterned African American quilts alongside the symmetrical quilts familiar to most white Americans? How much farther would we have to go in understanding the relationship between women, culture, and art in order to do this? Women's studies asks us to add new information, especially information about diversity, and to struggle with the difference it makes to have to process all this when things no longer add up in the same way.

Consider sex and sexuality, a third case. History and the social sciences, as I remember them and as they are often still taught, focus on the public events of our lives. They tell us what governments did, what religious institutions said we should do, what social conventions we create and follow. They rarely tell us about our private lives; about intimacy and interpersonal behavior; about how public conventions set down the possibilities for private behavior and how private activities modify, indeed challenge, public conventions. How have the twin descriptions that for every woman there is a man and for every man there is a woman affected our ability to value same-sex relationships—mothers and daughters, sisters, friends, role models, lovers? Why do we think that the course of our lives and the nature of our culture are more determined by what a small group of leaders proclaims than by the daily choices of most people as they allocate their resources and energies? How would history and the other social sciences look if we included the historical, social, and developmental study of sexuality at their center along with the study of more public topics? Women's studies asks us to revise our thinking about what constitutes full and appropriate information and think critically about the consequences of those choices.

The questions I have just posed, about Betsy Ross, quilts, and sexuality, illustrate how women's studies researchers develop a critical perspective and ask questions to provide more complete information for the formulation of social policy and personal values. The number of examples could go on and on. But I want to shift my focus here. I want to move from considering what questions are at the center of women's studies for feminist scholars and think about how students benefit from all of this activity. Women's studies is, above all else, student-centered.

What Does Women's Studies Do for Students?

Florence Howe, an early women's studies scholar who currently heads the Feminist Press, wrote that women's studies is the perfect liberal art.[2] She said it accomplishes five objectives:

- It is interdisciplinary and unifying.
- It teaches skills in critical analysis.
- It assumes a problem-solving stance.
- It clarifies the issue of value judgment in education.
- It promotes socially useful ends.

By naming issues central to women's lives and teaching about them, women's studies crosses disciplinary boundaries and brings new perspectives to bear on questions that were once unnamed. The issue of domestic violence comes immediately to mind. Not more than twenty years ago, the phrase "battered woman" was unknown. The practice, however, was not. But the idea that the family was not necessarily a safe, much less happy, place for all people was unspeakable. To understand the issues of domestic violence, students cannot rely on the insights of only one discipline. Sociology might tell them this problem exists in every income bracket, but they need history to tell them how privileging men and male authority seems to encourage domestic violence. Anthropology might explain that other societies do not have domestic violence, but they need literature to understand how people have been prevented from speaking about it in this culture. Policy analysts might tell them about programs for correcting it, but students need psychologists to help them understand who perpetuates battering and why. Economics helps them understand the circumstances in which women believe that enduring is preferable to risking lack of support. Philosophers have an enormous contribution to make in helping students make sense of the issue of domestic violence, weighing the claims and unifying the insights from across a disciplinary landscape.

I think my comments so far tonight have demonstrated how women's studies teaches skills in critical analysis. Let me reiterate the point by saying that students are very aware both of what it means to take in information that challenges current values and of how painful it is to be forced to think anew on one's own. There is always a point in the spring semester in the introductory Women's Studies course, along about week 6, when students start saying, "Gosh, ignorance was bliss." They'll come up to me and exclaim, "You've no idea how much easier it was when I didn't notice all of this! It's hard to have to figure out where I stand and to convince my friends who aren't in the class that it matters." The arrival of the swimsuit issue of *Sports Illustrated* always comes around this time; it provides a concentrated version of sexism that plunges every Women's Studies student, male and female, into a critical analysis of where they stand and why.

I would add here a word about men in women's studies. Male enrollments are rarely as high as female. Yet for the men who do engage in the critical thinking skills offered in women's studies, the rewards are many. One ongoing task in the women's studies agenda involves incorporating men into our constituencies while continuing to focus on women in the male-centered environment of the academy.

The most exciting aspect of women's studies from a student's point of view is that women's studies assumes a problem-solving stance. This approach to knowledge is the hallmark of the liberally educated person. In women's studies students repeatedly find problems defined, solutions proposed, personal positions developed. Let's take a very simple example. It is a rare young woman who, by the time she has reached her senior year in college, has not noticed that classroom dynamics are different for her than for her male counterparts. She may not come up with the analysis herself, but she will tell you, when queried, that she does not speak in class as often as the men or that, when she does, she is put down as pushy; that while she doesn't really care and can do the math problems just as readily as everyone else, all the talk about baseball that surrounds working with batting averages doesn't really interest her; and that when talk turns to social problems arising from single parenthood, she alternates between rage at the lack of understanding dominant in the culture and her own positive experiences of being part of an extended female family. I could give you a hundred examples of the ways in which students express to me what Bernice Sandler and her colleagues at the Association of American Colleges call the chilly classroom climate.[3] Suffice it to say that once classroom dynamics have been identified as ways in which seemingly objective knowledge is processed and made personal, female students almost always identify their silence and begin working on it. Most women simply do not have the same classroom experience as men; until the ways knowledge is transmitted are identified, the problem of why women and men develop different learning styles simply cannot be addressed.

Much that I have said this evening points to the fact that women's studies is in many ways an exercise in making things complicated. It desimplifies the world as we know it. This is particularly so for students. But in the act of making things complicated, women's studies clarifies the issue of value judgments in education. Women's studies is about the task of asking how we know what we know, who evaluates the knowledge, and what the consequences of such an evaluation scheme are. Nowhere is this clearer than in a college music curriculum. The basic introduction is often called the "masterworks" course, and it is just that—a review of the works of men. The composing and performing of women, contemporary as well as classical, is virtually unknown. Yet family records, the histories of academies and religious houses, and court accounts all suggest that women wrote, played, and sang. Why do we not now consider them worthy of study? How can we dismiss their importance to the cultural milieu? What values are at stake in dismissing the problems of shifting notions of "greatness"? What difference does it make in a student's education when the musical canon rarely includes women? What does it say about the concert agenda and recording-buying habits that this liberally educated person will pursue over a lifetime? And what does it say to the aspiring women composers, conductors, and performers about their chances?

I want to return to my own discipline of political science to discuss the last of Howe's points—that women's studies promotes socially useful ends. There has been a recent explosion of scholarship in feminist political theory about the question of what promotes citizenship and how the age-old ideas of citizenship preclude women. I would need another speech to explore this issue with you in any detail. Suffice it to say that rather than simply urging women to be more like men in their political activity, feminist scholars are now able to explain the ways in which political participation is grounded in rules and ideas that exclude women. It is not socially useful to simply urge women to do the self-defeating. It is socially useful to expose the gendered rules of the political game and begin working on their transformation.

T-shirts

I began with bulletin boards. Let me end with T-shirts. If there is a bulletin board in every academic building in the United States, there are surely at least half a dozen T-shirts in the wardrobe of every college student in the country. They say everything, from advertising the name of the schools you visit to promoting the events in which you participate. Hanes Beefy-T's are considered the best, and extra large is the preferred size these days. Two weeks ago Duke University's Women's Studies Program sponsored a sesquicentennial celebration. For three days the campus was filled with alumnae visitors, distinguished speakers, and eager students attending lectures and participating in workshops. Prior to the weekend, the students who live in the Women's Studies Dormitory held a contest and selected a T-shirt design. They sold them throughout the weekend to one and all, building up their programming funds. The front side symbolizes the Women's Studies enterprise. A magnifying glass, scientific tool and educational symbol in all the liberal arts, is used to bring the words *Women's Studies* into focus. The slogan on the back is Carolyn Heilbrun's statement, "Today's shocks are tomorrow's conventions." The shock of twenty years ago, that the study of women and gender systems was a legitimate endeavor, has largely passed. But the challenges of feminist scholarship to traditional assumptions in the liberal arts curriculum are still going strong. It is the challenging of those assumptions that I hope will become convention for liberal arts students of the future. Women's studies is necessary to keep the liberal arts growing, to aid them in conveying a more accurate and complete picture of the human enterprise, and to enable students to establish the integral links between learning, knowing, and living.

CHAPTER 7

How the Inquiry into Women's Studies Grew

When I am asked to reflect on how the women's studies enterprise began and grew, I find that at least three approaches tug at me for attention.

The research scholar in me wants to rush over to the library, do a literature search, and come up with the definitive answer and a healthy bibliography. Immersed as I am in women's studies, I realize I have never read or compiled a scholarly statement on the origins of the field. Yet I believe that I could find a well-researched history, thoughtfully analyzed, in book form, waiting for me to read.

The activist and administrator in me wants to collect accounts from colleagues, both local and national. It would be a relatively straightforward task, calling people up and asking them to recall how women's studies began on their campuses, then weaving the stories together to form a collective narrative.

As a feminist, I feel pulled to think back to when I first said, "I'm in women's studies," and to remember what experiences led me to identify with it. But I cannot actually remember. It feels like I've always been in women's studies—I cannot remember a time when it was not all that I thought about. Yet I know there was a time before women's studies, just as I know that women's studies is not as widespread as it appears to me.

I did utilize all three sources of information in preparing my remarks. Each made its own contribution to my evolving synthesis. An outline began to emerge in the process. And that is when I had a click, one of those moments of feminist truth that explains reality.

I recalled the first course I ever developed. In 1969, I began teaching with

This paper was first presented on April 20, 1988, at the tenth anniversary celebration of the Women's Studies Program at the College of Wooster.

a visiting appointment at Duke and the University of North Carolina at Chapel Hill, filling in for others, teaching courses they had created. In 1972 I became director of Continuing Education at Duke with an adjunct position in the Political Science Department. Here again, I was teaching inherited courses, mainly in international relations and African politics, which was my dissertation speciality.

The following year I approached the chair of my department and said I wanted to teach a course on Third World women. I was an Africanist by training and a complete stranger to the new scholarship on women. The phrase "women's studies" was not even in my vocabulary. But I knew that the United Nations Decade for Women was coming up. I was in touch with other women scholars who were beginning to talk about the need to learn from women around the world and to give priority to their situations. I knew some staff people in Congress working to get the Percy Amendment requiring the U.S. Agency for International Development to consider the impact of technical aid projects on women.

The chairperson looked at me as if I were from another planet and announced that the only way new courses entered the curriculum was when a distinguished research literature on the subject existed. I thought about the piles of mimeographed papers on the floor of my study at home. I looked at him and surprised even myself by confidently asserting that there was now an extensive research literature in existence on the subject of Third World women and development.

One might say I told a bald-faced lie. The few feminist scholars in the field were scrambling to locate reliable studies and to formulate a research agenda. But he never questioned me, assuming I must know what I was talking about, and said, "Yes, of course, then we ought to have the course." And we have ever since. I learned, in a split second, the necessity of claiming knowledge if women are to become empowered and to effect change.

We need to look around ourselves, remember our own experiences, document as much as we can through other sources, and say what we think. We created the record as we lived it; now we need to claim and interpret that record in order that the spaces which we have begun to create can exert an increasingly transformative force upon the institutions in which they are located.

At the Margins and in Opposition

Women's studies, like any development in the academy, has diverse origins and multiple realities. As I look back, trying to research the facts and re-create the circumstances in which women's studies began, three aspects of its beginnings in the late 1960s and 1970s stand out most sharply: we began at the margins, often in opposition; we began at the grassroots; and what we have created in the current cycle, in some twenty years, is a spectacular success, if not a miracle. Now what do I mean by each of these statements?

Women's studies needs to be thought of as the academic arm of the women's movement. For the purposes of this story, we can say it began in the late 1960s when women first entered the academy in large numbers as higher education experienced a growth spurt. It began when leaders in the women's liberation movement asked their academic sisters some very basic questions about political consciousness, organization, and power—and those in academics found there were no answers available. It began when women both in and out of the academy learned from what was happening to the civil rights movement and its agenda for African American studies. It began when academic women became involved in political action themselves, on campus and in the community, and rethought the nature of the research work they were conducting.

Initially, very simple questions could not be answered. These questions seem ridiculous to many of us now. Had women made contributions beyond the home? Were all women alike? When women were the subjects of inquiry, what was said about them? How was a field of inquiry distorted by partial information?

Many of us have vivid memories of the first time we encountered this new way of thinking, with its pointed questions and revealing answers. Morgan's *Sisterhood Is Powerful* and Gornick and Moran's *Women in Sexist Society*,[1] both published in 1971, served that purpose for many. For me, as an Africanist interested in Third World women, it was Rosaldo and Lamphere's *Women, Culture, and Society*, one of the first collections that took a cross-cultural perspective on women.[2] The paragraph I remember most clearly is this one:

> Aside from these [few exceptions], however, anthropologists writing about human culture have followed our own culture's ideological bias in treating women as relatively invisible and describing what are largely the activities and interests of men. In order to correct that bias, to alter our conceptions of the female, and to understand their source, what we need are new perspectives. Today, it seems reasonable to argue that the social world is the creation of both male and female actors, and that any full understanding of human society and any viable program for social change will have to incorporate the goals, thoughts, and activities of the "second sex." (p. 2)

Our opposition to the way women's reality was conceptualized led us to the three basic tasks of women's studies. First, we needed to add new information to what already existed. In the field of art history, we needed to ask why the women who painted, the women who served as patrons to male painters, and the women who were the objects of men's artistic gaze were never mentioned— yet we knew a great deal about every aspect of the male painter's personal and professional history. As we succeeded in gaining this new information, other issues arose: why was a landscape prized over a still life and why was painting but not quilting considered a form of artistic expression?

Second, we needed to correct existing ideas. In the field of politics, for example, researchers frequently document the way that young children are socialized into their civic roles. They look at the first authority figures available to them (police officer, president, etc.) and ask how children identify with those figures. Such research assumes that all children come to trust and emulate such figures. It rarely distinguishes between boys and girls; it almost never examines how intersections of race and gender influence the different ways in which certain children are discouraged from identifying with these figures. As a result, we have a set of ideas about political socialization that are only half true at best.

The third task facing women's studies was to rethink a number of basic assumptions and theories in light of this new and more complete information. The most familiar example is that of history, as we came to understand that the record of the past is more than a series of military, economic, and technological events carried out by men in public places. The historical record is also constituted by the stories of ordinary individual women negotiating their way through the life cycle and attempting to integrate their familial and civic concerns. With this new knowledge, history moved from being a list of battles to a more in-depth look at societal patterns and the choices women and men have made as they lived their lives and constructed their environments.

At the Grassroots

The women's studies movement called for change on at least three fronts—the individual, the institutional, and the ideological. On all three fronts, people in women's studies believe that we need to look closely at what we do, for it is only then that we can imagine alternatives. Assuming we know already what we are doing, they argue, will not lead to change.

Activists in the women's studies movement placed a particularly high value on equal access for individuals. They put a great deal of emphasis on the need to have women in the academy, especially women willing to teach students new ways of thinking. Without individual women teaching about women, taking up equity issues, and challenging institutional mores, women's studies could not have grown.

Activists in the women's studies movement demanded that institutions of higher education act affirmatively. They pushed their institutions to move beyond the conventional ways of doing things to alternative approaches that would encourage women seeking access. Committees formed, flyers appeared, team-taught courses made it into the schedule, curriculum requirements were modified, students were counseled, office space was found, small budgets were pieced together, and campuswide programs received public attention and support. Through literally hundreds of specific steps, institutions modified themselves in response to the requests of individuals and groups.

Activists in the women's studies movement further demanded that ideas be changed. If women were to be in the classroom and to have a positive experience there, what they learned had to be based in their experiences, represent a portion of their expressions, and reflect their expectations. Ultimately, those in women's studies asked piercing questions about how social structures and ideas came to be that way.

It is important to emphasize that all of these grassroots activities took place in relative isolation in the 1970s, without extensive national networks. Certainly, individuals knew one another and schools exchanged information. But the predominant force for change came from local efforts to create new information and drew on the energies and abilities of individuals committed to the process. Only later were the more formal trappings of professionalism put in place. These models became available to the many schools beginning programs in the 1980s and beyond.

Organizing for Change

While there is a dizzying array of ways in which these early organizational efforts were undertaken, there is a general pattern to the process. Drawing on roots that extend into the era before the late 1960s,[3] the growth of women's studies programs during the last twenty years constitutes nothing short of a spectacular example of educational change. The success of women's studies must be discussed as it evolved, from a campus-based perspective. Taking that view, we need to think in terms of courses, programs, and transformation efforts.

Courses

Individual women, beginning to research new problems, began teaching new courses. These innovations occurred both within single disciplines and more frequently across several. New course titles started to spring up, offered by women on the faculty. At Duke the earliest examples included courses on women and poverty with economist Juanita Kreps and the social history of American women with historian Anne Firor Scott. I taught the first course in a U.S. university on Third World women and social policy.

Other women, often graduate students and community members working in cooperation with faculty, came together to teach interdisciplinary, issue-centered courses. The introductory women's studies courses usually began in this fashion. Their focus was related to the climate of the specific campus, often covering those topics that did not receive treatment in other departments on campus. Their credibility was often related to the status and backing of the instructors as well as the resources the colleges and universities were willing to put forward. Where status and resources were lacking, difficult tasks became more impossible. The courses dealt explicitly with pedagogy and were inter-disciplinary and broad in scope. They incorporated the insights and writings of women outside the academy, encouraging students to use their knowledge in practical ways through internships and voluntary commitments so that they could learn about women by working with women.

Programs

Programs emerged from courses; while the pattern varies, some common threads can be found. Most typically, student groups pushed administrations into establishing committees to investigate the feasibility of setting up a program. Those initiatives were joined by the faculty women whose attention had turned to women, gender, and feminist theory as well as by the junior faculty coming out of graduate schools where these new scholarly developments had been introduced. In one-on-one interviews conducted by eighteen graduate students in my 1992 course on the foundations of women's studies, every member of the Women's Studies faculty who was surveyed had become concerned with women's issues initially through her personal and political involvements, not through her scholarly investigations. Once introduced to those queries, however, female scholars turned them into subjects for systematic research in their disciplines.

In 1976 Florence Howe studied fifteen programs and sketched their common characteristics.[4] Unlike many other academic units, women's studies programs had ongoing relationships with their local communities and quite specific political agendas. They all emphasized the advising and career concerns of the students enrolled in courses. Women's studies programs became intellectual as well as physical places to explore questions of praxis. Establishing a program was an indicator of institutional legitimacy that gave permanence to the activity. Slowly additional scholars claimed feminist scholarship as part of their work. And with all of these developments through courses and programs, concentrations, minors, majors, honors, graduate education, and tenure lines in women's studies followed.

Transformation Efforts

Having core courses plus courses on women and gender rationalized in a program structure meant that women's studies had to give attention to the relationship between continuing to develop itself and convincing the rest of the academic world to change too. One of the central early questions in women's studies was the either-or of "what next?" Some argued that Women's Studies would eventually disappear; as soon as enough was found out and transferred to its appropriate disciplinary home, the enterprise could fold. Others argued that women's studies should ignore other disciplines and work toward independence by pursuing its own methods, findings, and implications. Those early debates demonstrated to those in women's studies as well as in other fields that the task for women's studies would always be double-edged. Women's studies must continue to develop autonomously, for without space and resources progress could not continue. Yet it must continue to communicate with others about those developments; if women's studies had failed to establish relationships with other academic units, those units would not have benefited from the progress and might even have been hostile to the endeavor. In this dimension women's studies remains unique among many other interdisciplinary efforts.

Estimates suggest that well over 150 campuses now have some form of curriculum transformation effort, and the research literature on those efforts is growing. Each effort is, like much of women's studies, specific to its environment. Yet each effort shares some common characteristics. Faculty colleagues appear less resistant to adding new information than they are to rethinking the old. The enormous growth of women's studies is both a positive factor in making the inquiry appear central and a negative one in that approaching this literature appears daunting for a single individual. Colleges and universities with a tradition of concern for teaching and with a history of collective curricular efforts appear to fare slightly better when undertaking transformation projects; such institutions have already worked beyond the idea that each faculty member is an autonomous actor in the pursuit of truth. And undergraduate efforts are more readily undertaken by faculty than graduate efforts. At the graduate level, where the future of the professions is defined, tampering with the mores of the discipline appears most threatening. Graduate faculty reactions to the development of interdisciplinary endeavors vary. Some embrace the changes, others circle the wagons. This is a new problem for women's studies programs as the field takes on the characteristics of a discipline, a subject taken up in the final chapter of this collection.

Beyond the campus, in slightly more than ten years, a number of other professional developments have taken place that make campus-based efforts more effective. National associations have arisen. The National Women's Studies Association was created in 1977. Earlier many discipline-oriented associations like the Modern Language Association had formed units on feminist issues. Scholarly journals began appearing. *Signs* and *Feminist Studies* began in the middle of the 1970s; 1983 saw the founding of *Sage: A Scholarly Journal on Black Women*; by the late 1980s almost every discipline had developed a separate journal devoted to feminist scholarship. Foundation support was critical to these developments, for it was through the funding of research centers (now numbering some fifty) and transformation projects that the inquiry flourished.

Reflections

In my outline of how the women's studies inquiry grew, I have emphasized the process of creating ideas, organizations, and participants. I have not taken much time to describe what we are coming to know, focusing instead on how we came to be engaged in the process of knowing. I want to continue this emphasis on the process of women's studies by reflecting on what I think will concern us in the future. I have at least three reflections in mind.

First, women's studies is intimately connected to the realities of women in culture and society. As a result, women's studies will continue to struggle with a series of questions stemming from that connection. Here I am reflecting on some of the questions that people in women's studies ask themselves, the internal concerns of the enterprise.

How explicitly politically active can and should women's studies be? How can women's studies be an effective agent for change within the institutions of higher education where it is based yet not be co-opted by those institutions? What questions should be researched and taught in women's studies? Do particular perspectives and groups dominate its agendas? How can the emphasis on women be maintained while the diversity of women's experiences is recognized? How are its results presented to colleagues? to students? to the public?

Second, whatever its internal queries, women's studies poses external challenges to cultural values. It threatens many, inspires some, confuses others. The Western worldview has been challenged before, shaken, and redefined. Copernicus challenged the notion that the earth was the center of the universe. Darwin made us see that human beings were not creatures unto themselves but had evolved from the living world around them. Freud made us aware of the fact that our actions were not always controlled by our conscious will. And some who work with computers say that we are experiencing the dawning realization that human beings are not unique and irreplaceable, that machines with human characteristics can be made. Feminist inquiry poses such a challenge to conventional wisdom about people's place in the scheme of things, about the very meaning of the way in which life is organized. Why is male-female a primary distinction for us? How do we understand sexual similarities and differences? How ought culture and society, its values and institutions, be organized to reflect that understanding? What does all this mean for the way we live, the choices we make, the goals we have? And above all, particularly for students meeting feminist inquiry for the first time, where does it all lead? How do we balance the teaching of realities with the retention of optimism?

Third, not only is women's studies engaged in discussions about its internal directions and the challenges it poses culturally—it must deal simultaneously with both success and invisibility. I want to conclude with this third reflection, suggesting that the inquiry will continue to live with these tensions well into its third decade.

Women's studies is clearly successful. On my campus nearly 1,000 students per semester enroll in courses the program offers; some 25 percent of them are men. As the editor of a scholarly journal, I have a serious backlog of outstanding manuscripts with no end in sight. These are not isolated examples. By national estimates, almost three-quarters of a million students take 30,000 courses through more than 500 programs. *Signs,* the journal that I edit, is one leading example of dozens of similar publications.

Women's studies is also simultaneously invisible. When my colleagues in sociology organized a campuswide retrospective in 1988 to recognize the events of 1968, they managed not to mention women. The situation repeats itself outside the university as well. My twelve-year-old daughter took a social studies class on the 1960s and was required to interview a person who lived then. I was happy to be chosen, thought about it for several days after I'd heard the assignment, and offered what I thought were some pretty good comments on the impact of the birth control pill, Friedan's idea of the problem with no name, and how the Miss America Pageant was first boycotted. According to my daughter, my interview was "bad" because I did not talk about Vietnam, men like Martin Luther King, and the student protests. I spoke to her teacher, who became very defensive about "covering everything."

How are we to deal with these contradictory experiences? All of us know that we move in different communities, relate to different people, and respond to different cues. Yet how is it that at one moment women's studies is the center of our research, teaching, and commitment—the only thing that matters—and the next minute ignored and dismissed? I have no magic solution. I can only suggest that we acknowledge these multiple realities. We must evaluate each encounter and try to close the gap between those who know and those who resist knowing, those who will converse with us and those who cannot; we must be aware of the fact that the strength of the resistance may be an indicator of the impact that women's studies is having. Our frustration with ignorance about women's studies is a product of its success. Women's studies came into being without a recorded history and created its own; in the process of documenting our stories across time, place, ethnicities, and sexualities, we do indeed challenge the status quo. It is comfortable to ignore women's studies. And it is frustrating to be ignored. But the inquiry continues to grow because we continue to confront that ignorance and to use our frustrations for the benefit of us all.

Let me close by reflecting on the shifting metaphors of seeing, speaking, and listening that characterize the brief history of women's studies. It was common in the first decade of women's studies to use a sight metaphor. People talked about making the invisible visible—seeing women who had always existed but whose history and experiences had been ignored in presenting the human story. Implicit in the metaphor was the idea that seeing was believing. If we "saw" women, we would "see" them. If we studied them, we would let them into our institutions as students, hire them as faculty, elect them as our representatives, give our money to their needs. But seeing was not sufficient to the task at hand. Too often seeing certain women meant not seeing other women. To others, visibility appeared threatening and set a backlash in motion.

In the 1980s scholars in women's studies began to replace the sight metaphor with a metaphor emphasizing voice. They began to realize that unless women were talking and being talked about women could not bring about the institutional transformations they sought. These scholars began to talk about students, especially female students, gaining a voice to articulate their positions, their educational needs, and their goals as they understood them. At the close of the decade, gaining a voice replaced being seen as the dominant metaphor, for it described more precisely what the next steps needed to be.

I think the metaphor for the 1990s may well be one of listening. How do the visible, articulate women in North American society get the others in the conversation about education to listen? How do they break through the media-created stereotypes and create spaces in which different voices can be heard? A conversation requires talking and listening. Women and those in women's studies have been seen and are talking; campuses and higher education are only beginning to listen. The challenge for the 1990s will be getting heard.

Understanding
Women's
Diversities and
Commonalities

This forum, energetically organized by Ellen Ironsides and her colleagues, follows the outline of *Educating the Majority*.[1] My task is to explore with you the first section, looking in somewhat greater depth at the theme of diversity and commonalities. I am also assuming that the most effective way to approach this topic will be for me to share some perspectives with you and then for us to engage in a question-and-answer session to elaborate our ideas together.

Let me then outline three perspectives that we, as women in higher education, need to employ in thinking about diversity and commonality. I want to take an epistemological approach and think about our thinking on diversity. In doing so, I want to focus first on diversity, then on commonality. I also want to take the student point of view more frequently than an administrative or a faculty one.

Going beyond the Facts of Diversity

My first observation is that while we are increasingly confronted with the *facts* about diversity in higher education, our actions, ideas, programs, and structures lag far behind. We have all learned that college students are not only young, white, middle-class Protestant males. Even if our own student body does not include all the diversity that exists nationally, we acknowledge the importance of understanding the shifting ethnic and racial basis of our global population as we approach the end of the century.

Let me illustrate the complexity of incorporating new facts with ongoing

This paper was presented at the Women Administrators in North Carolina Higher Education Forum, held at the University of North Carolina at Chapel Hill on June 8, 1990.

practices by citing two examples that come from working closely with African American women students in my position as director of Women's Studies.

The first example concerns role models. When dealing with college women, both inside the classroom and on campus generally, we often say that students need role models to emulate, models who can mentor and inspire them in turn. We often claim that one of the reasons young women feel lost about their future is that they lack relevant female role models.

On the surface of it, the very fact that we recognize the importance of role models for women can be read as positive, a step toward acting on something we now know about female students. But I have never heard the role-model discussion proceed without an African American woman student protesting the terms of the debate. Almost without exception, she will say she has role models—her mother, her aunts, and her grandmother have managed remarkable achievements against the odds; she doesn't grasp why white women lack role models. The rich and rewarding discussions that ensue from such a recognition of difference and similarity are beyond the scope of this talk. Let me simply say that we come only part of the way in dealing with the fact of diversity by recognizing male-female differences and not recognizing differences among women. We strengthen rather than weaken women's causes when we speak to all women. We need to do it directly, by bringing up the subject and working through different women's contributions.

A second example reinforces this point. Last year I invited the dozen or so African American women in my introductory Women's Studies class to lunch at my house to talk with them about the way the class was meeting their needs and to solicit their suggestions. While the conversation ranged over many things, eating issues kept resurfacing, so we settled on them for an in-depth discussion. According to these young African American women, the preoccupation with diet that characterized many of their white fellow students was a real barrier to friendships. African American women and white women had quite different concepts of physical beauty, they said. For example, the women at lunch that day felt that a large figure was a powerful one and that size was positive; for white women this was rarely the case. Mealtimes, according to these students, could become cultural battlegrounds, with white women strategizing nonstop about how to eat less and African American women taking quite different positions on the subject. While African American women appreciated the emphasis in the counseling and student health services on anorexia and bulimia, they believed that it served only a portion of women students and ignored the health needs of *all* women.

I offer these examples not to criticize how little we in higher education have done to deal with diversity, but to suggest how much farther we have to go in putting into practice the facts we now have at our disposal. We must constantly keep our minds and practices open to the limitations of inherited ideas and the need to develop alternative ones.

Confronting the Hidden Curriculum

My second observation deals with curricular issues. It seems to me that when we do confront diversity, we often contain the discussion, as I did in my first observation. We try to digest the new fact and integrate the knowledge into our institutional practices and procedures. We are much less enthusiastic about confronting what the curriculum says about diversity. As administrators, we often back away from discussions with faculty about the content of their teaching, relying instead on the hope that our exhortations to appreciate diversity, coupled with changing practices outside the classroom, will somehow seep down the halls and into the rooms where the business of education is occurring. I don't think so. I think we have to deal explicitly—in appropriate ways, I hasten to add—with what gets taught and how it might be done. What we teach can be analyzed both directly and indirectly. Here again, let me offer some examples.

We are all familiar with the canon debates and related discussions about including material on people other than white men in both humanities and social science classes. The faculty has made significant progress in including new material. But if what Duke students tell me has any validity at all, we have a long way to go. Here's what they're saying:

- After the one lecture devoted to women in a semester-long course in religion, the professor jokes that he will get an award from the Women's Studies Program for how much he's done.
- Readings by and about women appear occasionally in history and literature classes but are critiqued more severely and dismissed as less theoretically weighty than material by men.
- Differences among women are either not discussed or lumped together into a race-class-and-gender day at the end of the course.
- References to women, particularly in political science and economics, are always negative. Women are the butt of jokes. Women are evaluated by a male standard and dismissed as lacking.

I could go on at great length about how diversity is handled in specific classroom situations, but for now it is enough to say that the mere mention of women, people of color, and other groups constitutes no more than a first step.

I hear my mother's voice: "It's not *what* you said but *how* you said it," she used to caution me.

These examples focused on the direct mention of various subjects in classroom settings. Now I want to address the hidden curriculum and the impact of indirect teaching on diversity. Let me focus for a moment on the natural sciences.

We are all aware of the movements in the sciences to recruit women and people of color. Encoded in these recruitment efforts, to my eye and ear, are two profound biases that ignore diversity. One has to do with age and the other with sexual orientation.

The majority of recruitment efforts are directed toward the young. Just as we seem to think (based on very illusory evidence) that all individuals are completely formed exclusively by mothers by the age of two or three, so we appear to assume that all science must be foregrounded by middle school. Is there no place for mature women in science? Is the scientific enterprise really that linear or continuous? I would argue that it is simply counterintuitive to say that only the young, caught early, can do science. I do not have the specific answers, but I must suggest that we investigate *science* rather than its *recruits* to find alternatives. This is the message of *Educating the Majority*, and it needs to be applied to natural science as well as other parts of the university.

When women and science programs are underway, there is an extreme heterosexual bias at work in so much of what goes on. If women are discussed in science, it is usually in informal settings that stress how to manage a career in science and a marriage. Academic advisers alternate between the assumption that women should go slower and be women (i.e., marry and have children) and the assumption that they should ignore being women (i.e., deny that they are family members). Do you have to be a mother to be a woman? Do all women want to marry? I often listen to these debates, assuming for the moment a lesbian identity, and find myself appalled by the general cultural lack of awareness to difference. I urge this exercise on each of us: assume an identity—based on sex, race, age, or ability—other than your present one and listen to what is being said. I think you will be shocked by both the direct and the indirect messages being put forth in our classrooms.

Attending to What Students Know

I have recently become interested in a third question, the basis of my last observation. It assumes that we are working to close the gap between what we know and what we do, that we are engaged in confronting diversity inside the classroom as well as outside of it. My third observation is that we need to pay more attention to who the students are; what they know and want to learn; and what values, assumptions, and experiences they bring to the learning enterprise and into which we pour information.

Of course, learning is a relational, interactive process, but I am saying more: that contemporary students—young and old, male and female, white people and people of color—have many ideas about themselves and the culture in which they live; we need to understand their ideas before we can effectively talk with them about diversity. Their experiences are not the same as ours, and it isn't just a matter of age. It has to do with their cohort and their historical context as opposed to ours.

For me, this observation grows out of being involved in curriculum transformation projects. As many of you know, women's studies programs devote considerable energy to working with faculty who are not feminist scholars and encouraging them to incorporate material on women into their courses. Similar efforts occur across all ethnic studies as well. When I step back and look at curriculum transformation efforts, I am struck by the fact that their emphasis is exclusively on content, with a dash of pedagogy for spice. They are constructed to instruct faculty about new material and to suggest how that new material might be presented. They do not ask who is receiving the material and how students' background, values, and ideas form the basis for receiving this new information.

My initial reaction to curriculum projects has been reinforced by a variety of other experiences. For example, following the developments in literary theory about reader response and the relationships between text and reader, I began to think about students as readers of the lecture and the lecture as text. This led me to ask what students heard in what faculty were saying.

I also began to listen to graduate students, all politically correct and well informed, complain about the undergraduates they teach. I contrast their complaints with what I hear undergraduates say about men, women, race, class, and gender, and I wonder whether the graduate students are talking about the same undergraduates who participate in the programs we sponsor and exhibit insightful, innovative analysis of their ideas and assumptions.

Finally, I consult with my colleagues in Women's Studies, and we analyze what students say in their journals and papers. These students are thinking carefully and deeply about issues of diversity and commonality, but it is often in ways very different from our own as professionals from the ages of thirty to eighty.

Unless we pay more attention to what students know and think, we will miss the opportunity to get ideas across to them. Let me illustrate by sharing some insights I have gained into students' thinking this past semester. Please note here that I am describing Duke students. Other sets of students at other schools would have other ideas and values. The idea that students have cultural maps onto which we are writing is what I want to emphasize in these examples.

In the introductory Women's Studies course in the first few weeks, I engage students in learning about sex-role socialization by assigning an exercise in gender-role violation. I ask them to name a behavior that they think is inappropriate for them, as a man or woman, and then to try out that behavior, just once, in public, with an observer. They write a brief paper describing what they did, why they chose to do it, what reactions they got, how they feel about it, and what the relationship is between their own ideas and the responses they received. I make only a few suggestions about what to do because I want them to figure out what they think.

The range of things they choose to do is endlessly fascinating and surprising. Some women pick up men in student bars; some men cry in front of pals. Women carry heavy objects in public while their male friends tag along empty-handed. The more adventuresome women sit on campus benches and rate men, read pornography, or funnel beer at fraternity parties.

Read together, two distinctive patterns emerge. First, these students understand how the sex-gender system operates in our culture in a very sophisticated way. They understand how it supports power differences. What they do not understand is why it came to be that way, how it perpetuates itself, or what can be done individually or collectively to change it. They lack historical as well as theoretical explanatory frameworks. They can name the cultural practices that mark maleness and femaleness with an acuteness that is painful to hear. Do we talk to them with an appreciation of how detailed their knowledge is? Do we understand how profoundly they lack an analysis of the workings of social and cultural systems that perpetuate differences? They don't remember the 1960s and the rise of feminism as a social movement. They do remember the conservatism of the 1980s and the backlash against feminism. They are confused by the contradictory messages they hear.

Second, students anticipate the gender-role exercise eagerly from the first day of class. They always think it will be fun and invest considerable energy in planning and staging their violations. As they engage in the project, they experience enormous confusion when they find that the reactions of their peers are overwhelmingly negative. Whether they commit these acts on campus or in the community, students experience censure for overstepping cultural boundaries. They then have to deal with the fact that they are not the free agents they thought they were. They get into deep discussions of the role of cultural and social expectations in forming individuals. Do we present material to them in ways that recognize the tensions they experience in being both agents and victims? Do we understand that they live in a relatively diverse community of dormitories and classes whose diversity we tend to minimize if not dismiss?

There are many ways to interpret the material I am generating from students; time prevents us from doing more than naming and illustrating the point. Let me simply restate it: in order to teach diversity and commonality effectively to students of every background, we need to pay more attention to what they know, discarding our templates of knowledge and formulating ways to teach the new scholarship on women and gender to students as they are in the 1990s.

Knowers, Knowing, and the Known

I think it is inappropriate to try to come to any general conclusion, for the very purpose of *Educating the Minority* and this forum is to open up questions for debate and engage each one of us personally in seeking answers. I have outlined three perspectives about diversity that I hope are instructive in thinking about the changing nature of higher education. I can summarize what I have said by reference to a schema that Mary Hawkesworth first developed in a *Signs* article and later elaborated in her book *Beyond Oppression*.[2] Mary said that we need to ask about knowers, knowing, and the known:

- Who are the *knowers*? Who has cultural license to generate knowledge? We are obviously seeing an expansion of the category of knowers.
- How does the process of *knowing* occur? How has knowing moved from the formal analysis of selected texts to the more multifaceted investigation of a wide range of experiences from diverse vantage points? What constitutes knowing?
- What is now *known*? Is it sufficient to the tasks before us?

It seems to me that when we talk about diversity in higher education, we are talking about encouraging new knowers and engaging in alternate ways of knowing so that what is known is more complete and more useful to all. How and when will we know that we have accomplished something? There is no certain way to know. I sense that our uncertainty will be replaced, at least partially, by the satisfaction that comes from getting a fuller picture.

PART THREE

Teaching

I
n this part of the book I take up the question of how I have put some of my insights about women, education, and institutional power into action in the classroom. I do that by analyzing in detail how the undergraduate and graduate core courses in Women's Studies create spaces that enable individual students to make new connections between themselves and their circumstances. My general aim is to explore the claim that women's studies makes a difference by asking exactly how? why? and with what results? All four chapters in this section grow out of research conducted in Women's Studies classes; each uses those classrooms as sites for ethnographic investigations.

Chapter 9 was written in 1990 when I first began to realize that unless I, as a teacher, knew more about undergraduates' understandings of gender dynamics, I would not be effective in conveying information or in developing perspectives. Chapter 10, on undergraduates as active agents in curriculum transformation, was completed in 1993 as I came to grips with how to conceptualize students as collaborators in the educational process. Chapter 11 was researched and written in 1991 to investigate the effect of the Women's Studies Program on undergraduates' ideas and activities. It takes me further into an understanding of what students know and how they use what they know in the classroom, on campus, and in their lives beyond the college walls. Chapter 12 focuses on graduate students and the ways in which they respond to unlearning and relearning scholarly material. Here I am able to take yet another step, examining the dynamic between what I teach and what they learn. The activities described in all four chapters occur in the classroom—for me a central site of observation and documentation. What I have learned in the classroom provides the empirical underpinnings for my reflections on administration that are the subject of Part 4.

Duke University is a private research university of some 11,000 graduate, undergraduate, and professional-school students. At the collegiate level it is a residential college specializing in the liberal arts. At the graduate level it is a high-powered institution training research scholars. As a select school, its students are drawn from among the most academically and financially privileged cohorts in the country. Few students are beyond traditional college age; 18 percent of first-year students were people of color in 1990. Figures for the graduate population are similar. The Women's Studies Program has grown into a strong and visible campus presence, enrolling over 1,000 students per semester in classes and sponsoring numerous lectures and projects. It works closely with the campus Women's Center, under the aegis of Student Affairs. The university also houses a center for research on women that is jointly operated with the University of North Carolina at Chapel Hill.

Like other coeducational colleges and universities, Duke presents a campus culture that is by no means favorable to women. Some practices and structures simply exclude women—revenue sports and womenless classes being the prime examples. Some aspects of campus life belittle or ignore women—such as fraternity domination of social life and departmental politics that preclude hiring women faculty. Other issues of direct relevance to women are simply evaded—eating disorders and interracial dating are not subjects of sustained attention in campus programming or classroom instruction. The campus culture here, as elsewhere in the United States, is relatively hegemonic, based on values inherited from an educational system that was designed for white male elites. Various campus groups and offices arise each year to address these issues and others. With energy and time, they do alter the campus climate, as the recent campaigns to present information on acquaintance rape have done. Such efforts, however, resonate with a dominant culture that mutes efforts at change, especially when that change is directed to reallocating power among groups based on gender, race, class, and sexuality.

Some have argued that Duke has been more effective than many other universities in creating a climate where women's studies flourishes. After the selection of Nannerl Keohane to become the university's first female president in 1993, discussion ensued about the circumstances that enabled a conservative southern research university to take a move that was widely considered bold. Drawing out clear lines of cause and effect is plainly impossible. What does seem possible is to explore the multiple initiatives on women's issues pursued by women's studies and others that create a climate where such decisions can be made. That is the task of the chapters in this part and the next one. What does appear to be true is that feminist scholarship has provided the backdrop against which other initiatives succeed. Thus, the successful operation of the program provides a structure into which feminist scholars, when recruited by some departments, move. The extensive offerings of the program mean that students gain a critical perspective with which to view classroom and campus events. And the positive synergy of outstanding research, ample teaching, and effective programming create a situation that wins administrative support, further reinforcing the program's efforts.

Women's Studies 103, entitled Introduction to Women's Studies, is offered at least once every year and consistently enrolls between sixty-five and one hundred undergraduate students. The class population tends to consist of predominantly white, upper-middle- and-middle class women. For the past several years, the class has included 10 percent people of color and 10 percent males.

Class time is divided between lectures, films, and discussions. Seven times during the semester, instead of meeting as whole, the class meets in small (ten to fifteen students) discussion groups facilitated by graduate teaching assistants. On the first day of class, students fill out an initial evaluation that is designed to discover their previous experience with women's issues and their expectations of the course. At mid-semester they fill out a similar evaluation; at the last regular class session they complete the standard university course evaluation form. In addition to readings and a final examination, students complete four major assignments, each of which requires them to perform a certain activity and then analyze in writing what they observed when they performed the activity. Upon completion, the assignments are extensively discussed and compared in the small group discussions.

The first assignment, which was described in Chapter 8, is a gender-role violation and explores how gender-role expectations affect personal interactions. The exercise requires the students to publicly undertake an action that they would normally consider inappropriate for themselves as women or men. They must have an observer stationed to watch both their own reactions and those of the people around them. In their papers they are asked to draw on their reading and lecture materials in order to speculate on why the gender norm exists and to examine the source of social controls.

In the second assignment, a curriculum evaluation, students move to the level of societal analysis. They fill out a questionnaire about two of their courses. The questionnaire is designed to reveal the underlying assumptions of a course and the existence of gender bias, if any is present. Questions range from the very specific ("How many photos and illustrations in the course material show women in positions of power or action? how many show men?") to essay questions requiring synthesis and analysis of the specific findings ("What are the strengths and weaknesses of the course in terms of providing a full perspective on women in its subject matter?").

The third project, an oral history interview, requires that students foreground questions of history, change, and continuity. Students must interview a woman who is at least twenty years their senior or over the age of sixty-five. After reflecting upon certain issues that they have come to understand through talking with her, they write a report analyzing how these issues reinforce, complement, or contradict what they have learned from classroom resources. A large percentage choose to interview their mothers.

Finally, students must perform an action project, an attempt to initiate change. Projects can be done in groups or individually; they may be quite public or essentially private. The emphasis of the assignment is not on the success or failure of the action but on the process of setting actions in motion as well as understanding both what constitutes social change and how change occurs for women. Their final paper must draw clear links between what they do and the historical efforts of women to change society as well as women's social roles.

Chapter 9 analyzes students' conceptions of gender, drawing on material from the first assignment. Chapter 10 examines students' assessments of gender content and dynamics in their classes, as derived from the second assignment. The ways that faculty understand their role in transmitting knowledge and defining classroom dynamics are the subject of Chapter 11. Here I argue that one way to increase the amount of material on women in the curriculum is to teach students to demand such material by taking students through the steps of researching what they are being taught; exploring with them why that is the case; and then helping them create the intellectual and interpersonal tools they need to do something about the situation. Chapter 11 studies the ways in which students gain a voice as women. The process of "coming to voice" is discussed largely in terms of their relationships with friends and family. These three chapters all draw on the undergraduate classroom for their data.

Chapter 12 looks at the graduate core course, A History of Feminist Thought (WST 211). Since 1985 the Women's Studies Program at Duke has offered a graduate program leading to a certificate in women's studies. To earn the certificate, students must take WST 211 as well as two other courses that extend their disciplinary work on women and gender.

This dual focus in the women's studies concentration reflects the context in which advanced study is pursued at Duke. Duke does not offer master's degrees in the traditional disciplines as free-standing degrees; nor does it offer a master's degree in women's studies. Moreover, feminist scholars at Duke offer within their own departments a rich variety of advanced theory courses that take up current debates as they emerge. Thus the Women's Studies community felt Duke needed a concentration that would include at least one course that would bring students from diverse departments together for multidisciplinary conversations, give them a historical perspective on the contours of contemporary work, and enable them to see how feminist inquiry entered the Anglo-American academy. The graduate core course emphasizes how the exclusion of material by women has shaped the construction of the academic disciplines we have inherited.

Both graduate and undergraduate students seek out Women's Studies as a place in which to approach issues that they want to explore not only within their course work but after graduation in their careers as well. Both express the need for a place where they can garner explanatory frameworks for their personal experiences. Both talk openly about their need to develop a voice that can express the questions they have and the answers they are discovering.

Undergraduates experience isolation most frequently when friends criticize the changes a student in Women's Studies is undergoing. While residential colleges often fuse the personal and social worlds of undergraduates, these students still have a wider university and many other places to turn for friendship and support for their emergent feminism. For graduate students, however, the department is their social and professional world. As a result, graduate students experience the issue of isolation more intensely.

As emergent professionals, graduate students are undergoing a socialization process that makes them feel vulnerable to attacks on feminist scholarship when they envision such inquiry as their "life's work." Graduate students often talk about lack of assistance, indifference, and even hostility from mentors who are unfamiliar with feminist frameworks. They also meet resistance in the undergraduate classes they teach from a younger generation that considers a feminist perspective unnecessary in today's world, where "everything has changed."

Living and working within this context, graduate students often find explorations into the history of feminist scholarship both critical and frightening. They know that without this material they cannot get the full benefit of their disciplinary journeys. Yet gaining a feminist perspective makes them angry, frustrated, and sometimes discouraged with how much remains to be done. Because feminist scholarship has developed so extensively within the past few decades, this upcoming generation of feminist scholars faces a vastly proliferating field with which it is difficult simply to keep up—much less keep up with other fields. Graduate students face another reality: that learning this new material requires them to unlearn some of the collegiate knowledge they have mastered and to which they cling when so many previous foundations are being shaken. When I first presented the material in Chapter 12 as a public lecture, I found the audience anxious to meet the foremothers who have preceded this generation, angered that these women have been neglected in inherited knowledge, excited to discover an intellectual heritage as distinguished as others they have studied, and fascinated by the process in which students and material interact.

Two of these four chapters are coauthored with graduate students. One of the most rewarding aspects of working with emergent scholars is the opportunity to teach them new material and to enable them to reflect on the multiple uses of that material. When working with graduate students in the classroom, I involve them in research projects that allow us to gauge more precisely what we are doing. Linking teaching and research about teaching is a new experience for graduate students at Duke. It fosters in them a sense of expertise and confidence that they take with them into the profession. And it contributes to the documentation of women's studies that is sorely needed if we are to take advantage of our heritage and improve our capacities in the future.

While it is evident that data from any one class, indeed any one university, are limited, I hope these chapters illustrate a way of approaching and utilizing the data at hand. I hope the discussion of these case materials fosters the practice of recording everyday activities and encourages other teachers, students, and administrators to find additional, parallel ways to investigate their own daily realities, their consequences, and their possibilities.

CHAPTER 9

"Just an Experiment for My Women's Studies Class"

Female Students and the Culture of Gender

Coauthored with Michelle LaRocque and Miriam Peskowitz

I n the early 1980s the new course Introduction to Women's Studies was designed at Duke University. Although it continues to change every semester, one feature, the exercise in gender-role violation, has remained constant. In originally designing the course, we benefited greatly from discussions with colleagues at other colleges and universities. One of the most helpful suggestions came from Dr. Barbara Risman of the Sociology Department at neighboring North Carolina State University. She described an exercise that had proved useful for her class on gender and family. In this exercise, students committed a gender-role violation and wrote an analysis of it. For example, a female student might ride the intercampus bus and insist that a male take her seat when it becomes crowded. Or she might try to control a conversation in a mixed group, turning the discussion toward women's concerns and keeping it there. By creating such scenarios, acting them out, and then analyzing them with the help of a planted observer, students could start to develop a critical perspective on gender roles, looking through the familiar to see cultural ideas and everyday practices in a new light. The idea sounded good, and the exercise was incorporated into the course.

In the years since, the exercise has assumed a central role in the course. Conducted at the beginning of the semester, it is a constant topic of interest throughout the semester. Students enroll anticipating the exercise as one of their first experiences in Women's Studies. The campus newspaper almost always refers to it, and occasionally it has been the subject of a full-length article. It was also chosen by an independent documentary filmmaker as a topic for a series on male-female relationships.

Whenever we describe the exercise to colleagues, they too are intrigued and ask for details. A faculty seminar on curriculum transformation studied the student papers that came from the exercise as a means of gauging student understanding of gender dynamics and the institutional forces underlying them. In short, what started out as a simple device to engage students in the study of women and gender has grown into a defining characteristic of the class on the Duke campus.

The fascination of students and professional colleagues with the exercise led us last year to explore more fully what has been going on. Those explorations are the basis of this essay. The paper is not about pedagogy as it is conventionally defined. Rather, we use this pedagogical exercise to theorize about the relation between the content of women's studies, the kinds of knowledge that students bring into the course, and students' dispositions toward understanding the material and experientially integrating it into their lives.

While we have not yet worked through all the implications of these explorations, we believe that by laying them out here we have taken a first step. We began by asking ourselves what intrigued students in the exercise. As we explain below, the opportunity to investigate the relationship between their experiences and the ideology surrounding those experiences appears to be a particularly valuable learning moment. Examining and demystifying relationships between social institutions and their surrounding ideology have been central activities in women's studies generally, both in teaching and in research. In this specific instance, students seize the opportunity to create scenarios about what they know, comparing their experiences with the research knowledge available in the form of readings as well as the general cultural knowledge conveyed to them through others' reactions to their actions. They connect the personal to the political, and in the process learn how to analyze institutions and themselves.

And other faculty members? Why do fellow colleagues continually seize upon this aspect of the course as something they want to adapt for their own courses? We theorize that the exercise accomplishes at least three things from the teacher's point of view. First, the exercise uncovers a good deal about how students conceptualize gender dynamics; it underscores the fact that students have a considerable amount of information about gender culture, if not about its antecedents and consequences. Second, the exercise dramatizes how much teachers need to teach to the varied ideas and experiences that students already possess, rather than assuming they lack any ideas about gender. Students are not "blank slates" regarding gender culture. Moreover, gender culture inter-relates with racial, ethnic, and religious backgrounds that must be integrated into descriptions of gender. Thus students come to the classroom with all sorts of constructed meanings of gender. By understanding and teaching to these constructs, we can help them think critically about gender and culture. Finally, the exercise models an approach to learning that lies at the base of women's studies: describing women's experiences in order to move from description to analysis and explanation of gender dynamics on a social and cultural level.

Below we describe the exercise, what the students do, and how they learn from it. We follow this description with some speculations on the gener-alizability of our experiences with this exercise. It is critical to recognize that we did not set up the exercise in order to analyze it. Quite the opposite: the fascination with the exercise by others over time has led us to think through what happens when we assign it and students undertake it. We seek to under-stand what the general interest in this specific exercise can reveal about teach-ing and learning in women's studies. The more we talked about what we were learning from the students' processes of learning, the more we saw the need to systematically record what we were observing. We want to reemphasize that while the exercise itself is exciting, most important are the students' responses and how these responses help us to theorize some pedagogical aspects of women's studies and feminist thought. In doing this, we seek to create a new discourse on teaching, learning, and thinking. We have chosen an essay format in which we put forward our observations and then analyze them as the most useful way to start thinking about our experiences and to invite others to join us with their own observations.

The students whose papers we analyze here took the course in the spring of 1990. We set aside the few papers from male students, concentrating instead on the responses of the seventy-nine female students. The students are drawn equally from all four years of the undergraduate college and represent some twenty majors. About half belong to sororities. Most of them come from middle- to upper-income households; for many, this economic position is a recent one. About 10 percent of the young women are African American, and perhaps another 5 percent identified themselves as members of non-European ethnic groups. None of the students identified their sexual preference in this assignment.

The students analyzed here stand in varying positions on a continuum running from nonfeminist to "curious about feminism" to feminist. Respond-ing to a questionnaire distributed on the first day of class, about one-half of the students identified themselves as feminists, most providing a definition that focused on the belief that individual women could "do anything they wanted to do." Yet when it came time to violate a gender-role norm, because each person was asked to come up with her own violation, the woman's self-identification as a feminist did not seem to make a difference in the ease or difficulty of the project. In all cases, because it was a very personal challenge, what started out as a simple and potentially fun assignment quickly became a complex, fearsome, thought-provoking, and often difficult task for them.

Because this paper constitutes the first research project to use the introductory class as a site for ethnographic investigation, in writing this paper we do not yet have the means to analyze the backgrounds of the students and match backgrounds with responses. Lacking such material, we focused on the data that the exercise made available to us, data that described the "college" culture in which they lived, a culture they perceived as relatively hegemonic in its norms and values. These students report that the culture exerts very strong influences over their behavior, particularly with respect to gender roles. As we shall see, the exercise identified specific aspects of the culture they found restrictive and subsequently began to question. This concrete awareness of how the gender system works in their own lives was reinforced by readings and presentations throughout the semester; this awareness became the basis for discussions in the class as a whole on the interrelationship of race, class, gender, and sexuality.

Helping students deal with the transition from their "ignorance" of the gender system to the all-too-painful and suddenly ubiquitous awareness of that system is a serious concern. Class films and assigned readings contain varied examples from different races, socioeconomic positions, and lifestyles. Campus and community activists from advocacy organizations (such as date rape projects and women's shelters) make presentations to demonstrate how people employ feminist frameworks in everyday life. Faculty from other departments lecture, illustrating how advanced courses further explore the intellectual investigations presented in an introductory interdisciplinary class. In addition, class discussions, both in the lectures and in small groups, focus on building connections with the insights first glimpsed in this exercise.

The Gender-Role Violations

Several years ago, when the assignment was first conceived and distributed, we had few specific notions of what exactly these female college students would see as female and male roles in social situations. Our only requirement was that they take along an observer, whose commentary plays an important part in their subsequent analysis of the experiment. Based on the violations performed by previous introductory classes, the project assignment sheet for the spring of 1990 suggested several violations. To a limited degree, these suggestions define a range of gender roles for the students. However, students were also given the option of devising their own violation, so long as it was not something they "already always did." In fact, more than half of the women created new violations.

Before describing in detail these students' choices of gender-role violations, we want to make clear that throughout this paper, we consciously use terms such as "male," "masculine," "female," and "feminine" to designate culturally held, socially constructed stereotypes rather than essentialized, ahistorical definitions of gender. It is, in fact, the whole point of this exercise to bring these stereotypes into the open so that students can analyze and critique their alleged universality, accuracy, and potency.

Imitating typical male actions was the rule for all of the violations. None of the women performed violations that explored or challenged stereotypically female behaviors, such as dressing up and putting on makeup before appearing in public. Their violations read as texts in which female college students assume notions of WASP maleness rather than as attempts to relinquish, modify, or even problematize notions of femaleness or explore alternative combinations of both.

The chosen violations divided easily into two broad categories. In the first category, the young women demonstrated a consciousness of men's actions in everyday campus life—activities which men do or which society condones for men and not for women. Those students who chose to concentrate on men's actions frequently performed acts that society generally considers disrespectful and rude in the abstract but appears to condone when performed publicly by men. On campus at least, men were seen as culturally empowered to swear, arrange their genitals in public, dress sloppily, smoke cigars, chew tobacco, drive offensively, funnel-drink, belch, fart, spit in public, and eat lots of food. For purposes of the assignment, women did the same. For example, in order to mimic male harassment of women, a group of female students occupied public benches on campus and shouted comments about the physical appearance of male passersby. Other women committed "chivalrous" acts for men: hauling heavy objects, carrying grocery bags to cars, starting a fight to protect a man's honor, and giving up a seat on a bus. Many of the female students tested male and female roles in heterosexual dating relationships. These young women bought men drinks, asked them to dance, requested their phone numbers, and initiated physical contact. Finally, some students performed violations which they believed displayed an open admission of, and interest in, sexuality. These women bought and read pornographic magazines, rented pornographic videos, and bought condoms.

In the second category, the students intentionally entered the physical spaces dominated by men and mimicked men's behavior once there. Here the students sometimes imitated male roles, but, more important, they did so in spaces not considered open to women. These "invasions" fall into two groups. Some women chose site-specific places in which they felt excluded or uncomfortable: the free-weight sections of gyms, pornographic video stores, football fields, on-campus basketball courts, certain spaces at a fraternity party (such as the funnel-drinking area where beer is poured down someone's throat through a funnel and the area behind the bar where beer is pumped from the keg), and pool halls. Other women targeted all-male domains not necessarily linked to a specific site by playing active and casually organized sports such as football, volleyball, and basketball or by dealing with cars and car maintenance. In all of these violations, the women focused on going where many men go and, once there, doing what many men typically do.

The activities these students chose to perform tells us about the wide variety of roles and actions that they considered to be gender-linked. The range and depth of information these female students had about male behaviors and attitudes is striking. Yet while identifying gender roles came fairly easily to these women, translating this knowledge into action was quite another matter. The young women's descriptions of their feelings gave us a sense of how pervasive and rigid they experience the constraints of hegemonic college gender culture to be in their everyday lives. The majority found this direct and conscious intervention into the culture more difficult than they expected. The following response is typical of those students who approached the activity thinking it would be easy and unproblematic: "We, especially myself, consider ourselves to be products of the '80s. We thought it would be difficult to find a gender role that we would feel uncomfortable breaking. Originally I was going to ask the young man [for a date] in person, but as the time grew nearer I became more and more uncomfortable. Even over the phone the discomfort persisted."

Some of the students tried to commit their violation in a place, or with a person, as remote as possible from their real lives: "We must confess that we chose to leave Durham to better secure our chances of not running into someone we knew because then I'm not sure if we could have gone through with it."

The women described in detail their emotional responses and feelings of discomfort while carrying out their violations. In general, they reported feeling "embarrassed," "uncomfortable," "awkward," "self-conscious," and "anxious." Others wrote that they felt "sleazy," "crude," "unattractive," and "unfeminine." This was particularly true of the women who bought pornography, smoked cigars, or mimicked what they considered to be rude and undignified male behaviors.

For the students who committed sports violations, fear of ridicule by the males present produced strong emotional responses, as this woman explained about her experiences in the pool hall: "For the first time in my life I understood the nature of objectification. To these men, we were Women; nothing else defined us, nothing else had any relevance to them. I felt immobilized with embarrassment, weak and defenseless against a wall of blind expectations."

Images of enforcement were present in their writings. Many of the women reported feeling "paranoid" while committing their gender-role violation, as though they were "doing something wrong," "committing a crime," or "breaking some special rule": "I had visions of condom police, a loud chorus of drugstore shoppers chanting in unison—'woman buying condoms on aisle seven.'" From a woman who smoked a cigar in a shopping mall: "What really surprised me was when I got butterflies in my stomach when a policeman approached me. He was just walking to the trash can, but I actually felt as though I had broken the law."

For some of these young women, the violation was made more difficult by the overt resistance, ridicule, or negative reactions of others. When analyzing their emotions, students reported in particular that encountering resistance gave rise to, or heightened, their feelings of embarrassment and self-consciousness: "When I performed this gender-role violation, I felt embarrassed and awkward. . . . These feelings were especially strong when I first put the [tobacco] chew into my mouth and when I had to spit; I felt very unattractive and crude. Although these emotions were originally self-imposed, once the men in the room noticed my discomfort and began to joke about it, my emotions intensified." One woman, who chose to bowl with the guys, try to win, and then boast about it, reported that her initial good feelings about winning were short-lived: "When I violated this gender norm and gloated over my victory, I felt pretty good about myself. I enjoyed acting this way about winning and did not feel embarrassed at all until they started openly criticizing my behavior. Then I felt very self-conscious. Although I tried to defend myself, I still felt sort of looked down upon, as if I had fallen out of favor."

When students met with resistance from friends, co-workers, or acquaintances, many of them felt that they had to apologize for or explain their behavior. This woman felt the need to explain her possession of a *Playgirl* magazine after her male friends announced they had just lost all respect for her: "At this point, I decided that I should explain the real reason for having the magazine before I lost three of my closest male friends. Even after fully explaining the experiment, however, I still felt uncomfortable and very afraid that my male friends would not really believe my story. I almost felt like I was a bad person, like there was something wrong with me for buying the magazine."

Despite the difficulties, some women students reported feeling "empowered" or "liberated" while committing their violations. This was particularly true of the women who bought condoms. One woman wrote about her third condom-buying outing: "When I violated this norm, I felt powerful. . . . I was in the position of power." Another woman was delighted by the demystifying experience of changing a car tire: "When I did have to change the tire, I felt I did just as good a job as any male would have done. I discovered that I could do it, and the male-dominated mystical aura to it disappeared; I had learned the truth!"

Sometimes the experience disrupted a student's sense of identity and compelled her to reevaluate prior conceptions of herself as a "liberated" and "modern" woman: "Before I did this assignment I would have been one of those women who said that I was 'liberated' and that I would not have had a problem with asking a man out or buying him a drink, but it appears that I am not quite as liberated as I would have liked to think."

Through reflections on their direct incursions into gender culture, these female college students discovered cultural gender prescriptions to be much more pervasive and rigid than they had previously thought. The violations clarified for them the extent to which gender norms construct and constrict everyday life. The violations further enabled them to contrast what they "know" on the basis of experience with what they act out because they "know" such behavior is expected of them. Read as snapshots of select college-age women in the early 1990s, the experiences and responses of these students suggest that, despite contemporary discussions about the breakdown of traditional male-female roles, barriers against changing gender norms remain strong. Students know the dominant gender culture and bring it with them to the classroom and the campus where it is reinforced. Tellingly, these students equated thinking about gender exclusively with imitating masculinity rather than experimenting with what constitutes female culture; thus confrontations with various culturally imposed gender roles proved confusing and frustrating.

Understanding Gender Culture

In addition to violating a chosen gender norm, the assignment required each student to consider why that norm exists and to speculate on the mechanisms that perpetuate it. Their reflections on these topics allow us to move beyond the initial snapshots to analyze how these students think cultural systems operate. In the initial explanatory attempts, the young women used their personal histories to figure out where they learned their ideas about gender and how these ideas affected them during the activity. At the sociocultural level students did two things. As required by the assignment, they used the initial class readings and lecture material to analyze both the content of gender norms and the processes by which these norms are established and perpetuated. Their attempts at explanation brought in a wide variety of sociocultural mythologies of gender.

The women students understood that forces of socialization existed. As the principal socializing force in these women's lives, these women often cited "family." This was particularly true with regard to norms governing sexuality and dating rituals: "Sex was a taboo subject in our household. I always felt ashamed by the prospect of my mother finding out about anything that happened to me sexually. I was taught, above all, that nice people just didn't discuss sex. And nice girls certainly don't buy condoms."

For some students, familial gender norms were linked specifically to ethnicity, religious background, and regional views of gender-appropriate behavior. As this student explains: "I was raised in a conservative southern home where you did not accept a date from someone if he called you and asked you out for that night; it was not proper. . . . Basically, I am the stereotypical southern belle. Because of the way I was raised, approaching a guy and buying him a drink was very difficult." Some students could locate no particular source for their ideas about gender; rather, they appealed to their "socialization as a female" or to "society" in order to assess their responses to their actions: "My self-imposed apprehension was a result of my socialization as a female. I felt awkward and silly because I knew it was 'improper' in society's eyes for me, a young woman, to seek employment at a gas station."

From these analyses it is clear that this group of female college students can identify some of the arenas and institutions in which gender-appropriate behaviors are learned. Yet it is also clear that they find it difficult to think about how the components of this process of socialization operate. The students initially had few ideas about *how* cultural gender roles are perpetuated or *how* knowledge about gender is acquired and reinforced. Their explorations of gender norms help us determine the kinds of information to which they have access and see the conceptual maps they employ to explain the processes by which gender systems are created and maintained.

Students cite many sources of information when trying to explain the cultural reasons for gender systems and the power relations embedded therein. Despite this variety of sources, their analyses fall into five broad categories: (1) dominant symbolic systems and cultural meanings; (2) the control of female sexuality; (3) economic factors and the assumed traditional division of labor between women and men; (4) the early socialization of boys and girls into culturally appropriate gender behavior; and (5) power dynamics between men and women.

The students used these categories as explanations in several ways. In some cases, a student offered just one of these categories as the social justification for the norm she violated. For example, one woman appealed to ideas about female sexuality to explain why it is a gender-role violation for a woman to buy condoms: men but not women are allowed to display publicly their sexual habits. Another woman explained heterosexual dating norms as a function of economic factors: "Males can justify the reasons for their earning higher wages than females through cultural outlets such as the tradition to buy the drink."

More commonly, however, a student attempted to "add on," offering a string of informational categories linked together into a narrative. One woman's discussion of buying pornography looked to cultural systems of religious values ("Moslems as well as very religious Jews and Catholics insist that women cover themselves in public"); moved from there to the social control of female sexuality through representation ("Usually the virtuous woman is portrayed with her eyes cast downward"); suggested further that childhood socialization also contributed ("The treatment of children from birth by parents and continued by teachers and peers fosters different patterns of behavior in boys and girls"); and finally returned to cultural meanings, this time in the form of media advertisements ("Advertisements are another manifestation and cause of the enculturation of the idea that women are more passive").

These narratives varied in coherence and explanatory power. Notably, each tried to forge a framework that would account for the perpetuation of gender norms by adding up several different explanations of which the student already possessed some knowledge. Other students, frustrated with figuring out the "reasons" and unable to find a framework that satisfactorily described the gender norm, claimed that no explanation existed.

Some students' inabilities to explain the processes by which gender norms are established and perpetuated were revealed in their tendency to fall back on unproblematized invocations of history. Despite the availability of many sources of information about gender-based ideas and behaviors, many students arrived ultimately at unicausal explanations of gender culture by identifying "history" as the principal causal mechanism:

> Historically, men have always pursued women, dating back to the days of chivalry when it was believed that women were creatures to be idolized and adored and men must win the love of a woman.

This has a historical basis rooted in the time when young women were sold into marriages.

The existence of the gender norm is associated in my mind with the olden days where men would retire to a separate room from the women after dinner to discuss "important" matters that women were not allowed to take part in.

The establishment of gender norms was here seen as an "event," something that occurred at some discrete if unspecified point in history. Gender norms were seen as obsolete, as vestigial and residual effects of something that once was:

. . . historically, to keep women in subordinate positions to men socially and economically as well. This is definitely an archaic holdover from the days when it was believed that women actually *were* inferior to men.

Historically, in our society women were considered sexual objects. . . . This idea has continued into our era, keeping women objectified, and therefore subordinate. For this reason men are free to make comments, whether complimentary or insulting, to women at any time.

Initially students did not interpret gender systems as dynamic, as continually created and re-created, as perpetuated through society, its institutions, and its representations. They did not generally see themselves, their families, friends, the college campus, or society in general as participating in the continuous remaking of gender norms. In their eyes, gender systems were static and fixed entities, just as in their choices of gender-role violations masculinity and femininity were seen to be fixed entities.

For these students, gender systems were things that exist "out there," external to the self. Gender systems were sometimes seen as things *imposed upon* individuals but rarely as things that individuals participate *in* or act upon: "If a person can be made to control his or her own body by an external force (even if this external force acts through internal restraints), then has not this control actually been removed from the individual? Furthermore, this process of suppression has insidious implications for the position of women in our society, for once a person's body can be controlled, how difficult is it to prevent the expression of the person's mind, and then the person's social and political needs?" Only rarely, in some of the explanations, did students recognize their own culpability and participation.

Students' statements show that they know their culture well and that the culture calls on them to accept stereotypical ideas about women and female-ness. The culture constructs their ignorance, not offering systematic explana-tory frameworks. The explanations held by these young women for how things work represent a significant challenge to feminist scholars who seek to teach today's students how to analyze, demystify, and change the power dynamics in gender systems. Understanding that students begin feminist inquiry data-rich—at times data-confused—but theory-poor is an important step in helping them recognize that they already possess data upon which to build explanatory frameworks and that these frameworks will be helpful to them in all aspects of their lives. Learning to sort through a variety of frameworks and identify what works for each person is, of course, the long-term goal of the exercise, the course, and of liberal and critical education itself. Rarely, however, do we have the data to analyze where students begin and how they formulate their expec-tations. This investigation into gender systems might well prove a more widely applicable model.

Teaching with Students' Experiences

The students' papers and their insights on the gender culture that forms their world have captivated and fascinated us. In this section, we want to articulate what we gain as teachers and how we change when we begin to take students' ideas seriously. Doing so also allows us to reflect upon what the students themselves learned through this project in experiential feminist learning and how their reflections need to inform in turn the future organization of wom-en's studies materials and learning.

The students' discussions of their gender-role violations offer us a picture of the culture in which they live. Our students are of college age; many have experiences, histories, cultural options, and feminist commitments that are very different from those of us who teach them women's studies. Identifying some of the students' categories for understanding sexual differences, gender hierarchies, and power relations gives us the bases for creating more effective and accurate ways to formulate the information and theory that we present. Simply put, listening to their papers lets us figure out where they start and lets us build on this starting point rather than passing it by. Paying attention to their starting points gives us insight into the relative advantages and disadvan-tages of the types of knowledge they bring with them into our classrooms.

To their advantage, students enter the classroom with stores of information about men and women. They tell us in remarkable detail what men and women do and refrain from doing; where they go and do not go; and what the cultural boundaries of masculinity and femininity are. The classroom they enter exists within a larger college or university context that offers them much formal and informal information about male and female roles. When the Women's Studies curriculum, or any curriculum, offers them the opportunity to analyze gender, that curriculum must recognize and build on the types of information they already have. What we need to do is help these young women develop ways to organize and reconceptualize the information they receive in their daily lives.

Related to this task is a disadvantage that stems from the multiple ways in which residential campuses fuse the personal and social world of each student. This fusion makes it difficult for students to distance themselves from their experiences in order to understand how gender culture operates. They are not accustomed to viewing the pieces of information they have about gender as parts of a cultural system. When working with such students, educators need to discuss frameworks that make visible both gender systems and the mechanisms of power, culture, and ideology underlying the systems of everyday life.

One of the guiding principles behind women's studies is that ideology about women and gender often contradicts the actual experiences of both women and men. The gender-role exercise sets up a space in which students can learn this lesson firsthand. The students began the introductory class with definite ideas about what constitutes gender-appropriate behavior. The gender-role exercise asked students to challenge actively some of these ideas and then to explore the relationship between their experience with gender roles and their understanding of them. It was the experience of a gap between their recently gained experience and their prior understanding that then motivated students to search for adequate explanations of their experiences with gender culture.

For the women students in this class, the exercise proved a pointed, and at times poignant, moment at which they began to question what they had previously taken for granted. By encouraging them to design and implement the exercise on the basis of their own assumptions about gender, the experience gave the students an opportunity to develop a critical perspective. The need for a critical perspective is heightened by the fact that the activity is done in public and with an observer, whose comments about the scenario are central pieces of information. Although one young woman reported telling a man for whom she had just bought a beer at a local night spot, "This was just an experiment for my Women's Studies class," the "experiments" were, in fact, also very real.

Carrying out these "experiments" forced students to confront not only external reactions to their behavior but to acknowledge and evaluate their own feelings about their behavior. Regardless of whether a behavior produced feelings of discomfort, frustration, or empowerment, the students learned that gender dynamics are a great deal more complex than they had imagined. Many students reported that the exercise encouraged them to identify other gaps between the cultural representations of women's lives and the realities of women's experiences. Finding a "lack of fit" inspired students to reflect upon themselves in relation to the cultural construction of gender-appropriate behaviors.

This critical perspective is, we think, a necessary condition if students are to look for and appropriate new information about women and to develop new frameworks that can interpret and assess gender culture. Of first importance, the exercise launched students into a questioning mode. Having experienced and, with varying success, tried to explain the dynamics of gender themselves, students grew increasingly eager for frameworks that gave them more satisfactory explanations than those previously available to them. This process of uncovering and unlearning necessitates that the students learn to theorize, analyze, and label gender and gender systems; this necessity continues as they begin to learn more about the lives and circumstances of all sorts of women in all sorts of places.

In assessing the students' experiences, we learned three specific things. First, as this essay has shown, we learned how these students reflect on gender. Second, we learned that in order to teach them about the dynamics of gender and power, we had to locate our theorizing in their experiences. Third, we learned that while the slogan "learning from our students" may seem deceptively simple, it pushed us outside some of the most familiar ways we have of assessing and drawing conclusions from data.

This essay offers a snapshot of some young women taking women's studies classes in the early 1990s. But more than that, in this essay we have traced our initial and exploratory attempts to analyze and interpret students' ideas as well as the stances they take. We hope that by doing so, we will inspire instructors at other universities and colleges to perform similar investigations so that women's studies as a discipline can continue conceptualizing ways of understanding students. An articulated process of self-reflection about the *interaction* between scholarship on women and gender and undergraduate learners of women's studies should strengthen both projects of feminist teaching and critical learning.

Assessing
Curriculum
Transformation
through Student
Observations

A long with developing women's studies as an autonomous academic discipline, feminist scholarship seeks to transform the curriculum of other disciplines. This transformation process involves not only including the materials, methodologies, and theories generated by the study of women and gender systems into ongoing departmental offerings but also engaging a field's paradigms from the various points of view adopted and experienced by real and therefore diverse women instead of some abstract ideal Woman.

Curriculum transformation activities are central to most women's studies programs and centers for research on women. These units send out information to their mailing lists; sponsor visitors; hold conferences, seminars, and institutes; and generally serve as a source of information on curriculum transformation for any interested party.

Most research literature on curriculum transformation focuses upon content and theory within a discipline (literature reviews, theoretical essays on paradigm shifts, suggestions for course revision, information on pedagogy), remaining satisfied with merely interjecting a multidisciplinary component. Such research takes the form of project reports, general overviews from individual faculty members recalling their own experiences, and essays that articulate the need for curriculum transformation.[1]

How much feminist scholarship is actually being taught in contemporary college classrooms? This deceptively simple question is frequently posed to me as a women's studies program director. I have no ready answer. Despite the tremendous energy currently being expended in these projects, there is no established norm that determines the amount and content of feminist research that courses could or should include. What constitutes "the appropriate amount" is a question that is not only currently unanswerable but, more significant, rarely discussed. Yet the question cuts straight into the politics surrounding curricular changes as well as into our understanding of the teaching-learning process.

Assessing how much material on women and gender is incorporated into courses constitutes a central task for those who wish to further the curriculum transformation process. Feminist scholars are just beginning to develop a research tradition that documents their ongoing, daily activities, including curriculum transformation. They have extensive individual experiences that enable them to describe anecdotally what is happening with colleagues and students. We've all heard about the occasional faculty member who jests that including a work by a woman on the syllabus qualifies him (it is usually a male instructor) for the Women's Studies faculty. The Women's Studies students in his class joke back, suggesting there is more to inclusion than that. Students new to feminist scholarship often report that Professor X is "great" because "We are reading two books by women this semester." Students who have done a fair amount of work in women's studies decry the syndrome of devoting a week at the end of the course to women—a week that often gets cut since "There is so much important material to cover and we are out of time." Graduate students note with frustration their professors' tendency to lump together race, class, and gender in one day devoted to a discussion of "difference." The following exchange is not atypical of my experience as director of Women's Studies.

I chat with a fourth-year graduate student in early modern European history who will be teaching a course on gender and costume next spring. I ask him to write a short article for the newsletter on what he is planning to do in that course—we both know that feminist scholars have avoided the issue of costume and fashion even though questions of dress often crop up in discussions of feminism. We agree that such an article would be both useful for him to formulate and great for the newsletter.

He then volunteers the information that a couple of years ago he could not have written such an article. Why, I ask. Well, he explains, he has always known about costume and fashion, having entered graduate school with an M.F.A. in design as well as years of theater experience. But he "didn't get the gender part." I press further: what made him consider gender in his analysis now when he had not done so previously? Besides course work and general reading in a department that respects feminist scholarship, he cites two additional experiences. First, while working as a teaching assistant for one of the Women's Studies faculty members last year, he learned how to use gender as an analytic tool and was astounded at how much more engaged his students became. Both those who "loved" the approach (more frequently women) and those who "resisted" the material made him realize that women and gender provide a way of presenting topics that speaks to most students. Their reactions, in turn, profoundly influenced his own analysis of the material. Then this year—here he groans audibly—he is a teaching assistant for another professor, a "real antifeminist" he claims, who constantly puts women down. He finds himself personally offended by the way this professor ignores recent scholarship and clings to ideas that many now find incomplete. Moreover, he has trouble generating debate in discussion sections because the students turn off to what the professor says. "It doesn't connect," they report. He concludes our conversation by saying that while he cannot explain curriculum transformation, he knows he has been experiencing it and would like to further explore the process by writing a newsletter article.

I use this graduate student's story because he is willing to admit what he did not previously know and what he has come to know. In similar conversations with faculty colleagues, one rarely gets such a direct account. Colleagues are more likely to discuss material they have just added to their syllabus by implying that they "just happened on it." Their conversations suggest that they do not deliberately seek out material on women, for that would be a "political" act (read "undesirable"). In addition, graduate students, as teachers in training, often ponder how effective they have been, wondering what students know and "how to reach them." By contrast, faculty have an established history of teaching and therefore find it easier to rely on their expertise than to actively explore what students know.

How then do we in women's studies go about studying the curriculum transformation process by learning what is happening in classrooms so that we can effectively intervene to further the process?

Studying Curriculum Transformation

If one were to listen only to the negative accounts of women's studies and ethnic studies that fill the popular press, one would assume that every class on every campus concentrates exclusively on this new material and completely ignores everything else. If one were to listen to women's studies faculty, curriculum transformation project leaders, graduate students specializing in some aspect of feminist work, or even supportive deans and chairs, one would think that the process of utilizing the new scholarship is limited to a few, isolated spots on campus and is slow at best.

Empirical accounts of what actually happens in classrooms across the country are rare. They are rare because documenting what is taught and investigating classroom dynamics violates academic norms. Yet the absence of a standard measure or established methodology forces us to rely exclusively on the reports and recommendations of faculty who have been involved in curriculum transformation projects.[2] Occasionally a project analyzes syllabi content or looks at book assignments.[3] Course evaluations, usually done at semester's end, rarely include questions about course content per se. Moreover, each of us knows that intentions, outlines, and readings constitute only part of a class. The background of the professor as well as the interests and characteristics of the semester's students combine with the broader social and cultural context to modify what happens in each class during every semester.

As a result, people working on curriculum transformation projects find themselves in a curious situation. The amount of material on women and gender grows. The most publicized reactions are negative. Yet because we lack an accepted, conventional way to assess what is actually being taught, we cannot answer the "how much" question in a precise way. More important, we cannot specify concrete strategies that would increase the amount of material being incorporated.

Faced with this predicament, I began to rethink an exercise I had been using in the introductory Women's Studies course at Duke. The exercise asked students to complete questionnaires and write a short essay analyzing what they were currently learning about women in two other courses that were not cross-listed with Women's Studies. Since I first used this exercise in the fall of 1984, a rich data base has been built: some 900 observations by 500 students on over 600 individual courses in 35 departments and programs at one university.

But these data raise methodological problems, particularly for scholars in the social sciences. "Good" research design calls for a theoretical question to be posed first; methods of collecting data to answer it are derived secondarily from the established tradition. In this case, the reverse occurred. Having designed an exercise for teaching purposes, over the years I realized that I was gathering information on a major educational policy issue—information not readily obtained in any other way.

Using the data raises a second problem: students' reports of their experiences are conventionally discounted as unreliable sources of information. As scholars, faculty members, and researchers, we imagine all the factors that influence students' responses; as a result, we dismiss their validity. While we must certainly interpret students' responses with caution, the need for some baseline information strikes me as more compelling than the advice to put aside these data and wait until a "more objective" study can be designed, implemented, and analyzed. Inspired by recent ethnographic work in cultural studies, I decided to write this paper as an investigation into students' ideas about curriculum transformation.

After all, it is in such points of tension between experience and institutional theory and practice that feminist theorists find the stuff of analysis. Women's studies faculty have long argued that discrediting experiences is one of the major ways in which new perspectives are squelched, facts and opinions denied, and the status quo maintained. Is it that studying what students observe about our handling of women and gender dynamics in classes is threatening and that we hide behind the screen of objective research design to quiet our fears?

Using Student Observations

Having thought about a way to study curriculum transformation through student observations, I found myself immobilized when I tried to write. Over three years I drafted numerous versions, three of which I circulated to colleagues for comments. At one point, I submitted the most recent version to professional journals, twice receiving external reviews and rejections. What I had to say was eagerly received in informal conversations in professional settings. Down on paper, however, fellow scholars found all sorts of objections to the observations being made.

When I thought about including a version of the paper in this collection of essays, I decided to address my dilemma directly. What was it about this paper that made it so difficult to write and why had none of the previous versions worked for scholarly audiences?

Thinking about this dilemma led me to reconsider what is involved in a project that studies curriculum transformation from the students' point of view. Such a project challenges two fundamental yet unspoken academic canons. First, each of us regards ourselves as an expert in our subject; we decide what is to be taught. Second, each of us thinks we control the classroom; we decide how that subject is to be presented and discussed. Just articulating these canons causes some to deny their existence. Yet the discomfort that surfaces when they are articulated suggests a sensitive area is being named.

Most professors research and teach largely without direct observation or comment from professional colleagues or students. When we do participate in curriculum discussions and projects, we focus on the abstract ideas we seek to convey rather than on the specific information and classroom dynamics that constitute the life of a course. (I have found this to be particularly true in the humanities and the social sciences.) In some cases, people interested in improving teaching techniques participate in videotaping sessions. They receive organizational and stylistic instruction that helps them convey material more effectively. But the question of what material to convey is not addressed and only rarely do these sessions attend to the gender dynamics associated with organizational or stylistic changes.

Asking students to collect information about the material on women and gender discussed in their classes and to analyze the way in which their classes handle that material reverses academic power hierarchies—it puts students in the position of those who know. The negative reactions of professionals are in contrast to the positive enthusiasm with which students greet this approach to curriculum transformation. They recognize almost intuitively that this exercise asks them to do something that is not usually done in a formal and systematic way. While many students informally discuss and compare what is said in their classes, most students never have the opportunity to convey the substance of these conversations through institutionally recognized means.

Investigating curriculum transformation through student observations violates professional mores while simultaneously speaking to unrecognized student needs. This recognition enabled me to locate this project within my own intellectual endeavors. That is, my emphasis as a researcher, administrator, and teacher has been to observe and then work to modify structures that appear limiting to women. Courses that lack material about women's diverse experiences limit women's abilities to know themselves. Such courses also hinder both men and women from understanding how gender operates in their worlds.

Collecting information that starts with what students think they are learning (regardless of what faculty think they are teaching) provides a different, albeit complementary, approach to the faculty-centered approach taken by most research on curriculum transformation. It is hardly surprising that this stance feels empowering to students and discomforting to faculty. Nor is it surprising that I have found writing about this project both complex and troublesome.

What Do Students Say?

When I began to teach Introduction to Women's Studies, I quickly learned that simply talking about the absence of women from what is taught in the curriculum is of limited effectiveness. Again and again students would claim, "But things are changing," and then cite an instance in which a professor mentioned a woman or women's concerns. Believing that learning is most effective when students can observe directly the phenomena in question, I developed a set of questions that they could apply to two other courses they were currently taking. The questions ask about the organization of the class; what the readings include; what comes up in discussions, either in lectures or in sections; and what the gender dynamics in the classroom are. I would ask them, after they had completed the questionnaire, to write a short essay analyzing their findings.

Students frequently receive the assignment and immediately object. "There is nothing in chemistry that has to do with gender!" "The teacher does not allow discussion in lecture." "My two other classes are drama classes that have no readings." I put aside their objections and insist that they just try: "Be an ethnographer, observe the culture of the classroom, and report back."

Part of the theoretical framework underlying the questionnaire came from the work of Peggy McIntosh.[4] She has delineated various phases of incorporating material about women: courses that never mention women; courses that occasionally mention those exceptional women who broke the usual (read male) patterns; courses that include a separate section on women; and courses that integrate women and gender so fully that the subject matter looks different. The ideas underlying the questionnaire also drew on Bernice Sandler's work at the Association of American Colleges.[5] She and her colleagues identified the research on classroom climate and found it to be a chilly one for women. Sandler lists the many ways of excluding women from the situations in which knowledge is transmitted—historically, linguistically, interactionally, and culturally.

Student questionnaires have been coded by sociology graduate students over the years and the results compiled annually. Table 1 profiles what students have said over a seven-year period. The most striking finding is that a substantial number of students find that their courses remain "womanless." In 1984, 33 percent reported that their classes outside Women's Studies never mentioned women; in 1991, 31 percent gave the same response. Student comments about such courses also remained essentially the same. In 1984 a history student said, "My seminar [in European history after 1939] ignores the important contributions, even the presence, of women in European history after 1939." Five years later another student said of a similar history seminar:

> Europe and the World since 1914 studies the significant events and people in Europe between the years 1914 and the present. It is highly significant that women in this course aren't portrayed as policymakers or even as a significant part of history. All eight of the books which constitute the reading material for this course fail completely to include any mention of women. When studied from the perspective of this course, women can be viewed as insignificant concerning the development and the course of European history since 1914.

Assessing Curriculum Transformation 139

Table 1. Student Assessments of the Material on Women in the Curricula of Non–Women's Studies Courses, 1984–1991

Category of Response	Year of Survey						
	1984 (%)	1985 (%)	1987 (%)	1988 (%)	1989 (%)	1990 (%)	1991 (%)
Womanless	33	23	21	29	28	31	31
Women treated as exceptional or as problem	44	59	25	28	24	23	14
exceptional			14	10	15	14	7
problem			11	17	9	9	7
Women treated separately or comparatively	25	18	54	43	48	46	55
separately			14	9	12	11	22
comparatively			40	34	36	29	26
mixed evaluations						6	

Note: In the 1984 and 1985 surveys, evaluations were based on three categories. In subsequent surveys, there were five. In 1990, several students distinguished between sections of the course taught by different instructors or organized in different ways (teacher-led versus student-led, for example). There are no data for 1986 because the course was not taught that year.

A second finding was that the number of students who found that their courses fell in the middle range of McIntosh's classifications decreased. In the first two years, students reported that when women were mentioned at all, women were presented as exceptions to what was understood about men or as problems to the analytic scheme. Here is one student's comment from 1984:

We don't read women authors and we don't really talk about female characters. When we do talk about how exceptional they were, it is suggested that most women aren't like that. If we do spend any time on one or more, they are talked about as an anomaly and then dismissed. For example, throughout the assigned readings, women are almost never mentioned except as the wife of a great leader (and even this is rare). In class women are mentioned and quickly dismissed with, "You know how things were back then, women had no real lives." However, interestingly enough, the most recent class period dealt directly with women. In the lecture, the professor told of the radical women (*radical* not being negative; the same term was used to refer to the men of the day) who cut their hair short and wore blue spectacles. The professor continued and discussed some of the actions they took to gain a sense of self-identity and freedom. These women were successful in their struggle for independence, yet not a single specific name was given. This I found particularly biased and unfair; for every previous reform movement mentioned in class, a list of the most influential (male) participants was written on the board. "These women" (whoever they may be) remain unidentified in our class, in our notes, and worst of all in our minds. Why is it that for any other major event I can immediately associate a name with its occurrence? Why are "these women" not worth mentioning?

Student reports suggest that, over time, the number of courses that treated women as exceptions or as problems decreased—from 44 percent to 14 percent. Significantly, the tone in which students analyzed such classes grew sharper. The following description of a political science course was written in 1990: "My political science professor always assumes men do politics and if he ever mentions women, he always does it in a complaining way, talking about how they don't fit the theory he is explaining. He then dismisses the importance of women to this explanation. He never questions his explanation. I have come to see through my Women's Studies courses that there are errors in his ways of describing politics, but it would be pretty hard to explain that to him!"

A third trend in student observations of curriculum transformation suggests the amount of material on women being integrated has increased. By 1991, students claim that as many as 55 percent of their courses incorporate women in some way. In 1984, students found only 25 percent of their courses incorporated women in any way.

Just as women studies faculty have no standard measure for the appropriate amount of material to be incorporated in a course, so student standards for what constitutes "integration" vary enormously. A 1989 student said that in her survey course "women are portrayed as an integrated part of the art world and the class also pays attention to several female artists, emphasizing their unique contribution in the realm of feminism." For a 1988 anthropology student, however, integration means more: "The class lectures that we have had reveal very little bias toward one sex or the other; in general I think it would be fair to say that the professor treats males and females equally in the course material. As we discussed clans and lineages, we looked at inheritance, descent, and other things through women and through men." For a third student, one taking an English course in 1990, neither the mere mention of women nor "equal treatment" constitutes integration. For her, it was necessary to reflect on the broader consequences of historically excluding women from knowledge. She claims that "this class has rebuked the notion that the experiences of women are somehow less important or inferior to those of men and was almost a beacon of inspiration in a society where this notion is rarely accepted."

As I compared the rankings each student gave their courses with the short narratives they wrote, a similar pattern emerged. Students tend to "credit" or give a "high" ranking to any mention of women or gender in a class. Yet after they have completed the questionnaire (which they are told to do first), the essay portion of the evaluation, in which they analyze their findings, becomes noticeably less generous.

In their essays students are more likely to recall specific episodes that they consider negative. Frequently they make excuses for faculty: "He went to graduate school a long time ago before these things were written." "He cannot be expected to be an expert in everything, and this is just one of the things he doesn't know." "It is hard to get everything into a single semester." "The professor knows best, and if he doesn't include it, he must have a good reason." Yet at the same time they find excuses, they voice expectations: "I really wondered what the women were doing." "I want to know if women would have written it this way." "I cannot imagine that the women thought about it just like the men did." "I wish I knew more about how these women combined marriage and family with their careers so that I could do the same." "I'd like to know how she spoke up to him so I can imitate her."

In their papers students both recognize that faculty possess the authority to define knowledge and express a desire to see a connection between what they are studying and the professional and personal questions they are experiencing. In this gap between what students have usually expected and what they have come to want feminist analysis finds its audience.

What Kinds of Information on Women Are Being Incorporated into the Curriculum?

After five years of asking students to sketch out how much material on women they are receiving, in 1989 I began asking them to consider a second question as well: what kind of information is it? I asked them six questions, each of which represents a different approach to curriculum transformation. Were women's "traditional" roles the focus? Were women mentioned only when they made "outstanding" contributions? Were women's own descriptions of their lives included? Were women's situations related to society, economics, and politics? Were differences in the perspectives and power between women and men discussed? And, most significant, were differences among women considered? Whether courses consider differences among women is indicative of whether courses have begun to deconstruct culturally received notions of the ideal woman in favor of authorizing the experiences of "real" women.

To convey the patterns in students' responses, I created a scale, set forth in Table 2. Students rated course readings, class lectures, and class discussions on each of the six questions with a yes or no. The number of positive responses to each question for 1989 and 1990 were added together. A cumulative score was then given to every department according to each of the six approaches to curriculum transformation. Ratings for readings, lectures, and discussions were congruent in every case, never varying by more than 10 percent. The department ratings for each type of transformation were grouped quantitatively according to the amount of course material with curriculum transformation: one-quarter or less; from one-quarter to one-half; from one-half to three-quarters; and, finally, three-quarters or more.

Thus the data reveal six specific approaches to curriculum transformation and their distribution across departments. The first approach to curriculum transformation, emphasizing traditional roles, clearly makes the minimum amount of change. A discussion of differences, the sixth approach, represents quite extensive change. Read from top to bottom as well as left to right across the columns, Table 2 maps the terrain of change. This progression of six approaches in no way suggests that attending to differences among women should or can be left until last. Quite the contrary. Courses that do not attend to the experiences of women of color or lesbians, for example, fail to impart information about women; they deal exclusively with the abstract, ideal woman rather than giving primacy to real women's experiences.

To summarize the findings indicated by Table 2 in a sentence: more courses in more departments do the minimum amount of transformation and fewer courses in fewer departments do the maximum. While the pattern is hardly surprising, understanding the breakdown in each of the six approaches can help us interpret more fully the student evaluations recorded in the preceding section. It is important to note that the unit of analysis here has shifted from the course to departments, a move made necessary by the large number of observations and the fact that we work with course titles rather than individual faculty names.

In the narratives students wrote to accompany their ratings of classes, students explore what is said about women and gender. Mentioning traditional roles without questioning that categorization is perhaps the simplest and most frequent way in which material on women can be included in a course. Many courses in most departments—with the exception of the natural sciences and sociology—appear to do this. How women are thought about "traditionally" troubles students, as this student's description of her French class makes clear:

Table 2. Curriculum Materials on Women and Gender, by Department, According to Student Rankings, 1989 and 1990

Types of Material	Distribution of Material in Departmental Courses			
	¼ or less	¼ to ½	½ to ¾	¾ or more
Women's traditional roles	Sciences Sociology	Music Public Policy Sciences Political Science Religion	Art History Psychology	Anthropology English Languages
Women's outstanding contributions	Public Policy Sciences Sociology	Languages Political Science Sciences	Anthropology Art English History Psychology Religion	Music
Women's own descriptions of their lives	Art Music Public Policy Sciences Religion Sciences Sociology	Anthropology History Languages Political Science Psychology	English	
Relationship of women's lives to social, economic, and political systems	Sciences	Art Music Public Policy Sciences Political Science Psychology Religion Sociology	English Languages History	Anthropology
Differences between the positions, power, and perspectives of women and men	Sciences	Art Music Public Policy Sciences Political Science Religion Sociology	English Languages History Psychology	Anthropology
Differences between minority and majority women	Art Languages Music Public Policy Sciences Political Science Religion Sciences Sociology	English History Psychology	Anthropology	

Note: Data are from twelve departments. There were too few observations from the other twenty-three smaller departments and multidisciplinary programs to be included.

The purpose of this class is to discuss several different aspects of French culture and everyday life. By reading various newspaper and magazine articles . . . in the text, the class members discuss the topics assigned by the professor. Although I first believed that it was impossible for a French class to be sexist, I discovered in my survey that my class consists of discussion based only on the dominant role of men in French society. The professor has chosen to portray French women in a submissive role by simply skipping articles referring to strong women and emphasizing only those articles that depict women as housekeepers and mothers.

She reports the following example:

The first chapter of the text focuses on the changing French family. The chapter consists of various articles about the dual role of parenthood, the changing role of the liberated woman, and the destruction of the typically close-knit family. But whereas the editors of the text chose to publish articles which depict several views of women, our class read only two articles from that chapter. These two articles portrayed the working woman as the reason for the separation of parents from their children and one survey which recorded how often husbands help their wives with housework. The professor completely neglected discussing the other articles which presented such subjects as a woman author's depiction of the modern French woman. Similarly, an article in a later chapter that we read detailed the shopping practices of French women. Thus, the professor has chosen either to skip the female-oriented articles in the text or to discuss those articles which describe a traditional, subservient woman.

When women are noted as "outstanding," what is said about them? This question proved provocative for one student in the music survey course. She began by observing that both her textbook and the lectures included few listings for women musicians before the 1960s:

One exception I found to this pattern came in the form of Clara Wieck Schumann, who had eight pages listed next to her name. My curiosity piqued, I decided to read the pages listed, thinking that the topic of those pages would be Clara Schumann. Instead, I found that she was the wife of the musical genius Robert Schumann. When Robert died, she became the lover of Brahms, another well-known and accomplished musician. Little was said of her musical talent other than the fact that she was a musical prodigy at nine but later had difficulty raising seven children as an adult. Would she have had so many page numbers after her name had she not been the wife and lover of two great musicians? Probably not. After the

1960s, I found that more female musicians were listed (e.g., Donna Summer, Madonna, Sheila E., Tina Turner, etc.)—but still with only one or two pages listed by their name. However, compared with my physics text, the Masterworks of Music text is a paragon of gender equality. At least this text acknowledges the fact that great female musicians have become more recognized in recent history.

Using women's own descriptions of their lives is a third way material about women can be included in courses. Fundamental to the enterprise of feminist scholarship is the idea that we must listen directly to women themselves, not simply to their male observers and interpreters. Table 2 suggests that even fewer courses in fewer departments take this approach. Students' responses to this question suggest that they are sensitive to the need to hear directly from women themselves and find this way of incorporating material particularly effective.

A student in English put it this way:

I learned a great deal about why gender roles exist and persist. Not only are male authors more visible than female authors, causing us to believe that there are actually more male authors than female authors, but we are fed information about women through the eyes of dominant canonized male authors. We are trained to see women and men as they are depicted in the literature we read because we have accepted this literature as a true reflection of society. We accept that what happens to women in literature happens in real life, so when every single novel with a female protagonist ends and the woman is either dead or married, we believe this to be the way things are and we don't question the stereotyped message we are sent. Until women's literature is more widespread and visible, we will not begin to see the side of women that only female authors can depict. Until female characters' lives begin to actually reflect our own, we will not accept our own experiences as true.

Over and over again, students claimed that the relationship of men's and women's lives to the social, economic, and political systems in which they live as well as to the differences between the positions, perspectives, and powers available to women and men were not discussed as frequently as they need to be. Listed as the fourth and fifth categories in Table 2, this material is evident in even fewer courses in fewer departments and at lower levels. When courses deal with social relationships and with power dynamics, students are full of praise, as the following two statements suggest.

Art 70 [a the survey of art from the Renaissance to the present] is the epitome of how a subject dominated by males can still be taught to eradicate the gender bias that it faces. Our teacher's exemplary approach to art explains why women have been left out of art and why they are depicted the way they are in each work of art. The teacher also requires reading out of a text that is dedicated to female artists throughout history. Rather than separating the course into male artists and female artists, the professor integrates the subject matter by presenting works by females, showing the different view they give. This enables the student to look outside of art, into society, to see how the different sexes view the world. The student learns how the controller of culture (art) can influence the beliefs and perceptions that society has about groups within it. Specifically, we learn why women artists have been left out of art history books by our patriarchal society.

The first book we read in my history class contained the letters written between a Nuremburg husband and wife of the sixteenth century and shows the life of a woman in her own voice. The entire class was surprised by the amount of control she had over her life and that of her husband. The professor warned us against falling prey to the myths of women's lack of status and described the reality of her position within the community and the household. In class, women are presented as an integral part of the formation of German history in the Renaissance and the Reformation.

The final question students are asked to consider is whether or not the class deals with differences among women, particularly between women of different racial and ethnic backgrounds. Students claim that most courses in most departments do not. It is significant that they rarely commented on this topic in the essays that accompanied their questionnaires. Their silence suggests that very little material on women of color is part of their education. The following comment, which describes a class exploring the literature of colonialism, shows that when such information is included, its impact is powerful:

What is valuable is the class discussions, in which we can relate the sexism to the racism that is found in the novels. We have also been able to draw parallels and to reach conclusions about the relationships between men and women, between the conquerors and the conquered, between the participants and the nonparticipants, and between the powered and the disempowered. By discussing women's issues in this class, we have been able to consider important questions about the ideology of imperialism and to decide whether or not this ideology was justifiable.

When given the opportunity to assess what kind of material on women and gender systems appear in their classes, students appear to be keen observers of the teaching and learning process. In contrast to the way in which they appear to rank a course favorably and then describe it in less favorable terms, students appear to have a clearer sense of what is and what ought to be included when asked to describe the ways in which the material is presented. In this part of the exercise, they acknowledge the absence of specific kinds of information and see the consequences of its lack.

How Do Gender Dynamics in the Classroom Relate to Curriculum Transformation?

The exercise on curriculum transformation was first developed to explore whether material on women and gender was included in the information that professors provide. In the last three years, the exercise has been expanded to analyze the kind of information being given. Both the "how much" and the "what kind" questions concern readings, lectures, and discussions—all formal aspects of what is being said about the subject at hand. In the last two years, as the influence that interpersonal relations exert upon learning has become a more widely discussed topic on this campus, as on many others, I have begun to ask students to consider a third question: Do the patterns of interaction in the classroom reflect gender dynamics and, if they do, how are these interactions related to their acquisition of material?

The students' understanding of these dynamics can be quite sharp. The following comment about an ethics class comes from a student with little background in women's studies:

> So far, my ethics class has been a very alienating experience for me and many of my women friends in the class. The professor is male, and although women constitute a strong majority of the class, the discussion is dominated by men. The men dominate the discussion because almost everything they say is readily affirmed by the professor, while the women have to fight to get their views acknowledged by the professor as valid. The main readings are written by males for and about males, and all of the readings are discussed from that viewpoint—that is, all of the readings are discussed within the framework set out at the beginning by the key authors, Kierkegaard and Peck. . . . If I were to base my assumptions about women in society solely on this course, I would assume that women are weak, immoral, neurotic, sexual objects whose role and position in society is to be inferior to man in every way. No contemporary women's issues about the life cycle are discussed; for example, abortion, child care,

women in the workplace, and other issues of relevance to women are never discussed.

Men, too, learn to see the process of exclusion, as this comment from a male student suggests:

> The presentation of ideas in my statistics lecture and sectional meetings is somewhat unfair to the female gender. My professor and T.A. both have a tendency to use a narrow selection of practice problems. In fact, I would estimate that 90 percent of the problems in the probabilities section deal with some form of gambling, whether it be poker or rolling the dice. Playing cards and other forms of gambling have historically been associated with men. Using only one type of example which is biased toward men promotes an attitude that the study of statistics is inherently biased. Last week while I was doing some of the practice problems for the probabilities test with some friends, one of the girls in our study group pointed out that she was having trouble with the problems *because* she did not know anything about these gambling games. Suddenly I realized that these problems assumed some working knowledge about playing cards and other games. This revelation reinforced the idea that a great deal of gender bias exists in academic disciplines, including my statistics and economics courses.

In 1991 I took the classroom analysis of this project a step farther. Until that time I had read and returned their papers individually; I then presented the data to the class in a subsequent lecture. This lecture was always well received; in response to the patterns I summarized, many students recounted additional experiences. Last year I decided to ask for seven student volunteers (in a class of one hundred) who would analyze the class findings rather than write an individual paper. After my teaching assistants and I read and graded each individual paper, we handed over blind copies of the questionnaires and narratives to the student committee of seven and asked them to make sense of their classmates' findings. The students wrote a report, distributed copies to the class, made an oral presentation, and wrote an op-ed piece for the student paper.

In their group report, the student committee went farther than I had previously gone. In addition to examining specific classroom dynamics, the student committee spelled out what such dynamics meant and took a firm stance against much of what they saw. The following paragraphs from their group report document what they found and what they believe should be the norm:

Most of the class expected to discover what they already felt—women have every advantage at Duke that men have. But after the reports were completed, many students realized for the first time that being male or female affects their Duke education. Even though overt discrimination technically is gone, the students discovered the many ways in which women are still at a disadvantage in the Duke classroom.

For instance, in a majority of the classes surveyed (which ranged widely in subjects and fell under fourteen different departments), men were called on more by the professor and were interrupted less than women. In some classes the professor would encourage the men to speak out and guide them to a correct answer, while instantly correcting a wrong answer from a female student. In one class, the professor always called on a male student first, regardless of who raised their hands. In another, the professor knew all the male students' names and called each "Mr. ——." The one female student in the class was always referred to as "the young lady." . . .

Some female students said even fellow classmates make a point of dismissing their feminine voices, treating them as intellectually inferior. As a result, the female student often feels what she is saying really isn't important. Eventually, she refrains from entering classroom discussions altogether, only perpetuating the problem. . . .

We (professors and students alike) have learned to accept these discrepancies because they have been presented to us as the norm. However, "normalcy" does not make tradition valid. Acceptance of this norm is not only sexist, it is dangerous. . . .

Of course, not all Duke classrooms have a chilly climate. Many Duke professors present an adequate representation of both sexes and encourage all students to participate in class. In their reports, students expressed pleasant surprise and relief when they found such egalitarian classes. However, the very fact that the students showed surprise and overly commended a completely nonsexist professor says something in itself. This type of class should not be the exception but the norm.

As one student pointed out, "We hear of education as necessary, as enlightening, as powerful, but we must also consider that education may be repressive and even powerfully manipulative." Our class realized that in subtle (and sometimes not so subtle) ways the classes we are attending do not provide an equal education for women students. . . . Duke students need to gain a new perspective on student-professor relations. It is true that professors are in a position of authority while we students are the subjects. However, we are also the consumers, and to an extent our opinions can make a difference in what is taught at Duke and how it is taught.

Students consistently report that the amount of material which includes women and gender issues continues to grow. Yet this growth is matched by growing expectations on their part. Once exposed to the new scholarship on women, students recognize its value and demand more of it. While they give their teachers better "grades" than they did in the past, students also have deepened their understanding of curriculum transformation; they are asking that more be done.

Some Duke students appear also to be intervening directly in order to ensure that curriculum transformation occurs. In essays and classroom comments, students frequently report that they deliberately encourage professors who "mention" women by asking them to say more. At other times, they actively resist the silence that meets their questions about women by persisting with further questions about where they might turn to learn more.

Often such questions lead to spirited discussions. In one particularly painful episode, a student reported criticizing one of the books on revolution that her class was reading because its author never mentioned women's roles. The author of the book happened to be a Duke faculty member; many students in the class began attacking her for attacking him—"a really nice man," they claimed. She struggled with articulating a feminist critique while making a distinction between ideas and person, two issues that had previously received no attention in class and whose discussion she soon found herself leading.

Whatever the initial reactions to students' interventions, it is clear to them and to me that their questions have an impact. Sometimes they tell about discussions later in the semester, which return to women and handle the issue in greater depth. Often a faculty member will inform me that his or her class this semester "has a lot of Women's Studies students and they are quite vocal in class." Occasionally, debates in classes have taken on a second life outside the class itself. In the case of the student I mentioned above, both her entire dorm as well as several of us in Women's Studies followed the course of her seminar as it struggled to take in a feminist perspective. Daily accounts of the shifting positions of each character were as intriguing as any television serial—only I am quite sure we learned a great deal more.

From a student point of view, the way in which women and gender are presented and discussed appears as important as their mere mention as topics, if not more so. Such student observations suggest that individual faculty members function as "gatekeepers" of knowledge to a much greater degree than disciplines or departments do. Just because English literature in general is a field with a great deal of feminist scholarship, and the Duke department in particular has a strong representation of such scholarship, does not mean that any given course in the English Department will include material on women or exhibit classroom dynamics designed to bring women actively into the learning process. While faculty must have feminist scholarship available to them as well as a campus climate that encourages them to use that scholarship, availability and climate are not enough. Increasing student demand for such information is an overlooked but effective means to encourage curriculum transformation. Students require active preparation and encouragement if they are to be able to transfer information learned in the context of a women's studies class into other courses.

The exercise in curriculum transformation grew from a small assignment designed to help students think through what they are being taught into a project designed to help them analyze what they are learning and then actively engage them in the process of modifying and sharing what they are learning with fellow students in other classes. But that step of active engagement in another class does not automatically take place. Without an explanatory framework that describes the absence of material on women and gender in the curriculum, students will not demand fuller knowledge.

The idea that what a student knows is both valid and valuable confronts the convention that instructors know best and are "in charge" of the classroom. The pervasiveness of this view is difficult to fully appreciate. All of the student quotes refer to the fact that students are relatively powerless in the classroom to alter either material or interaction. Only when this powerlessness is named and analyzed and strategies for overcoming it are debated can students begin to think they are entitled to ask for more—and they might just get it.

Finding a Voice, Taking a Position

Coauthored with

Silvia Tandeciarz

and Kathryn West

Documenting Learning in Women's Studies

Accdording to many students who take women's studies courses, these classes involve much more than intriguing or cutting-edge scholarship. Students claim women's studies helps them understand questions, feelings, and discomforts they had long experienced but previously lacked a validated way of explaining. They believe what they learn is valuable and productive, both personally and professionally. One student described the process this way in the spring of 1991:

> I have had an interest in rap groups since I read about them in Introduction to Women's Studies. I wrote in a paper for WST 103 that I felt as though that class had been a kind of "rap group" for me. We discussed many ideas that fascinated me. I constantly tried to apply what I learned in that class to actual events in my life. Suddenly so many of my own experiences were explained in a framework that I could understand and analyze. The personal was political and my personal life was directly affected by politics. Since this discovery, I have become more and more active in women's groups on campus. The "rap group" of WST 103 moved me to action.

While she, like others on the campus grapevine, frequently affirms both the difference and the power of women's studies, little has been done to document the steps that constitute the process of this learning experience.[1]

In this essay we seek to delineate some specific steps through which one set of undergraduates engaged in women's studies material. Following the trajectories of selected students in the introductory Women's Studies course at Duke (WST 103), we listened carefully to how students describe (1) what goes on in Women's Studies classrooms; (2) what and how they learn; and (3) how their newly developed understanding impacts their lives, both in and out of academic settings. We wanted to learn how different students develop a cognitive framework affected by an awareness of gender roles. To do this, we explored how each student learns to use historical, sociological, cultural, psychological, and experiential knowledge in order to think about gender issues.

We were initially sparked to investigate these questions by the most recent work of Carol Gilligan.[2] Gilligan focuses on how young girls approaching adolescence become silenced by cultural norms and how that silencing affects both their public and private lives (as girls and later as women). She articulates the need for interventions in young girls' lives as they approach adolescence if young girls are to speak about their own experiences and perspectives with confidence. We believe our investigations into the impact of women's studies on college students illustrate such an intervention at work in the stage of late adolescence, when young women confront an Anglo-American hegemonic college culture that derives from institutions designed to serve young white males of elite European backgrounds. While all young women negotiate college with a distinctive set of conditions stemming from racial and ethnic background, family history, and their own adolescent socialization experiences, we believe that each young woman meets a campus culture that mutes differences from the privileged norm. By setting up a space in which young women can pursue their education as women, the women's studies classroom enables women to rewrite their scripts—whatever those scripts might have been.

Our Study

After teaching or serving as research assistants for WST 103 during the 1990–91 academic year, we compiled dossiers on all sixty-five students who had taken the course the previous year. We interviewed the twenty-two students for whom we had a complete file consisting of initial, mid-semester, and final course evaluations; all four class assignments (gender-role violation, curriculum evaluation, oral history review, and action project); and the final exam.[3] Conducted one year after they completed the class, the interviews covered students' experiences during the class itself, what they had been doing or thinking about women-centered questions in the intervening year, and their assessment of the course's impact on them as individuals. We limited the interviews to those students for whom we had complete written documentation because we wanted to compare their later reflections with their earlier statements.

As we studied these materials, we found ourselves referring again and again to certain students due to the quality of their comments as well as their in-depth articulation of their experiences both in and out of the classroom. Four of the twenty-two students we interviewed seemed to exemplify especially powerfully the voices of hundreds of women we have heard describing their experiences as Women's Studies students. This group consisted of Karen, Beth, Jenny, and Anne.[4]

Karen is a sophomore psychology and history major with no previous experience in Women's Studies courses; she enrolled in the course over the explicit objections of her family. Beth is a sophomore chemistry major with no previous experience in Women's Studies courses; her mother encouraged her to take the course. Jenny is a sophomore history major with one previous course in Women's Studies; she was encouraged by her family to take the course. Anne is a junior biological anthropology and history major with no previous experience in Women's Studies courses. She reported feeling somewhat awkward about enrolling in the course because, while she believes that "in an age where women on average earn a third less than men and women can't be safe walking alone at night, I think a woman would have to have her head 'buried in the sand' not to be a feminist," she was worried that she would not be "accepted" as a feminist due to her stance on abortion.

Like so many students who decide to take a Women's Studies course, this group of four reported facing both external and internal conflicts. The initial evaluation asks the following question: "Someone says, 'Are you one of those feminists?' What does it mean? And how do you respond?" In responding to this question, three of the four noted the widespread confusion over the meaning of *feminist*, expressing anger and frustration at the derogatory tone of "Are you one of those feminists?" As with well over half of the respondents in recent courses, two of these women chose to answer yes but to provide their own definition of feminism.

Students come to Women's Studies with many different needs. They meet their needs with those tools provided in class that could be grafted onto their own situations. However that learning occurs, certain approaches are shared in common: a desire to gain a general knowledge of women's studies and feminist issues; a desire for a better understanding of themselves as women; a search for how gender relates to other defining characteristics in their lives (race, class, religion, region, and sexuality, among others); ideas on how to become more involved in working to change inequality; and a desire for frameworks that tie together previous courses, life experiences, and feelings about women's issues.

Clearly these four students do not represent all the students in the class, much less every student at Duke or in women's studies courses nationwide. All four are young, white, middle-class women. The twenty-two students for whom we had full documentation did not include women of color or men. Moreover, if any of these women (either in the larger set of twenty-two or among these four) were exploring nonheterosexual identities, they did not volunteer this information and we did not ask. We started with students, not teachers. We asked what they took away from their encounters with feminist scholarship, not what we had given them. And we asked how this scholarship had changed their perspectives; we did not want to measure, by tests, what we thought they should have retained. A more varied set of students will allow us to further delineate steps in this process. Here we only begin, well aware that the steps will differ for others but certain that documenting students' perceptions of their experiences is a necessary and long-overdue perspective on the learning process. We believe this perspective is critical to furthering the discipline of women's studies.

Gilligan and the Path from Silence to Voice

Listening to the voices of these four college-age women as well as their eighteen colleagues, we were struck by the similarity of their experiences and feelings to those of the adolescent girls described in the recent work of Carol Gilligan and the women of the Harvard Project on the Psychology of Women and the Development of Girls. Gilligan describes the developmental stage of eleven- to sixteen-year-olds as a time in which young girls face containment and repression: "The connection between inside and outside becomes explicitly a focus of attention when girls reach adolescence and become subjected to a kind of voice and ear training, designed to make it clear what voices people like to listen to in girls and what girls can say without being called, in today's vernacular, 'stupid,' or 'rude.' On a daily basis, girls receive lessons on what they can let out and what they must keep in, if they do not want to be spoken about by others as mad or bad or simply told they are wrong."[5]

For the young women in our larger sample, the time of late adolescence—coinciding with a physical separation from the family, a move to college, and a bid for independence (albeit differently defined)—appears to heighten the issues with which Gilligan's young girls dealt. When young women enter college (particularly those who go away to school), they experience a period of identity transformation and establishment. All the various social institutions of which these students were a part before college are now controlled by their universities. Moreover, male norms they might have encountered in elementary school and high school become much more pervasive in college. On many campuses, and particularly at Duke, social life gravitates around fraternities. Women come up against a wall of Western culture that excludes them, puts them in the position of object, and denies them the right to be heard as women. Whereas as children they may have escaped from one institution or space to another to find themselves and nurture those aspects of the self that were being silenced, in residential colleges these two worlds become one; escaping to find a room or voice of one's own proves increasingly difficult. The world of education and their personal worlds become fused, resisting earlier ties of family, community, and religion.[6] Like the newly adolescent girls Gilligan studied, women confronting college seem to develop various forms of double vision and voice as they attempt to negotiate structures of power that discount their experiences and perceptions.

A critical aspect in these times of identity formation and transformation centers around the concept of voice. When adolescent girls face a crisis, many take refuge in silence. When they reach college, these women tend to experience a lack of voice. Such women often enroll in women's studies courses because they feel they are missing something. Yet limiting the concept of voice to something young women lack is far too simple. After all, not any voice will do. The dominant culture requires that a young woman's voice be of a particular kind if she is to be heard. Too much strength is as likely to remain unheard as not enough strength. Having been nurtured in families where women are assumed to play strong roles, many African American women on campus report that while they know how to voice a position, they experience difficulty getting their positions heard on campuses where the gender norm for women is one of subservience and accommodation. Finding a voice as a person of color confronts the norm that females do not have a voice. While we do not now have a complete file of documents for any of the women of color who participated in the class, their undocumented comments (delivered both inside and outside class) lead us to believe that Women's Studies functions in a similar way for them by providing space and explanations for why they cannot get their voices heard.

In her conclusion to "Joining the Resistance," Gilligan writes of "voices of the underground," speaking under the sign of repression, struggling with "knowledge which is fragile, reaching out for connections" (p. 527). A majority of the women who enroll in WST 103 want to be in the position of a subject, which we define as a position with a voice that can be heard. They feel uncomfortable in the position of woman as object they see depicted all around them in popular culture (although for many this realization remains a gut-level response or intuition rather than an intellectual realization). In Women's Studies courses these young women find reinforcement for knowledge that is fragile; they find connections that do not require them to stifle what they know that they know. The combination of past (and present) experiences, class readings, and class discussions generates vocabularies and explanatory frameworks that provide a space in which many young women can voice both experience and analysis.[7]

The assignments for WST 103 force students to confront the college world; many of the activities in the gender-role exercise involve talking (and learning to hear), as do the oral history interviews and often the action projects. Through these assignments students develop the ability to interpret the world around them in terms of gender socialization; they learn to see how such socialization affects both people's actions and the expectations with which people live. In the process of gaining new knowledge about gender dynamics, many women find themselves able to articulate feelings that they had previously experienced very strongly but could not voice. By voicing what they see or know, they externalize a conflict that might have remained internalized and self-destructive. The skill of self-articulation, in turn, leads to new feelings of self-confidence, empowerment, and understanding.

Involvement in Women's Studies courses provides many of these young women with the opportunity to experience a dilemma similar to that of their early adolescence and, what is most significant, to experience it differently. They not only are able to understand and avoid the mechanisms of such silencing, but also can often uncover much that was repressed in an earlier period of identity formation. In the space set up by Women's Studies classrooms, these young women determine which issues and experiences from an earlier time they choose to undo.

It is no secret that women's studies programs are committed to change—to transforming the dominant cultural views and representations of women, to providing a base of support for women fighting institutionalized discriminatory policies, to helping students validate fragile knowledge, and to encouraging a politicization of self. The students we interviewed helped us explain what is different about such a classroom, what students get out of it, and how they learn. Finding a voice and getting heard as they take a position with respect to certain issues are two ways these students have been able to change their realities; these steps are only a beginning but, we feel, a deeply transformative one. Listening to the larger group of twenty-two and to the sample four as they spoke about finding a voice and getting their positions heard suggests that women's studies may well answer another question posed by Gilligan: "How can girls both enter and stay outside of, be educated in and then change, what has been for centuries a man's world?" (p. 509).

Our Findings: What the Students Say

In discussing their engagement with Women's Studies, most students describe a process of developing self-esteem and self-confidence, strengthening their sense of identity, and finding a voice. These things do not happen in a linear fashion. Different women begin and end the course at different positions. In addition, while one student may carry her gender awareness into some areas of her life, she may decline to carry it into all domains simultaneously. Insights about a particular past or present incident lead to self-validation and the ability to speak up about that incident or to voice opposition when a similar one occurs. At the same time, speaking up at some moment of tension may lead to growing self-esteem and validation, which can further the ability to understand and analyze. What these students describe is not necessarily a sequential three-step process of experiencing insight, feeling validation, and speaking up about it, but rather an intermingling of those experiences in ongoing exploration and growth. For the sake of clarity, we will concentrate on the four students and describe our findings in terms of a process that begins with experiencing a wall of obstacles to self-expression and development for women, moves into an understanding and analysis of those obstacles, and leads to a search for and implementation of ways through the "wall."

Experiencing the "Wall"

In this section we discuss experiences and encounters these four Women's Studies students reported that made them feel disempowered or silenced. These encounters were not always followed by immediate analysis or under-standing; instead, students would later apply frameworks and knowledge acquired in the Women's Studies classroom in order to cope with, overcome, and grow from such incidents rather than feel crushed by them.

In her curriculum evaluation project report, Jenny describes a classroom where "the professor has chosen to either skip the female-oriented articles in the text or discuss those articles which describe the traditional submissive woman." Although Jenny is angered by her French professor's selection, she says: "I remained quiet although I knew I should have suggested to the professor that we consider the other articles published in the same chapter. I think I was intimidated for two reasons. First, I feared that with the language barrier, I would not accurately express my opinion. Second, I subconsciously worried that the professor, a native Frenchman, might deem me a class troublemaker. I understand that this behavior [remaining silent] typifies the majority of women at colleges and universities." Would Jenny have spoken up in her broken French, despite feeling inadequate, had she been less afraid of offending her professor and jeopardizing the knowledge she might gain from the teacher-student relationship? Would she have spoken up if the person making this selection had been a fellow student instead of the professor—if the power relations had been altered? Our guess is that had the circumstances been more conducive to encouraging her perspective, Jenny would have protested the order of things. But to keep from being branded a "troublemaker"—not wanting to sacrifice her relationship for her beliefs—Jenny remained silent.

In her final course evaluation Beth also mentions an encounter in which a professor made her feel inadequate and embarrassed. She describes the incident as one in which her organic chemistry professor marked her test answer wrong even though it was the same as the one her textbook provided. When she went to speak to him during office hours, her professor said he did not have time for her questions and that the book was wrong; he then kicked her out of his office and invited in the next student. Beth felt humiliated and was so embarrassed about the incident that she didn't want to tell other people about it. Hence she felt isolated, as if it was her problem: there was something wrong with her that made her professor treat her this way. Prompted by discussions in her Women's Studies course, however, she discovered that similar incidents had happened to other women in the class. Together they were able to see the problem as one that involved gender discrimination. By the time of her final course evaluation, Beth could see her professor as a "real jerk" who "never wanted to discuss this with her." Although Beth never confronted her professor with such a charge, talking with other women about what was happening in the classroom made her feel less isolated and more in control; she regained her sense of self-esteem and her confidence in her abilities by being able to read the event as his problem, not hers. She was able to overcome a situation that initially had served to silence her, to make her feel inadequate, and to make her feel alone.

This event, which happened late in the semester during which Beth took WST 103, ties in directly with her comments in the curriculum evaluation project. There Beth states:

> In the physics class, women are thought of as taking the class more for a requirement than for a challenge. However, men are portrayed as being in their natural environment, as physics has been male-dominated for years. These male students are in the male environment of both teacher and text. This trend of males being in their natural environment while at work extends beyond college into the professional world, especially in the science professions. Society has acknowledged that men fit the mold of scientist, but is only beginning to acknowledge this role for females.

Having seen this early on as a result of the curriculum evaluation assignment, Beth was better equipped to deal with her chemistry professor when the situation arose. The two events—the planned assignment and the unplanned interaction in her professor's office—worked together to give Beth a sense of how gender influences power relations, the importance of developing support networks (whether with fellow female students or colleagues in the workplace), and the importance of having women role models in positions of power to change the stereotypes that discriminate against women.

In the final course evaluation, Anne also speaks of an incident that she began to understand only much later, after having taken the course. She recounts what happened following a presentation on date rape she attended with her boyfriend: "[The course] really shed light on the time when my ex-boyfriend pushed me down on the bed and said he could do all sorts of nasty things to me. I had never read about power relations before. How men feel they need a sense of power over women. Things he said and did made much more sense after that [being introduced to power analysis]. It didn't make it right, but I could recognize the dynamics he was working from. I recognize that in a lot of male friends—how they want to be domineering in conversations, stuff like that." At this time Anne has begun to recognize what she could only react to previously. The ability to recognize and name behavior that disturbs her becomes empowering, even when ready-made solutions are not available to deal with every problem.

Anne reports another eye-opening incident very early in the course when she writes about her primatology class in the curriculum evaluation project: "When discussing human evolution or humans as primates, Simons (the author) speaks of 'mankind' and 'man.' When diagrammatically showing bipedal walking, he shows a man walking. . . . One description of women exists in the book, an exception; women are described as having a less efficient walk than men because of the width of the pelvis. I'm not arguing against this as an anatomical fact, simply that it is a judgment which holds men up as the standard and women as the anomaly." In contrast to her final exam for WST 103, in which Anne vents a great deal of anger recalling this episode, her account here is largely neutral. She protests what she knows is wrong with this perspective, but feels she does not know enough to argue against an "anatomical fact." She therefore says nothing about it in primatology and limits herself to raising it as an issue in her curriculum evaluation project. In her comment, however, one can glimpse the beginning of a critique, a crack in the wall of knowledge, that may grow into a space for resistance, a space for her different and heretofore marginalized voice.

In the final course evaluation, Anne describes the same incident much more eloquently: "I thought there could be nothing gender-specific about biological anthropology. I thought it was totally dry, unbiased, scientific stuff. This caused me to look beyond the first reading. For instance, a description of the pelvic structure of a certain mammal went on to claim that women walk less efficiently. It was saying biased things in a 'scientific' way." Here Anne takes a position and is sure about the sexist nature of such a statement. She can furthermore see how power is encoded in merely sounding "scientific"; and instead of feeling silenced by her lack of knowledge and discomfort with the language being used, she can move beyond such circumstantial evidence to challenge the underlying message.

Understanding and Analyzing the "Wall"

Toward the beginning of WST 103, Jenny describes encountering a kind of "wall" with her new boyfriend. It is a relationship she will return to and write about throughout the semester; focusing on her trajectory through this relationship shows how one student works through issues raised both by women's studies and by encounters outside the classroom. While each student will develop his or her own coping mechanisms and will arrive at different solutions, we think that by focusing on one or two students in depth, we might better specify some steps in the process of arriving at solutions through a women's studies intervention.

For her gender-role exercise Jenny chooses to ask her new boyfriend out to dinner and to surprise him by paying for the date. She explains: "Recently I began dating a man, dare I call him a man or a guy, whom I met last month. We have begun a very conservative relationship which follows what many people would generalize as old-fashioned in which he asks me out and pays for the date. . . . Robbie's reaction to this 'gender violation' shocked me, and consequently we have learned more about our personalities from this experience." When the waiter brings the bill and Jennie takes it, she reports being "astonished" by Robbie's reaction:

> Not only was Robbie speechless, but the waiter almost started laughing and looked to see Robbie's expression. Robbie adamantly protested and said, "No girlfriend of Robbie —— will ever pay for a date if I can help it!" At first I thought Robbie was joking and that he was actually happy that I offered to pay the tab, but instead, Robbie appeared mortified by my actions. I firmly said that I felt an obligation to him when he paid for every date and that I wanted to try to even things out a bit. Although this "violation" was embarrassing to Robbie, once I started this activity I planned on carrying it through, much to his dismay. The rest of the night ended in a virtual argument about our respective roles in our relationship.

At this stage of the game, Jenny is shocked and astonished at her boyfriend's reaction, which to her seems quite extreme. She interprets it as resulting from the ways they have been socialized, preferring to view it as a learning experience which, through mutual understanding, will bring them closer.

One way Jenny negotiates differences between them will be "to verbally state my feelings to Robbie or any other man about my desire for equality, yet my need for security in relationships." In other words, one way to get over this wall will be to voice her needs and hope she meets with sympathetic ears. It is a step that does not wholly comfort her, however, as she cannot foresee how it will work out. She explains: "It would be too easy to conclude that I have now created an ideal relationship; that would be impossible, for I have been raised in a conflicting atmosphere which has reinforced independence and dependence. But I hope that I will push myself to contradict the submissive stereotype of women and concentrate on creating an equilibrium in my life that balances my sometimes aggressive behavior with an often unacceptable need for passivity." Jenny is aware that her own upbringing is full of contradictions: she has been taught to be passive at times (to win love, be accepted) and has been praised for her "aggressive" behavior at others. How can she combine the two into a strong sense of self, feeling confident and at the same time loved?

Jenny prioritizes communication. She is not willing to accept Robbie's desire that she play a passive role in the relationship, but she believes that they can get beyond this if they truly understand and care about one another. The knowledge she is gaining through women's studies thus seems to serve as a potential vehicle for deeper understanding and closeness, legitimizing her feelings while also offering a way ("Let's talk about class") to bring them up. Hence Jenny chooses to forgive Robbie his attitude—"He can't help it, really"— and decides to assert herself more. If by the end of the course she has determined that Robbie is the wrong man for her—she is not willing to sacrifice herself for the sake of this relationship, as it becomes clear she would have to do with him—this choice, or even its possibility, is not at all clear to her at this time. What happened in between the gender-role exercise and the final course evaluation?

In her final exam for WST 103, Jenny mentions another conversation with Robbie. The exam question asks, "A friend says to you, 'Sexism just doesn't really exist anymore. Modern women can do whatever they want to. Discrimination against women doesn't happen any longer.' How would you respond?" Jenny responds as follows:

When I first read this question . . . , one specific thought came into my mind, and that was a particular discussion I recently had with a man, my boyfriend. I was explaining to him that I was definitely a feminist, and I also described to him the goals for my future. Although we are not discussing our future plans right now, Rob interpreted my opinions [by] responding defensively with this remark, "Jenny, you are not a feminist, you are a woman who wants equality." At first I thought the discussion would end at that, but I would like to base this essay on his additional remark, "I think it's great that women want equality by having a career and a good education, and I want my wife to have these things, too, but when it comes to having children and a home, I want my wife to be there for her children." I think these ideas are symbolic not only of Rob, but of many men. The focus of this essay is that people want to appear open and nonsexist, yet when it comes right down to it, women are expected to find their greatest fulfillment through maintaining a family, not by their own personal success.

Jenny does not come right out and say that Robbie is sexist, but she certainly implies that his attitude about what he expects from his wife is sexist. This is a switch for her: she is no longer making excuses for him; she simply wants to argue with his position and chooses the forum of this exam to do so. There are at least two significant aspects to this incident: the interrelatedness of this course with Jenny's everyday life (she is using material from both to arrive at her own position) and the distancing from Robbie that is made possible by finding a safe space outside the relationship to examine what goes on inside it. It is clear that Jenny is upset by this incident. It also seems she is still not being heard. The voice she has developed through Women's Studies, her ability to articulate what is wrong with Robbie's position, is not translating into closeness with Robbie. He is still telling her what she is—"not a feminist"—while refusing to examine his own position.

In the course of defending her point in this exam, Jenny states:

> What Rob does not consider is the fact that many women simply do not desire motherhood, nor do they desire the work involved in having children. Rob is caught up in the general belief that women's ultimate satisfaction will not come from succeeding in the work force, but through the accomplishment of raising a family. . . . I don't think Rob has ever considered that motherhood can be a major intrusion in a woman's life. He seems to represent the ideology expressed in Freeman's definition of the "Motherhood Mystique" that motherhood is always a joyous, fulfilling occasion. Little does he understand that some mothers feel as if they are imprisoned by family life.

Her remarks indicate that, from her present perspective, whatever has led Robbie to believe these things is inconsequential: he is just plain wrong and needs to have his eyes opened.

Jenny then goes on to talk about her own mother's experience of raising her children without the help of her executive husband (something she explored in the oral history interview), saying, "I was unable to believe that she had remained in the marriage." She writes, "The example of my mother helped me realize that I cannot please everyone and that, as an educated young woman, I must not feel intimidated by competitive success." Her statement here strongly rejects the notion of sacrificing one's self and one's knowledge for a relationship, leaving her empowered to say, I simply cannot please everyone so I will please myself. Nevertheless, some remnants of guilt remain: "Until girls are taught that the ideal goal for them is not necessarily motherhood, they will be riddled with guilt for desiring the 'barren' lifestyle of an education and a career."

This "guilt" to which Jenny refers signals the double bind she clearly articulates, not only throughout the course but especially one year later. As she explains, she has been socialized one way and has been exposed to different options through schooling; she is consequently faced with inconsistencies in her own behavior as well as with conflicts generated by the clash between her newly acquired feminist perspective and a world pervaded by sexist attitudes. She feels torn by the desire to explore what might bring her fulfillment and the desire to be accepted.

This conflict is underscored when she returns to the subject of motherhood one year after the course. At this time she has broken up with Robbie. She explains:

> [Women's Studies was] part of the reason I broke up with my boyfriend. I had a hard time toward the end of the class keeping things in perspective. I loved my boyfriend, but he made jokes about Women's Studies—this was important to me and he ridiculed, belittled it. Professor O'Barr suggested that I talk about certain issues with him, but it didn't work. He didn't support any of this. It was hard to realize how unsupportive Robbie was being. [The breakup] was what had to happen, though. In a relationship, a person has to respect what she does as much as she respects him. My boyfriend was from the South, he made cutting comments all the time. It was very hard to live down the stereotypes of Women's Studies. I have a strong personality and was not willing to change for him. He is the oldest male—think what that means in terms of southern mentality. I had a better GPA and he was defensive about it. I felt I was totally compromising what was right for me. He put restrictions on me without me realizing it, and I didn't get any support from him.

The same issue that she once thought they could overcome through mutual understanding has finally driven them apart. Continuing to analyze the breakup as being partially due to North-South cultural distinctions and different socialization, Jenny no longer makes excuses for him. Nor is she willing to mold herself to his liking. She simply will not allow herself to be stifled, even when this means losing a person who meant a great deal to her. Rather than allowing herself to be silenced and become depressed, Jenny found support for her feelings and position in the Women's Studies classroom. Had Rob been able to join her and work through that space with her, perhaps they could have remained together in a healthier relationship. As it turns out, however, Women's Studies served as the tangible wedge that would keep them apart, while sustaining Jenny in her unpopular, unconventional beliefs.

Losing Robbie, however, has affected the way Jenny feels about herself and her engagement with feminist issues. When she discusses motherhood in the final course evaluation, her stance seems much less radical than the position she took in her final exam. She has decided she will drop her career for a few years to raise her children. She says she "wouldn't be happy" with herself if she didn't pursue a career after the first few years; but she also feels it is mainly her responsibility (because "woman has a more nurturing personality, even if it's socially constructed") to create a strong family base. While in the final exam Jenny argues quite vehemently—if in theory—that women might not even want children, when it comes to making a personal call, she still feels that she needs to do both—be a mother and have a career. She has arrived at a position, a kind of compromise between two extremes (all motherhood, all career). But she seems, more eloquently, to be stuck right in the middle of the dilemma, still wrestling with the questions: to what extent do I sacrifice my self for a relationship? and how do I manage to get rid of my guilt?

Moreover, she seems deeply hurt by the failure of this relationship. It might have been easier to change for Robbie; at least she might have had someone instead of being alone. She talks in her interview about the movie *Pretty Woman* (many students did) and her reaction to it. She says, "I had a hard time watching it. I was split ethically: I know it's wrong, but maybe I want to be treated that way." Jenny is signaling part of her confusion: while attracted to the way "pretty woman" is treated (i.e., she, too, wants to be loved), she finds herself reacting negatively to what "pretty woman" must do to win that love (transform herself completely). While as a fantasy it seems attractive, in reality following in "pretty woman's" footsteps would mean losing herself and would cause her too much pain.

Similarly, summing up the impact of Women's Studies in her life, she says:

> It helped me be proud of myself, to think independence is OK and not to
> be afraid of the future, of not being married in five years. I'm a smart

woman, qualified, I can live in this world and be just fine. It made me stand up for myself and not take shit from people like my boyfriend. I don't have to marry this guy. But still, I'm bothered by the fact that I judge my self-worth through having a man on my arm. It's definitely scary. I don't know how long it will be until I fall in love again. My parents don't pressure me, but I'm scared. I keep thinking I'll never ever meet anybody.

Jenny articulates both a desire to be "liberated," a strong and independent feminist (as she would define this), and an insecurity that makes her judge her self-worth by her relation to men. Women's Studies has helped her deal with the possibility that she might not find "the right man" as soon as she had anticipated, and it has enabled her to build an identity that is not dependent on such a relationship. Yet at this point she is not sure to what extent she is "a creation of Women's Studies, a monster" (as she described her feelings the spring she took the course) and to what extent she has developed her own voice, her own sense of self. She has made decisions, broken off bad relationships, found new ways of interacting with her sorority and her family, and she feels strong. But she also feels at war with herself; she still struggles with the sense of loss involved in having a voice.

Beth handles her engagement with the "wall" in a different way. Unlike Jenny, who struggles with her identity and who understands her own position (and the position of others) as the effect of socialization and learning, Beth sees the intervention of Women's Studies as eye-opening only to the extent that it has shown her what she's up against. Beth's main insight deals with how to talk to people so they will listen; she does not delve deeper into the human psyche to try to figure out why someone might be treating her in a particular way. For Beth it is enough to be aware of the existence of sexism so that she can be better equipped in preparing for battle.

As early as the curriculum evaluation project, Beth suggests that women are responsible for changing sexist institutions. She states, "At least this text acknowledges the fact that great female musicians have become more recognized in recent history. This more equitable representation might be due to having more women coauthor the text (sixteen times more)." If more women enter the power structures that keep them marginalized, these power structures would be transformed—hence, Beth suggests, it is up to women to fight discrimination. Beth continues: "My impression, of course, is that there were and always will be exceptional female musicians, but because they eventually must carry the burden of motherhood and societal pressures, their genius is not able to fully develop. Because the female musician's talent is not fully developed, her works or accomplishments are overshadowed by those of greater works created by male musicians." In this passage Beth does not question the standards that have been established to judge "great" works; nor does she suggest that women may not be well known because of a sexist bias in judging their work. She accepts the institutionalized criteria for greatness and explains why more women have not achieved it. Rather than questioning or challenging the rules of the game, Beth accepts them and decides to play better.

Consequently she begins to feel overwhelmed. In her final course evaluation she describes feeling "really upset, mad for a while. There was a stage when thinking about women's issues just got me more upset. I felt I couldn't change anything fast. Now I've come to terms with this. I just can't expect instant solutions or people to open their ears." She reiterates the need for role models in the sciences and other institutions and focuses on how she can make a difference. Her way of coping remains highly individualistic.

One of her solutions for dealing with the problem of institutionalized sexism, which she says she learned to recognize through Women's Studies, is learning how to talk so people, especially men, will listen. In her final exam she writes: "In the past, I thought using statistics—like 'women make 66 cents for a man's dollar, it's a fact'—would work. But somehow, and I believe it is because statistics are very impersonal in general, statistics did not seem to be very effective in supporting my argument. I have, therefore, adopted the personal approach, which involves using clear-cut examples/issues from the community . . . as [examples] of discrimination against women. Here would be my ideal approach to a male Duke student." Aware that she cannot expect immediate sympathy, Beth changes the way she talks to people so that they will hear what she has to say. It is in learning how to talk differently—more specifically, to articulate precisely where she sees discrimination happening—that she puts most of her energy. Women's Studies thus has provided her with a tool for her own self-empowerment as a woman: she can see better, and she can explain what she sees so people will listen. This is both in keeping with her idea that it is up to her—and women—to change things (it is not society's responsibility); and, at the same time, it is an effort to change a social structure that she finds oppressive.

This effort does not provide Beth with a new or radically different sense of identity. As she explains in her final course evaluation, writing to her congressman isn't something that "she wouldn't do already. . . . Women's Studies just gave me the impetus to do it. And I'm glad I did it." Whereas before she might have chosen to brush aside women's issues, she is less likely to do so after the course. But, finally, what shines through in Beth's thought and writing is a sense of realism. What Beth "knows" is that "people won't necessarily listen. If you want to change things, you have to give it your all. It won't just happen." She goes on to say, "I'm aware of how hard it is to make a difference. It's very disillusioning to think a guy equal to me can get so much farther. Now I feel I've just got to do what I want to do. I don't feel more empowered by the knowledge I've acquired. I feel there's more realism involved. It will take a lot to change things." At this intersection, Beth is not interested in analyzing the connections between the problems she has encountered, social structures, and herself; for her, it is a question of how better to navigate these waters. She must become stronger in herself, work harder, learn to talk to people, and find the role models that might make access to masculinist structures easier.

For Karen, much of the "wall" is made up of the conservative religious views of her family. Karen's comments suggest a conscious quest to find a way through or around the wall. In her initial evaluation Karen says, "My family is very conservative and feels that this [course] is a waste of time, but it is something that I am very interested in and concerned about." She describes herself as "interested in feminism but . . . unsure about a lot of the issues." In addition, she expresses a desire "to become more articulate about issues that concern me and the feelings that I have about these issues. I have a hard time explaining them to my parents or my male friends."

When interviewed a year later, Karen begins with, "I think my parents are really conventional. I came to Duke innocent and naive about lots of things." Her choice of words, her worry over being understood, and the number of issues touched on in these few sentences reveal the strong emotional impact and sense of dislocation these events created for her: "I was looking for something I believed in, aside from what my parents taught me. Does that make sense? There were a lot of changes going on for me [in my] sophomore year. The course did help build my self-confidence." Parents, date rape, environmental concerns, moral beliefs, religion, logic, identity, and self-confidence created a complex of interrelated, crucial, and immediate concerns for Karen.

As part of her quest for a foundation of her own, Karen interviewed her mother for her oral history project. She sees her mother's life as shaped primarily by religion and her mother's refusal to support the women's movement as a direct result of her religious beliefs—despite her mother's agreement with several feminist positions (including the problem of the media's objectification of women and the injustice of wage discrepancies). The last paragraph of Karen's interview report begins, "Although I do not agree with many of my mother's ideas about gender roles, I do understand that her religion is very important to her and to millions of others around the world." She ends with, "We must understand religion and its influence and importance, then try to change these beliefs to fit a feminist perspective." A year later, when describing the interview with her mother, Karen says, "I've always had uneasy feelings about the place of women in the religion of my family. [My oral history project] helped me rethink my mother's views of Christianity and move away from them." Karen feels that maintaining peaceful ties with her family will be an ongoing struggle; at the time of the interview, she was particularly upset with her family's willingness to accept the strictures of the Christian organization for which her sister works. After marrying another member of the same organization, her sister is allowed to work only part-time. If she has children, she will be forced to work only a limited number of hours on a volunteer basis. Karen seems in many ways to have given up on maintaining some connections; she describes how hard it is for her now to talk to her sister and how she has decided to not pursue or continue friendships with people who refuse to respect her feelings.

In one sense Karen found a concrete solution to her dilemma: "We read the coolest article during the class, on finding/believing in a goddess, having a religion that believes in the strength of women. It celebrates cycles, connections to nature. . . . I find myself thinking yes, I'm a strong person, and thinking about that article." However, she also says that she has not really followed up on her interest in the article by consistently practicing its suggestions. Nevertheless, Karen believes she has moved into a position from which she can feel confident about and able to vocalize her beliefs and feelings most of the time: "My family believes a woman is the one who should take care of the children, because of their religious values. I don't want to have children unless it's going to be shared—fifty-fifty." At another point, she says, "I don't feel like I want to be a mom like my mom. I didn't know how to articulate those feelings before— now I do." Encouraged in her perception that her discomfort with her family's religious stance is legitimate, Karen has been able to come into her own, express her view, and confront the sense of loss that accompanies her newfound independence and strength. While women's issues are not necessarily the primary focus of her activities, engagement with them permeates her existence: "I have used my feminist beliefs to become a woman leader in environmental movements."

Searching for and Implementing Ways through the "Wall"

Evidence for the ways in which students encounter problems and employ this naming process is most clearly seen in students' action projects, which ask them to identify an issue and attempt to change it. Karen's account is typical. For her action project, she decides to confront her friends who cheer at commercials that combine beer and women. She describes the typical scene:

"Yeah, all right, beer and babes!" "There's the beer, now where are the hot babes!?!" "Sweet babes!" I have heard these phrases many times while watching television with some of my male friends. My friends cheered this way for commercials, especially beer commercials, which included beautiful women. They chanted for the "two B's." This habit had increasingly grated on my nerves, so I finally decided to do something about it. For my action project, I chose to discuss with them the presentation of women in advertising and their reactions to these advertisements. I hoped to change their actions by altering their perception of the advertisements.

Getting her friends to see why this behavior is so offensive to her was not something Karen felt equipped to do before the Women's Studies class because she felt she could not articulate what was wrong with their behavior or why it made her feel bad or why they should stop. Only after having discussed the representation of women in the media, issues of pornography, socialization, and the effect of representations of women on her own self-esteem does Karen feel able to construct a coherent enough argument to defend herself and her objection. In order to feel she has a legitimate voice, she needs to arm herself with frameworks and explanations that will make her resistance possible. And still she is not sure whether people—even those close to her—will listen.

In her final course evaluation one year later, Karen weighs the results of her endeavor and sees her success as mixed. She says, "It felt good to tell them, but I don't know if it really did a thing except make me want to distance myself from some of them. It hurt the friends closest to me, and I think it hit home with a couple of them. With the majority it just pissed them off."

For other students the solutions they find to being women in a culture that devalues women are more subtle and less dependent upon external reactions for continuity. Students report, "I just do it," and try to reinterpret rather than control the reactions. Concerns over appearance come most frequently to mind here. This is what Anne wrote in her action paper:

> At one time, I envied the "ideal" body image and saw it as worthwhile to emulate as closely as possible, but I soon realized that this envy was misplaced. Society's standards of beauty are perpetuated by the media, and outside of it they have no inherent value whatsoever. Society's standard of beauty is an image, and, like all "images," this image is an illusion—a delusion—that looking a particular way is acceptable and desirable as opposed to having a different appearance. Such an attitude can be physically and mentally derogatory to those who do not match the stereotype.

Anne gives evidence here of a switch in her thinking. Supported by critiques articulated in the Women's Studies classroom, she experiences a sense of freedom in knowing that she does not have to be like those magazines tell her to be.

Anne takes her ideas about appearance and her willingness to experiment with definitions of female beauty a step farther during the follow-up interviews. She says that she now has trouble thinking about things in terms of "gender-role violations." "One gender-role violation I commit is that I don't own a hair dryer—I go out with wet hair just like the guys. I don't worry about my appearance much unless I'm interviewing or just feel like dressing up." The residual effect of what constitutes appropriate female behavior is still clearly here for Anne, yet she is determined to be her own person in at least some situations and to enjoy doing so.

Karen, when asked whether she was struggling with any contradictions that the course failed to resolve, also cites appearance. "Thinking I should get in shape or lose weight, then thinking about Kilbourne[8] and feeling, no, I should feel good about the way I am. I haven't gotten entirely past all that." Jenny, on the other hand, decides it is not something she wants to get past. For Jenny, the struggle has centered around how to be a feminist in intellectual terms and what she perceives as feminine in personal terms. In her final course interview Jenny reported finding the materials presented in class difficult. "It's thrown at you every day. . . . I couldn't verbalize how I felt. Now I can express it more. . . . I have achieved leadership positions at Duke that made me feel empowered. For example, the women at the Women's Center have to respect me because I work there and am involved." She feels she gets respect for her abilities, even though she continues to dress in a traditional way. "I feel," she says, "like I've disproved the myth of a Women's Studies certificate earner by being like I am." The cultural expectations weigh as heavily on one as on the others, but each chooses a different alternative. Karen realizes she is still struggling with it on some levels but does so consciously. Anne confronts the beauty-standards question by rejecting it, whereas Jenny reconciles it for herself and forces others to do the same. While their responses vary, their analyses are similar. They each assume a position and articulate it—they find a solution rather than remaining confused or passive.

Of course, while these newfound voices and self-determined positions are exhilarating, inspiring, and self-affirming, they are not always easy to maintain. Voices that insist on being heard can be disruptive, challenging, dangerous, even alienating, and may sometimes result in pain, loss, and disapproval. For Jenny, holding on to her voice and a strong sense of self may mean giving up what she felt could be a long-term romantic relationship. In another case, a student describes her interest in women's issues as an "ongoing issue with her boyfriend," but says that her ability to argue with him is an advantage gained from the introductory Women's Studies course. Beth describes conflicts with family, particularly her mother, over her new position. Her mother felt she chose to be a housewife; Beth feels this choice was valid, but her mother decides that Beth no longer respects her. Beth also found herself frustrated by the difficulty of change and says she had one crisis after another during the course of the semester. While she values the awareness she gained, she wanted more solutions. "It took me several months to repair my [normally] optimistic outlook." When asked whether she felt more or less empowered after taking the course, another student replied, "It made me feel weaker—like giving up. But stronger because I have lots of knowledge and can argue with people. Before, in high school, I didn't think about it. In college, people would say things that upset me, but I had no voice. Now I have data, and [that's made me] more confident." Karen notes an external conflict she had to negotiate while taking the class: "A friend and I . . . took the class together [and] heard things like, 'They're taking Women's Studies together—you know what that means.' It was frustrating to have to deal with their reactions to me wanting to explore myself. It made me really examine who I wanted to be friends with." Another student describes the conflict eloquently. While she says the course was one of the best of her college career, she also notes that "it would be so much easier to not know these things. I'm pretty much past that now, but still torn some-times. . . . It's really hard . . . no way all this can be changed." Once more, Carol Gilligan's description of conflict among adolescent girls resonates: "If girls know what they know and bring themselves into relationships, they will be in conflict with prevailing authorities. If girls do not know what they know and take themselves out of relationships, they will be in conflict with themselves" (p. 529).

While many of the students seem to have trouble imagining what their lives will be like after college, Anne carries her analysis of her experiences into an assessment of what trying to have a career as a woman will be like. In her final exam, she refers to the workplace as the "site of sexual harassment, site of discrimination." She remembers her oral history interview, when she was told that "new male doctors resented advice from female nurses, even when the nurses had been there for years and knew the patients, the dynamics of the hospital, the working conditions." Her interview subject was a doctor of medi-cal psychology who had spent many years as a nurse, having been discouraged in college from becoming a doctor. Anne was particularly disappointed to discover that some of this discouragement had come from a female doctor who continually told the young student how difficult it all was. Anne views this as the most disturbing of all the discouragements her interviewee experienced: "I agree with Adrienne Rich in believing that women have primary responsibility to encourage other women in the face of opposition from men, and that such encouragement is the only way in which such opposition will be fully overcome." Anne also demonstrates a strong desire to name things for what they are: "Though she [the interviewee] obviously felt resentful of these biases, she shied away from the term 'harassment' to describe the relationship between doctors and nurses. I consider any type of sex-related or class-related bias which makes working at a job more difficult to be a form of harassment, but she seems not to have so broad a definition of the word." Naming the experience, we suggest, is crucial to Anne's taking a position and reinforcing it. Naming sexual harassment puts the behavior in a framework that legitimizes her experience and interpretation, allowing her to rise above it. It is by developing this ability to see and name that we believe the Women's Studies intervention becomes transformative: the experience can be lived differently, Anne's sense of self protected, her viewpoint legitimized.

One reason Anne responds so strongly to her interviewee's career experiences is that she herself has experienced career discrimination:

Last summer I worked at a field camp collecting fossils, where I expressed my desire to become a paleontologist to one of the professors. He snorted and replied, "Why don't you decide to go to the moon, it's just about as impossible." Yet . . . he still found time to encourage, help, and "teach the ropes" to the two male field assistants; the other female field assistant was virtually ignored. . . . No explanation was given for [discouraging me] . . . he knew nothing about me, having only met me a couple of hours before and politely inquired as to my career interests—as if the fact that an undergraduate would take off to Wyoming for a summer to collect fossils was no evidence of possible career interest! Anyway, the point is that, in the workplace, women find their presence discouraged, their career goals belittled.

Despite this discouragement, Anne has gotten over the "wall." She rejects the American myth that merit is all it takes to succeed; such a position could lower her self-esteem, making her feel she was not capable of pursuing the career of her choice. She sees that others sometimes try to put her (as well as other women) in a certain position due to gender, and she is determined "to always challenge the status quo. . . . If people don't buy [it], it will have to change."

As these women draw on a combination of past experiences and emotions, classroom learning, course readings, and associations with other women in order to negotiate their own position vis-à-vis women's issues, they also find themselves rethinking their stance on other social concerns. Sometimes they reverse their previous position, sometimes they develop a different perspective that shifts (without reversing) their position, but most often they seem to incorporate and integrate various parts of their belief system, old and new.

Anne came to the course feeling conflict over the intersection of feminist beliefs and abortion. She considered herself a feminist because she felt it wrong that women cannot safely walk the streets alone and that significant pay inequities exist, but worried that feminists would not welcome her due to her pro-life stance. Over the course of the semester, Anne came to discover that not only are there other feminists who choose a pro-life position, but that new knowledge made her question whether she wanted to maintain that position. She says, "I kind of became pro-choice through the course because it made me realize the gender and race aspects of the [abortion] issue. I discovered it wasn't as simple as I had thought. Rich people will have them anyway, but poor people will get illegal abortions and die from them." She says later in her interview that while she is now pro-choice, she will never be entirely comfortable with abortion. Her position shifts in response to the broadening of her knowledge base, but the process is one of growth, not a complete upheaval of the old to be replaced by the new.

In another intersection of women's and other social issues, Anne describes herself as someone who was very homophobic, like her parents and her friends in high school. She was in the process of rethinking that position when she took the course and now says, "I can't believe I thought that way. I think back to my freshman year and I feel disgusted." Yet Anne, a firm believer in education, isn't stopping with that. She has given her father things to read about homophobia in our society—she mentioned Adrienne Rich's *On Lies, Secrets, and Silence* and Virginia Woolf's *A Room of One's Own.*[9] She recognizes that people see things differently according to the position from which they approach an issue. She feels the answer is to educate, to provide people with more information and more perspectives so that they can productively rethink their position.

Karen sees many intersections between women's issues and other social issues; in the course of her interview, she mentions at different points race, class, sexual orientation, the environment, and age discrimination. A leader in the environmental movement, she expresses worry over how to be involved with and work for the various things she is concerned about: "I feel like I'm kind of passive because I'm not involved in the Women's Center, even though I feel very strongly about it. I have spent my energy on environmental issues. I have used my feminist beliefs to become a woman leader in environmental movements. I talk with friends about this—we feel like we've narrowed down what we work for—and sometimes feel we should be working for poverty, date rape, etc.—but it seems there's only so much you can do. You only have so much energy. It would be too much of a drain to take on everything." Yet while Karen voices the concern of many contemporary young people, women and men, over how to juggle all their personal and social goals, she has thought carefully about what her concerns are; made thoroughly considered choices about where and how she will expend her energies; and, with the help of Women's Studies, developed the self-knowledge and ability for self-expression necessary to pursue those goals.

Both Karen and Anne see education as the way to change unfair gender stereotyping. When Karen implemented her protest against "beer and babes" commercials, she chose a strategy similar to that of the trajectory of the introductory class. She began with the personal level, explaining that she felt their comments were degrading to her. She then addressed the social picture, pointing out that their excitement over these commercials was degrading to women in general because they objectified women by placing them on the same level as beer. She also pointed out to them how they were being manipulated by the commercials and how the effect was a huge social problem, the myth that women like to be treated as sexual objects. "I decided to discuss two different levels of sexism; their reactions to the ads and the actual commercials. I hoped to change their actions by altering their perception of the advertisements. . . . I am not sure if I changed their attitudes, but I do know that they avoid these types of comments while I am around."

For Anne, when it comes to change, self-reconstitution is not enough. Like many other students, she wants to see change at the level of society. Anne's journey to this position is indicative of the road that many travel. In her final exam she writes, "But individual rights aren't the problem—objectification, subordination, discrimination, violence, and male domination are the problems." With this statement in her analysis, she is signaling something crucial. Anne has come to understand that it is not enough to grant individual rights to someone if the social dimensions are not addressed. This statement signifies that Anne understands herself and the issues she discusses in relation to society; she is not a "free" individual with guaranteed rights. Gilligan traces a similar dynamic in the lives of adolescent girls: "the tendency . . . for a resistance which is essentially political—an insistence on knowing what one knows and a willingness to be outspoken—to turn into a psychological resistance: a reluctance to know what one knows and a fear that such knowledge, if spoken, will endanger relationships and threaten survival" (p. 502). For Anne and many other Women's Studies students, this dynamic has taken an additional, freeing turn; Anne's "psychological" exploration of herself and her society has led to a new political awareness. It is the recognition that her so-called personal problem is society's problem.

Anne's recognition is not intellectual alone. She sees its ramifications in her everyday circumstances and realizes that she shares these circumstances with many other women. Later in the same exam, she writes, "I cannot run alone and I can't travel alone—the fear of rape curtails every woman's freedom. Occasionally I've ridden my bike alone at night and felt—well, yes, a little fear, but also a nagging guilt which I could not place. I realized that social pressures teach women that it is up to them to be careful, not up to men to stop the problem, and that by feeling guilt for my action, I was giving in to repercussions of social conditioning." Anne sees that social conditioning is formative of her identity, her feelings, her actions, and her guilt. Gilligan believes that if adolescent girls' healthy resistance to suppressing knowledge can stay in the open and remain political rather than turning inward to become psychologically corrosive, their resistance "can work to bring a new order of living into the world" (p. 533). Women's Studies has helped Anne articulate what is wrong with the "big picture" and see her problem not as a personal one about which she might feel ashamed, but as a sociocultural one. In differing ways and to different degrees, this realization is true for Jenny, Beth, and Karen as well. These students, and many of those we were not able to discuss in depth here, have gained a political awareness that has allowed them to use their knowledge and to turn their resistance outward. This step is crucial in transforming their sense of self and in developing a basis on which to act in the future.

Getting into
the Conversation

Feminist Thought and
the Transformation
of Knowledge

After more than ten years of teaching a graduate seminar called A History of Feminist Thought, it continues to be an intellectually challenging endeavor. Each year I am faced with wonderful new sources growing out of the burgeoning feminist research literature. I engage with graduate students from diverse departments, backgrounds, and perspectives; they bring quick minds and deep commitments to our discussions. Teaching the course has proved challenging in another way as well: whenever people find out that I teach the history of feminist thought, they stumble a bit. Most acknowledge they have never considered that feminist thought might have a history before the past couple of decades. Then they ask me what we cover. The subject of these remarks grows out of my answer to this question: what is there to talk about in the history of feminist thought? and why are people other than students interested in knowing the answer?

To explore this history, however, I must begin by mentioning what the class does not talk about—or, rather, what we only touch on as it relates to our subject matter. We do not talk about women's history per se. That is, I do not try to reconstruct the material and cultural positions of all women over time. While it is important to know some women's history, our emphasis is not directly on recovering women's experiences for the historical record.

Nor do we talk about the history of men's ideas concerning women. There is

A version of this essay was first presented as part of a series of reunion weekend programs sponsored by the Office of Alumni Affairs at Duke University and held September 19, October 3, and October 31, 1991. I also used these remarks as the basis of a series of public lectures I gave as a Fulbright Scholar at the Autonomous University of Barcelona in November 1991.

a vast literature on women's nature, most of it written by men, beginning with the Greeks and continuing into the present day. It is important to know what men, half of every human society, thought women were and ought to be. However, the seminar's emphasis is not on what men said.

What then is left to talk about? We talk about women's reflections on women—what different women, living in different time periods and various Western societies, have said and written about women's circumstances. We begin long before the rise of modern feminism in the nineteenth century, and we finish with the recent creation of women's studies as an academic enterprise.

While the questions vary with the history and circumstances of the questioner as well as with the composition of each class, every student acknowledges the fact that women have a problematic relationship to society and to their position in it. The history of feminist thought is about understanding women's circumstances, what women have thought about them, and, perhaps most significant, how they have proposed to alter them. My goal in working through the history of feminist thought with you this morning is to suggest that women's diverse reflections upon women challenge the very core of Western knowledge as this knowledge has been created and passed on to us at the present time.

To do so, I braid three sources together. First, I use the records we have of women in the past: their letters and diaries; the essays, plays, and poems they wrote; the speeches they gave; what was written about them. Second, I intertwine my own understanding of how ideas emerge within the interaction of text and student, ideas that yield incisive analyses of contemporary issues. Third, I rely heavily upon the words of the students themselves as they encounter these foremothers for the first time.

I have taken students' words from a learning log in which they write weekly entries. The log serves many different purposes for each student. It contains a personal account of the ideas students are encountering in the class readings. It analyzes how those ideas relate to cherished beliefs, previous understanding, and other current classes and experiences. It records what each student thought and how that student's thinking changes as the result of readings, discussions, and reflections. But most of all the log is a wish list of all the books to be read and ideas to be pursued after the present course, "when I have time."

Each student works his or her own way through the readings, learning log, and class discussions. Because the course focuses on rethinking academic knowledge as it is presently constructed, what any given individual student will learn in the course of the class depends on his or her background. I have organized my analysis around some patterns that demonstrate how students use the space provided by the course to unlearn some ideas and reformulate others. In one section I highlight the writings of one student, Michelle LaRocque, to illustrate how she engaged the material to rethink prior understanding.

I will begin this chapter as I begin the course, where European history has conventionally begun—with Greek civilization—and move into the "New World" with the emergence of Anglo-America. This approach replicates the way in which traditional academic disciplines have developed the historical record and taught what was deemed important in the past. This is how women's studies began—with the need to rethink the academic canon we have inherited. One of the most difficult aspects of this unlearning process involves unlearning the misconception that we can simply correct former absences by adding women into the received chronology. When women are fully integrated into the canon, history no longer adds up in the same tidy way. Thus, while the course proceeds within conventionally defined periods, I focus on selective themes that link past and present in a not-so-tidy fashion. History is not any more tidy than women's lives; chronological movement is not equivalent to developmental progress for women.

Back Then . . .

We begin the seminar by talking about women most students have never heard of; the fact that so many of us are unfamiliar with these women makes us all uncomfortable. This discomfort is particularly acute for graduate students, who are pursuing advanced work that should cover "everything." It suggests that what we know about the past might be incomplete in some fundamental sense. Not only are women missing; also missing is the improved picture of the past that including all women would provide. One of the first "missing women" we encounter is Hypatia.

An Athenian philosopher, Hypatia was appointed to direct the Neoplatonic School in Alexandria in A.D. 400 at the age of thirty. Such an accomplishment was extraordinary for a woman and particularly noteworthy because she was not part of the rapidly growing Christian leadership of the city. A new source-book on women philosophers describes her as follows: "Her reputation was incredible. Students flocked to her from everywhere, and letters reached her simply addressed to 'The Muse' or 'The Philosopher.' According to one of her pupils [whose written records we have] . . . she was at the time considered to be the greatest living exponent of Platonic, Aristotelian, and Neoplatonic philosophy."[1] Until the last few decades of feminist scholarship, Hypatia's influence on philosophy was unknown. Her claims to fame could be briefly summed up in two anecdotes recorded in the eighteenth century: how she hurled the equivalent of a used sanitary napkin in the face of a student suitor with the words, "This is what you love, young fool, and not anything that is beautiful"; and how she was mutilated and murdered by the archbishop of Alexandria in a bitter contest over political influence in the city.

Even these two anecdotes are not common knowledge. When students learn that Hypatia protested harassment and assumed leadership in the face of opposition, they begin to wonder who and what else they've been missing. They are emboldened by her story. The sense that it-has-happened-before mixes with the knowledge that she-has-been-forgotten in an uneasy combination.

This uncomfortable mix of the suppression of women and the neglect of their achievements hovers over our discussions as we confront the possibility that the story of women's lives from past to present is not one of steady improvement but one in which setbacks are as common as advances. A look at women in medieval times confirms our suspicions.

Contemporary social historians are recovering the stories of the lives of women in the past. What they are discovering challenges any idea of linear progress for women. In the medieval period women's opportunities appear quite extensive. Religious houses, major European social institutions, are run by and for both women and men. Women have property rights as well as a relatively secure marital status. And this is a world in which the sexual division of labor is fluid; men and women perform similar tasks, and gender is not a primary social demarker. The idea that medieval women exercised a degree of power intrigues many students, and they demand to know what happened to diminish such power. Behind their question is a clear contemporary concern: if women once had such power and then lost it, are our fortunes likewise in jeopardy?

They find in the history of the Middle Ages (the time of the commercial rise of Italian city-states) some highly instructive information about various ways in which social arrangements change the conditions under which women live. As dowry practices are re-designed to enhance the accumulation of wealth in families for commercial purposes, dowries fail to protect women as they once did. The growing bureaucracy and power of the Roman Catholic Church restricts the roles and responsibilities of women. And the recovery of classical texts, particularly Aristotle as promulgated by Thomas Aquinas, has major effects on women.

The research of social historian Susan Stuard on gender dichotomies offers one set of explanations that students find useful as they struggle to understand how women came to assume such fixed and negative characteristics:

This system of assigning qualities by sex, with women usually assigned the more negative traits, had not enjoyed much popularity in the early Middle Ages, however, nor had it been politic when abbesses, queens, and other powerful women distributed so much patronage. . . .

When polarities became fashionable in the 12th century, they stimulated imaginations and provided apt images for theological debates. . . . Lay people, even the illiterate, could grasp polarities and employ them as unquestioned assumptions, sanctioned by theologians. . . . This new definition of women passed on an inherited system of notions that remained largely unexamined, in which the polar construct remained constant while any particular comparison (men are at rest, women are moving) could be constructed to fit new circumstances. . . . Authorities in many fields of knowledge used notions of gender to simplify schemes of thought. They provided rationales for expedient acts using the opposition of female to male as justification. Europeans began to speak of "woman" as a category rather than of women as they knew them. This tendency became an overriding consideration in justifying women's roles, responsibilities, rights, and their place in Christian society.[2]

Students draw some very specific lessons from this brief exposure to medieval material. They learn that no single factor determines women's status. Rather they come to understand that many different social arrangements interact to determine ideas about gender as well as women's place. They learn that those experiencing the changes are not necessarily aware of the full impact of the changes at the time. And they learn that women's position is an excellent indicator of the nature of a society, for how women are seen and see themselves tells us a good deal about what a society values and ignores. Social and cultural arrangements simultaneously reflect and reinforce women's circumstances. Women themselves act both to support and to resist the positions they hold in complex and varied ways.

At this point in the explorations students want to know how women of the time understood what was happening to them. Fortunately, we now have available to us the writings of Renaissance women, made accessible by the scholarly work of the late historian Joan Kelly.[3] I cite but one example here for illustrative purposes. Christine de Pisan, who lived from 1364 to 1430, was the first female professional writer in France and the first woman of the late Middle Ages to champion her sex—a feminist forerunner, if you will. Born to an Italian academic family that worked at the court, she was widowed at twenty-five and began writing to support herself. Over the next fifty years, she wrote extensively. *The Book of the City of Ladies* (1404–5) is the work best known today. She began what Kelly calls the *querelles des femmes*, or war of women, a four-hundred-year-old tradition of writing about women by women in Europe prior to the French Revolution. We have now recovered a large number of those writings, spanning geographical boundaries, and the material is remarkable.

These women write about women and sexual politics; they react to changes in the views of women and want to make both men and women conscious of these changes. Like modern-day feminists, these women's investigations focus on two concerns. First, by looking at their own situations, these feminist fore-mothers recognized that men's statements about women's inferiority could not be validated. The disparagement of women, as de Pisan and others came to see, was literally "man-made," a projection of men about women that had no base in women's actual lives—however universal men's statements claimed to be. Second, the women of the *querelles des femmes* looked back in history to find powerful and educated women of previous centuries, using their stories to refute current claims that women could not be educated or govern. What is interesting about this tradition is that the women scholars did not attack men as individuals but men's ideas about women and the intellectual traditions that men were developing.

The excitement that students experience when they learn about their fore-mothers and about the critical perspectives that these women had developed some five hundred years ago is palpable in the classroom. The idea that women have analyzed their situations with such preciseness and that they resisted, using their "pens as swords" to fight intellectual wars, leads the students to take up these women as teachers, mentors, and role models. Indeed, one student wrote, "Just a note, why are we calling her Christine [in class discussions]? You wouldn't run around calling Shakespeare Will, so why the chumminess here?" I suggest this chumminess occurs because de Pisan speaks to these feminist students with a relevance and directness that make her seem a friend, someone whose goals and concerns they share.

What Can Be Done?

Women philosophers in ancient Greece, medieval women exercising some control over property, women writers of the Renaissance angered by the gap between what people said about women and what women actually achieved— it is all a bit much for students who are accustomed to feeling moderately comfortable with what they have been taught. What happened to these women and their ideas, the students demand? Why are all these women not common knowledge?

As a class, we move next to the eighteenth and nineteenth centuries. Here the number of primary sources by women and secondary sources about them is vast. Because we can sample only a few, let me focus upon four examples, each from a particular time, as they are understood by one student, Michelle LaRocque.[4] By following her thought processes, we can see the ways in which adding women's voices to the conversation can transform analysis. I want to look at the Enlightenment through a glimpse of Mary Wollstonecraft and her ideas about education. I want to approach the reform era by highlighting differences between the work of well-known political activists (such as Elizabeth Cady Stanton and Susan B. Anthony) and the alternative strategies of less well known activists like Matilda Joslyn Gage. I want to look at the work of African American women reformers in the nineteenth century in order to stress that white middle-class women were not the only women engaged in feminist thought and action. Finally, I want to show how concern with political reform in the middle of the nineteenth century gave way to an economic emphasis as the twentieth century emerged.

While there are enormous differences both across a two-hundred-year time span and within the writings of thousands of women, there are some questions that can help us make sense of this diversity. For instance, where did these reformers locate the source of women's difference? of their oppression? What did they suggest would change those circumstances? Depending on how each woman answered those questions, many others soon follow. Were analysis and explanation the most effective route to change? How effective were public acts of resistance? Should women reform the home or the world or both? Would women, kept outside the formal institutions of society, be more likely to achieve their goals if they tried to get into those institutions or was critique from outside their best chance? Did all women share the same goals for change?

Mary Wollstonecraft's *A Vindication of the Rights of Women* usually proves a shock to the class.[5] An Englishwoman born in 1759, she became famous for her spirited essays that attacked other figures of the day (particularly Edmund Burke, Talleyrand, and Rousseau). The success of her popular pamphlets led her to write a sustained analysis, the book-length *A Vindication*, which argues that women should learn (or be taught) to fulfill their potential and to fight the roots of their subjection. A daughter of the Enlightenment who values reason as the basis for thought and action, she describes the education of women in her society as follows: "Women are told from their infancy, and taught by the example of their mothers, that a little knowledge of human weakness, justly termed cunning, softness of temper, *outward* obedience, and a scrupulous attention to a puerile kind of propriety, will obtain for them the protection of a man; and should they be beautiful, everything else is needless, for, at least, twenty years of their lives" (p. 44).

Noting the limitations of the polarities that had become so popular centuries before, Michelle listens to Wollstonecraft's insights and applies them to contemporary issues of physical beauty, advertising, and eating disorders:

We see in Mary Wollstonecraft the recognition that [the woman who concentrates only on her body] destroys not only her reason, and not only her self, but her very body as well. When I listen to her descriptions of the genteel women who have become slaves to their bodies, I cannot help but be reminded of the contemporary phenomena of anorexia and bulimia: "I once knew a weak woman of fashion, who was more than commonly proud of her delicacy and sensibility. She thought a distinguishing taste and puny appetite the height of all human perfection and acted accordingly" [p. 57]; and "What can be a more melancholy sight to a thinking mind than to look into numerous carriages that drive helterskelter about the metropolis in a morning full of pale-faced creatures who are flying from themselves" [p. 68].

Although weakness per se is not now the feminine ideal, the woman with an eating disorder . . . is destroying her body in much the same way as these women who cultivated physical weakness. What is interesting is that a picture emerges of woman's body as a battleground—being simultaneously a means of power and the source of her oppression. That beauty brings power through acceptability and social recognition, and it is the same beauty that serves to restrict her by directing all mental efforts to consideration of the latest cosmetics and weakening her body when weakness is the feminine ideal and when "thin is in" (and "thin" is thinner than a human being is meant to be).

What we learn from this, and perhaps what some of the Enlightenment feminists did not realize, is that the solution to the man/woman as mind/body dichotomy is not simply to assert the power of woman's mind. This, of course, is necessary. But if we look at woman's body itself as the site of a power struggle, then we see that reappropriating the body is as crucial as reappropriating the mind. Indeed, we see that the mind/body dichotomy itself must be resolved. It is not enough to have power *through* one's body, there must also be power *over* one's body. And power over one's body means that the "end" for one's body—that is, one's *self*—must come from internal rather than external motivations.

Wollstonecraft's hard-hitting analysis inspires many students. They are excited to learn that more than a century ago women were thinking in systematic ways about gender and its construction. Other students get impatient when they read her. Yes, they acknowledge, she had things figured out. But what did she do? Did any women get beyond theorizing and take action against oppression? The short answer is yes.

The names of Elizabeth Cady Stanton and Susan B. Anthony have become increasingly familiar as the new scholarship on women has spread through schools, organizations, and the media. We know that women began to organize to get the vote, to reform social and political practices, and to influence the course of daily life through their study and action. These middle-class women of the mid-nineteenth century believed strongly in women's power to right wrong through activities informed by careful study. They certainly faced opposition, often fierce, but they did so firm in the belief that it was they who were implementing democratic ideals and practices, not their critics. They became relentless in their energy and commitment to women's suffrage, for they believed that in the vote rested power. Unlike their Enlightenment foremothers, for whom lack of education had been the stumbling block to full civic and cultural life, these reformers believed that access to political decision making held the key to women's emancipation and society's betterment.

In 1876, some fifty years before a constitutional amendment allowed women to vote, Elizabeth Cady Stanton, Susan B. Anthony, and Matilda Joslyn Gage began to write a six-volume *History of Women's Suffrage*. Believing that their long struggles would culminate in change, they sought to record the process throughout. One section of the first volume records their best retorts to objections to votes for women. These two paragraphs sound as if they could have come from yesterday's newspaper:

But, "in the settlement of national difficulties," it is said, "the last resort is war; shall we summon our wives and mothers to the battle-field?" Women have led armies in all ages, have held positions in the army and navy for years in disguise. Some fought, bled, and died on the battle-field in our late war. They performed severe labors in the hospitals and sanitary department. Wisdom would dictate a division of labor in war as well as in peace, assigning each their appropriate department.

Numerous classes of men who enjoy their political rights are exempt from military duty. All men over forty-five, all who suffer mental or physical disability, such as the loss of an eye or a forefinger; clergymen, physicians, Quakers, school-teachers, professors, and presidents of colleges, judges, legislators, congressmen, State prison officials, and all county, State and National officers; fathers, brothers, or sons having certain relatives dependent on them for support—all of these summed up in every State in the Union make millions of voters thus exempted.

In view of this fact there is no force in the pleas, that "if women vote they must fight." Moreover, war is not the normal state of the human family in its higher development, but merely a feature of barbarism lasting on through the transition of the race, from the savage to the scholar.[6]

While most nineteenth-century activists emphasized changing the influence of women by giving them the vote, others identified additional obstacles to women's emancipation. They saw the possibility that even when women were no longer excluded from society's decision-making bodies, they could still be prohibited from influence because they lacked the ability to think and speak for themselves. Matilda Joslyn Gage represents one such advocate of change outside the political arena. Originally active alongside Stanton and Anthony in the suffrage movement, Gage began to assume a more radical stance as she researched women of the past. Eventually she broke with her peers, going on to write *Women, Church and State*. Written in 1893, *Women, Church and State* rails against the church for "aiding, abetting and providing a system to ensure women's subordination": "The most stupendous system of organized robbery known has been that of the church towards women. . . . The whole theory regarding women, under Christianity, has been based upon the conception that she had no right to live for herself alone. Her duty to others has continuously been placed before her and her training has ever been that of self-sacrifice."[7] Rejecting the idea that men are governed by reason and women by emotion, Gage says: "It is men at their political conventions, sporting events and in war and rape, who totally let go of their emotional control in a way that women have never done. It is man who has exhibited the wildest passions—the most ungovernable frenzy; it is man who has shown himself less controlled by reason than is possible for women under the most adverse circumstances" (p. 243).

While Gage's radicalism has distanced her voice from the mainstream history of women reformers that feminist scholars have recently begun to narrate, Gage nevertheless managed something of a cultural end run. Gage was the aunt of Frank Baum, author of the Oz books; we have in his central character, Dorothy, a very independent woman. Literary scholars have demonstrated Baum's debt to his aunt and the reformers of their time. Even when we make allowances for the more modern interpretations that have made their way into the Judy Garland version of the story, Dorothy can be read as the woman Matilda Joslyn Gage sought—a woman who has a voice, a person who rebels against social institutions that restrain her, and a leading character who figures out a way to get what she wants. Generations of young girls have identified with Dorothy and found in her the hero missing in so much children's literature. It is no accident that she has this appeal, for her foremother was one of the most radical theorists of the nineteenth century, whose message moved into the cultural center in a distinctive way. From margin to center—isn't that the way new ideas travel? And aren't most propositions that are made by women about women and on behalf of women initially dismissed as too extreme? Do they then go on to become popular, as Gage's ideas did, via Dorothy-like figures?

Additional Alternatives to What Can Be Done

Students reading across these nineteenth-century figures begin to explore the very different solutions by which these women sought to answer the question, "What can be done?" Students observe that while some women sought to modify institutions by working within them, others increasingly worked outside those institutions to create alternatives. They note that there is no single cause of women's difference or subordination but rather a configuration of many influences. As they try to figure out the pattern and the best way to eradicate it, they become aware of the differences in proposed solutions.

Yet the history of feminist thought explores an awareness of differences among women that involve much more than differences among white middle-class reformers. As students read the writings of relatively well known nineteenth-century African American women reformers (such as Julia Cooper, Ida B. Wells, and Pauline Hopkins) as well as virtually unknown African American women (usually slaves), students learn that African American women activists had a different understanding of what constituted "feminist action." They learn not only that African American women reformers proposed strategies different from their white female counterparts, but also that significant differences exist *among* these African American writers. As Michelle puts it:

> The original pieces that we read by Cooper, Wells, and Hopkins all seemed quite different from one another. Also, their being on the "outside" of the tradition that we've been reading, and not having much sense of the history of Reconstruction—I didn't even know that any African American women were educated at the time, I figured just a handful of African American men had access to education—it was hard for me to fit things together.
>
> Reclaiming a history for African Americans was clearly important to

Hopkins and Julia Cooper. Both recognize that they are the heirs of a past "not of their own making." Hopkins showed, through her fiction, that African Americans must understand their past in order to work toward a future. She tried to teach her readership that they were the descendants of a great and ancient civilization. . . . Hopkins feared that African Americans would be annihilated in America if mob rule and lynching became accepted practices through the United States. She felt that giving testimony, in her fiction, to an African American presence in history could help to ensure a continued African American presence, by making readers aware of their heritage and by giving testimony to the truth of the African American.

Michelle cites Julia Cooper's valuable point: "It is the curse of minorities in this power-worshipping world that either from fear or from an uncertain policy of expedience they distrust their own standards and hesitate to give voice to their deeper convictions, submitting supinely to estimates and characterizations of themselves as handed down by a not unprejudiced majority."[8]

Students find themselves confronting differences in solutions yet again as we study turn-of-the-century discussions about the relationship between women and economics. Until near the end of the nineteenth century, feminists concentrated their energies on education, politics, law, and religion. As the century comes to a close, feminists become increasingly concerned with economic issues. Both women of color and white women found themselves struggling to secure decent employment outside the home. The poverty of new immigrant groups and the suffering of their families became a national social issue. The shift to women's roles as consumers for the nuclear family is just around the corner. What is the relationship of women to economics and how are they to influence economic systems? Charlotte Perkins Gilman and Jane Addams have two quite different responses. Yet their reasoning rests on a shared argument that the public and private spheres of men and women were simply no longer workable categories by which to organize social arrangements. Michelle assesses the two authors in terms of contemporary debates about abortion, violence against women, and child care policy.

The writings of Jane Addams and Charlotte Perkins Gilman offer alternative views of how the creation of a more human world will come about.[9] It can be seen most clearly in their views toward domestic life, especially housekeeping and the family. Addams conceptualized the city as "enlarged housekeeping," thus extending woman's traditional role into the traditionally male world of economics and politics.

In one sense, this call for women to be the "housekeepers" of the workplace and city does not seem like a radical proposal. On the face of it, it appears to limit women to their traditional sphere by associating women with domesticity. But I think that there is a way to understand Addams's proposal as a radical one, for it calls for an end to the dichotomies of public/private and industrial/domestic. Thinking of the city as one large domestic enterprise means that the public and the private are indeed the "same thing." What Addams has in mind is transforming the city. Recognizing that the enemies of the modern industrial city are "within" rather than "without" requires changes in both thinking about and governing the city.

Charlotte Perkins Gilman locates housekeeping as one of the primary sources of women's oppression, since women do not receive the economic value of their domestic labor. Furthermore, she claims, the domestic service of the wife is more restrictive than motherhood: "It is not motherhood that keeps the housewife on her feet from dawn to dark; it is house service, not child service" [p. 576]. According to Gilman, economic independence for women necessarily involves a change in the home and family relation. Gilman proposes a system of communal living—a communal house for women with families—where the domestic workers would be hired jointly by the families. According to Gilman, this would transform the present situation in which the wife is the "private servant" of the family.

Gilman's emphasis is upon making domestic relations explicitly economic, whereas Addams's goal is to make economic relations more "domestic." Gilman's goal is to transform the domestic sphere, Addams's is to transform the economic sphere; yet both are aiming for a reconciliation of the two spheres. Their goals, then, are similar, though the directions of movement are in opposition. The important point that emerges from both proposals, and what distinguishes them from the thinking of the woman's rights movement, is that it is not simply enough to "put" women into the economy, one must make domestic concerns an explicit *part* of the economy. Their common claim is that only by integrating the female and male spheres of action will it be possible to create a world free of oppression for both women and men.

As the semester nears its end, the number of ideas we have tackled seems almost overwhelming. How do women develop a critical perspective on the conditions of their lives that allows them to see how class, race, region, religion, and sexuality all influence their situations? What are the multiple sources of discrimination in society? How is it best to attack them? Are women complicit in their own oppression? Why is it so difficult to bring about change, irrespective of the strategy employed? And how can the whole entangled situation of women, culture, and society be understood? explained? altered?

"Othering" and Feminist Responses

Just when it seems that we could draw an intricate and comprehensive outline, albeit with a lot of question marks, we confront an additional and confounding issue. We confront the work of the early twentieth-century theorists who see women's circumstances not as the fault of men or women but as a system of interaction between men and women in which psychological as well as economic, political, cultural, and religious underpinnings overlap.

The class is introduced to the dilemma by the works of Virginia Woolf and Simone de Beauvoir. These two authors directly address questions about individual autonomy versus systemic influences; both see social construction as the cause of oppression. Their writings are so rich, diverse, and extensive it seems difficult to choose a single central theme. Yet, unlike their predecessors, these twentieth-century writers emphasize gender interactions and the interrelationships among oppressions.

Here is how Michelle utilizes the works of Beauvoir and Woolf to expand her own systemic analysis of how oppression works:

In thinking about the condition of women, Simone de Beauvoir and Virginia Woolf ask a question that had not been previously raised: What is it that men get out of asserting that women are inferior? True, Christine de Pisan had tried to discover the motivations behind the misogynist biases of many male writers and thinkers, but de Pisan was more concerned with efficient causes. She thus explained their misogyny in terms of the personal and psychological factors that led individual men to their views of women. Beauvoir and Woolf, on the other hand, are looking for the "final causes," so to speak. They ask *why* men insist that women are inferior, where "why?" means "what for?" They want to know what benefits men, in general, receive from their assertions that women are inferior.

Woolf and Beauvoir both focus upon the relational aspect of women's inferiority. Both arrive at this focus after noting the anger and hostility that is found in the writings of men who are attempting to "prove" the inferiority of women. Reflecting upon her journey to the library and her research into writings about women (which are all by men), Woolf comments: "All that I had retrieved from that morning's work had been the one fact of anger. The professors—I lumped them together thus—were angry." But, she asks, why were they angry?[10]

Woolf concludes that the professor is angry for a reason that is not obvious: "Possibly when the professor insisted a little too emphatically upon the inferiority of women, he was concerned not with their inferiority, but with his own superiority" [pp. 34–35]. Given that life is difficult and calls for courage, strength, and, most of all, self-confidence, one way to generate these qualities is by thinking that others are inferior to oneself.

Beauvoir also ties the hostility found in men's attempts to prove women inferior to a more fundamental concern with their own status: "This hostility may at times be well-founded, often it is gratuitous; but in truth it more or less successfully conceals a desire for self-justification."[11] According to Beauvoir, "Otherness" is a fundamental category of human thought. Drawing on Hegel's insights into the master/slave relationship, Beauvoir explains that we find in consciousness itself a fundamental hostility toward every other consciousness. The subject can be posed only through being opposed; thus, no group (in this case, men) ever sets itself up as the One without at once setting up the Other (women) over against itself.

Many students experience that "click" of recognition when they read Beauvoir's and Woolf's compelling depictions of how this "Othering" process works. Through all our readings, we have found a continual classification of biological females as cultural women. In the contemporary world gender constitutes a fundamental marker that determines power, status, satisfaction, tasks, even identity itself.

Recent works by women of color have brought the process of "Othering" quite powerfully to the future feminist agenda by insisting upon the multiple ways in which race and class separate women as Other from one another as well as from men. Of all the African American theorists students encounter, bell hooks appears to have the greatest impact. hooks argues that because women are socialized to the same values as men, gaining power within the existing social structure undermines rather than strengthens women's ability to change the system. According to hooks, when women are increasingly invested in the system, they use their resources to maintain rather than transform it. hooks claims she, as an African American, sees social relations differently from middle-class white women: "Living as we did—on the edge—we developed a particular way of seeing reality. We looked both from the outside in and from the inside out. We focused our attention on the center as well as on the margin. We understood both."[12] hooks is clear that her ability to hold an "oppositional worldview" stems from a survival strategy, but she does not claim that only those who are marginal can see in this way. Identities for her do not produce worldviews but give different kinds of access to different ways of looking at the world.

For students, hooks shows a way out of the you-can-only-see-from-your-own-point-of-view conundrum and the despair that ensues when that position is adopted. They often quote her: "Feminism is the struggle to end sexist oppression. Its aim is not to benefit solely any specific group of women, any particular race or class of women. It does not privilege women over men. It has the power to transform, in a meaningful way, all our lives" (p. 26). Many students embrace the shift hooks makes when she moves from saying "I am a feminist" to "I advocate feminism." This means that anyone can advocate feminism. It means that the priority is not on who one is but on what one thinks and on what one does. This shift transforms debates about who should do what into a set of political priorities that can be engaged—from either side.

Students talk frequently about power—power struggles in their departments, their own initial attempts at feeling empowered, the disempowering nature of much of education. With its clear analysis of how power works, hooks's writing is a welcome clarification in a world that is often utterly confusing. The fact that hooks uses her African American experience to lead them into greater clarity is not lost on the white middle-class student majority. Through the writings of bell hooks as well as other women of color, students begin to approach one pressing issue for future feminist scholarship. Because the traditions within which we in the academy work are profoundly male, white, and European, the history of feminist thought tackles those traditions by focusing upon how women resemble those men either in terms of class, race, or sexual orientation. This approach constitutes a specific and conscious choice that enables us to call into question the canonical traditions that are said to represent the "truth" of "the past." But future scholarship is already located in more diverse settings. The interrelationship of gender and race, gender and class, gender and sexual orientation, gender and age, gender and ethnicity, gender and ability—every combination yields a permutation that must not be glossed over.

The second issue that points students toward the future concerns the origins of women's studies, the process of bringing feminist scholarship into the academy, and current efforts at curriculum transformation (which themselves result from the extensive research of the past two and a half decades). Graduate students in their mid-twenties, enrolled in programs in the 1990s, were born just as feminism as a social movement emerged. They were in preschool when women not quite a generation ahead of them were setting up the first women's studies courses. By the time they got to grade school, legislative changes were in place; there was an optimism abroad that further change for all women would follow automatically. By the time they got to high school and college, many encountered courses on women or survey courses that included material on women and gender issues. For them, the long process of struggle that resulted in these outcomes is distant at best.

Tracing the story of feminist scholarship—its names, dates, places, and events—brings the process alive. It brings to the forefront the realization that they are the first generational cohort with the opportunity to specialize in feminist scholarship. And it increases their determination to sustain the process of keeping women at the center of attention this time around.

Organizing

E ach chapter in this final section examines a different project in which I went about turning ideas into actions. These efforts at organizing and educating for social change reflect two facets of my beliefs: structures that affect women are embedded in the larger social fabric, and that very social fabric must change for women's possibilities to be sustained; only political pressure, in its multiple forms, can bring either structural or ideological change. In discussing how I go about building institutions and communities, I have emphasized the centrality of space, both physical and psychological, to the process of change. As these stories show, space is an indispensable precondition, for it enables transformations in ideas and approaches to develop.

The chapters in Part 4 were written in the order in which they were lived. Chapter 13 draws on the perspectives I gained during the five years (from 1985 through 1990) I edited *Signs: Journal of Women in Culture and Society*. Chapter 14 describes how the Women's Studies Program at Duke built an endowment between 1986 and 1992. Taking Women's Studies extramural illuminates the connections that can be fostered between the academy and its alumnae supporters for feminist purposes. Chapter 15 centers on a project with undergraduates called WARP that Women's Studies undertook with the Duke Women's Center in 1991–92. Designed to create space that enabled students to explore the meaning of what they were learning in class, the project grew into a space where undergraduate women, rethinking the parameters of the personal and political, came to empowerment through the experience of talk. Chapter 16 grew out of a faculty development workshop, designed originally to further curriculum transformation and now focused on the inherited academic traditions of teaching and learning that mute attempts to change gender relationships. The workshop began in 1989. The final chapter, Chapter 17, looks at some characteristics of women's studies itself that will shape its history and its undertakings into the future.

Writing these chapters for this essay collection over the past year brought to the fore central tenets of building feminist institutions and community. They are tenets I had embraced but rarely articulated or explored. The chapter on alumnae funding was the easiest to write, for the tenets by which I operated were both straightforward and strong. I worked collectively with a group of people, and we were practiced in articulating our goals. We faced some indifference and opposition, forces that served to sharpen our sense of direction and determination along the way. The chapter on journal editing came into being almost as smoothly. Working from a feminist perspective where a view from the margin is second nature, I found it fascinating to assume a second marginal position, that of editor, and to use both to analyze the institutional dynamics I saw at work in the academy. The chapter on WARP, the student project, was the most enjoyable to develop because I realized anew the vitality, intelligence, and commitment that many students bring to the educational enterprise. Faced with some two hundred pages of carefully constructed student thoughts, I reveled in what I had learned with them and because of them. And the final chapter on the historical and conceptual contours of women's studies flowed in conversation with colleagues as we worked through common projects and talked together about the future, sitting in the very rooms described in the opening pages of this book.

The chapter that stumped me was the chapter on teaching. I fussed with it for over three months, never satisfied with its contours. Always in the back of my mind was the recognition that teaching is what I had been trained to do and had done for more than twenty years with considerable positive feedback. In the front of my mind was the fact that the alumnae of Duke University had honored me in 1991 by establishing a teaching endowment in my name. According to the empirical evidence, teaching was something I knew and did well.

Yet describing how I thought about teaching and how it needed to be altered was more difficult than any of the other projects. I came to understand that I lacked a language for describing the practices of teaching and learning and that I was trying to develop the language within a tradition and in an environment that works against such attempts. I turned to the active listening skills that I have used throughout my career and employed them again to think about teaching.

My insightful research assistant, a graduate student in the Department of Religion, Ann Burlein, reminded me of my own patterns. Typically, she said, I reorient my thinking and doing when faced with a problem. I then follow the practices that are the structuring principles of this essay collection, listening and observing, followed by efforts to explain and to instruct. I do not pull back, she concluded, until I have set in motion new organizational structures and perspectives to sustain the issues I see evolving. Employing feminist ideas and practices to alter student-teacher relationships is both the most recent and the most difficult of the challenges I have undertaken. And that is probably why I had the most difficulty writing the chapter on teaching and learning—and why I ultimately found it the most satisfying!

What Is It Like
to Edit *Signs?*

F rom 1985 through 1990 I edited a scholarly journal, *Signs: Journal of Women in Culture and Society.* Scholarly editing is not an art graduate students are taught. Most faculty serve as editors only once in their careers, usually long after having been readers and authors. Editing a scholarly journal gave me insights into feminist scholarship and into the workings of contemporary universities rarely glimpsed from other vantage points. In this essay I explore a question that was frequently put to me during those five years—"What is it like to edit *Signs?*"— by reflecting on some of the lessons I took away from the experience.

The Journal Signs

Signs is a quarterly interdisciplinary journal of feminist scholarship that publishes both original research and theoretical essays. Running approximately 225 pages, each issue contains a dozen or so articles as well as book reviews. About one in three issues revolves around a particular theme. Circulation hovers at 6,000, making *Signs* one of the largest scholarly journals in any field.

Signs originated in 1975 at the initiative of Jean Sacks, then director of the Journals Division at the University of Chicago Press. Working closely with the leading feminist scholars emerging during the first part of the decade, she established a scholarly publication that would foster the new scholarship on women. Catharine Stimpson was its founding editor; the journal was housed first at Barnard and then at Rutgers. After five years *Signs* rotated to a group of scholars at Stanford, where it was edited by Barbara Gelpi. As 1985 approached, the University of Chicago Press decided to regularize the five-year rotation process and issued a call for proposals, much as funding agencies do.

In the summer of 1984 several feminist scholars associated with the newly formed Center for Research on Women at Duke and the University of North

Carolina at Chapel Hill received a letter from the University of Chicago Press inquiring into their individual or collective interest in housing *Signs*. Support from the university in the form of released time for the editor was a prime consideration. At that point I had just become director of Women's Studies; my colleagues and I believed I could use my position as director to secure an additional staff person for the program as well as negotiate half-time off to edit the journal. For the next month we talked among ourselves about how we would organize such an endeavor, who might be involved, and what our chances might be of securing the journal.

Two colleagues and I took the initiative and wrote the proposal to Chicago in the space of a few days. It was July and hot as only the South can be. Because Women's Studies had not yet been given any secretarial help, I found myself running between offices and typing madly. I reached the post office just minutes before it was closing for the Fourth of July holiday and sent the proposal off. Driving home, I reflected on what I had just done. Was it wise to push for *Signs*? Did we have the time, talent, or resources for an undertaking of this scope? What would we gain? Did I really want an affirmative answer?

A month later I received a call from Jean Sacks late one Friday afternoon. She said our proposal had received top ranking from the scholars across the country who had reviewed it; now she wanted to talk to me. No, she said, she did not need to talk to anyone else other than my dean to ensure that I could be released half-time. She launched into a series of tough questions that constituted a job interview—questions about who I was, what I thought, and how I made difficult decisions. I talked about my enthusiasm for administration, my commitment to the growth and diversification of feminist scholarship, and what I understood to be my reputation as an effective leader. Then, rather abruptly, she announced I was the new editor of *Signs* and hung up. I sat for a long time, stunned and alone in my office that afternoon, thinking about what had just happened. I vacillated between wishing I had missed the post office deadline and knowing that this development could solidify the building of feminist scholarship on campus. Those feelings only intensified the following Monday when I learned that Jean had announced her retirement that same afternoon.

Journal publishing is something academics learn by doing—there is no how-to reading list, no training other than the hands-on experience. We spent one year of start-up time on the telephone with the editorial office at Stanford and with the Journals Division at Chicago. Barbara Gelpi and her staff were unfailing in their constant attention to our every question. Similarly, Robert Sherrill and his staff at Chicago reviewed policies and procedures again and again until the system began to sink in with us. We conducted a national search for the managing editor, Mary Wyer. She then led a local search for the assistant editor. Salaries for the two staff people came directly from the University of Chicago Press, as did all office setup costs. My full salary continued to be paid by the university, its subsidy to the publishing enterprise. With staff in place, Mary and I traveled to both offices; these trips helped us put faces with recommendations as we figured out what to do next.

After a year of preliminary work in which a board of associate editors was selected, employees hired, policies and procedures put in place, and a new office equipped, we began to both review new manuscripts and prepare our first issue from pieces forwarded to us by the Stanford office. From 1985 through 1990 we published the journal out of an office on the Duke campus. The staff read every individual article that came into the office. We then sent about 75 percent of those articles to one of the associate editors. About half of these, in turn, were sent to scholars around the country for detailed review and evaluation. No more than 15 percent of the submissions we received were eventually accepted for publication. Manuscript decisions were made by the board of associate editors; drawn from Duke, the University of North Carolina at Chapel Hill, and other nearby schools, the board met as a group about every two months. In addition to getting the journal out four times a year, we compiled six books, collections of previously published articles around an emergent issue in feminist scholarship. In late 1989 the process of rotation began again as we oversaw the transfer of the journal to the University of Minnesota.

During those five years, I learned a great deal about publishing academic journals, feminist scholarship, and the workings of students, scholars, and universities. I can now say that the most fundamental lesson I learned is to go ahead and get the proposal in, no matter how hot the afternoon or how late the hour.

Ruminating on five years of the most demanding intellectual and political work I have ever known, I identify three clusters of ideas that I developed as I learned to wear the lens of an editor. One cluster relates to the ways that extant academic practices are shaped by feminist scholarship. A second and closely intertwined issue concerns how a journal's practices in turn can shape both feminist scholarship and traditional disciplines. Both of these clusters involve a deepening sense of "feminist process." A third cluster of ideas draws out the several ways in which the production of feminist scholarship influences daily campus life. In each of the three instances, collaboration proved the key to accomplishment, be it collaboration in the review process, collaboration between professional editors and scholars, or collaboration with the general campus community. That collaboration continues, even though *Signs* is no longer a daily presence at Duke. Its influence continues to echo over the campus.

Changing Traditional Academic Culture

Looking back through the *Signs* years, I am struck with how often the conventional wisdom of the traditional academy was inadequate to the more complex tasks before us. Again and again we found ourselves engaged in unlearning some of the ways in which we had been trained as well as learning alternative ways to proceed.

Conventional wisdom would have it that brilliant minds, cloistered in solitude, arrive at great thoughts and present them in polished form for the world to acclaim. Wrong. We quickly learned that a collaborative approach brought out the best in the scholarship before us. This was particularly true of feminist scholarship that must meet the standards of many different disciplines as well as tackle problems that have neither standard methodologies nor well-accepted explanatory frameworks. Some of the best pieces we published were the result of elaborate consultations among editorial staff, reviewers, associate editors, and authors—consultations that often lasted months if not years.

One particular piece stands out in my memory. The author, a young scholar, had come upon an important piece of a historical puzzle and described it in an article submitted to us. She did not know the literature of the surrounding disciplines; she was working at a small and isolated college without colleagues or a library; she had attended a graduate program where none of her mentors were likely to be of help on this project. To make matters worse, her topic was one in which the *Signs* board lacked background. But we sensed she was on to something and began a networking process that lasted the better part of two years. We suggested books to read, people to call; we went over several versions informally before beginning the formal review process; when the manuscript was formally reviewed and passed by the board, we felt justified in congratulating ourselves as well as the author! An extraordinary situation, this article became a benchmark for us. Will we have to go to those lengths on this one? we would ask ourselves in other circumstances. Yet we also knew this situation represented what we all hoped could become a feminist standard of the collaborative process.

When we assigned a manuscript for review, we were conscious that we were making political choices every time we gave a manuscript to an associate editor, chose an external reviewer, asked for interpretations of reviews from other board members. We wanted the input of the best minds, but we also knew that every mind comes attached to a scholarly position; we had to balance positions as well as expertise. We asked ourselves what we needed from reviewers and how their perspectives related to the arguments made in the article. We knew that only by treating our process explicitly would we be able to recognize merit in the pieces under consideration. Our primary task was not to find out what was wrong with a manuscript, but to identify what was right and build on that core. Any other stance would have stymied the development of the field, a field that faced enough external detractors as it was.

When reviews on an article came back, both were read by the staff (sometimes also by the associate editor working with us) and almost always sent back to the author for revision. A revised article went through the same process: back to the associate editor, back to the reviewers, then to the staff and additional editors who built the case for publication. The final step was to take the case for publication to the bimonthly meeting of the full board, which made a publication decision based upon the reviews, a summary of the article, and the arguments put forward by the sponsors. At this stage, documentation on an article ran to at least ten single-spaced pages. This documentation contained a series of carefully developed arguments that would eventually make their way into the final article through the editorial process.

Every step in the process required collaboration, not competition. How could one person understand what the other said and help strengthen it? How could we improve scholarship in ways that would also enable the article to speak to a broad, interdisciplinary audience? Why was one piece more important than another and therefore should merit space in the journal's pages? How could we work with the author to incorporate these perspectives into a final product that would appear in the journal?

The initial view that most of us brought to *Signs* was that of an author. We believed articles should be written by qualified scholars who worked from an interesting thesis which they supported by good evidence and presented in a comprehensible, if not lively, manner. While we had all asked colleagues to read drafts and make suggestions, we expected that an author must demonstrate his or her ability to produce alone. Imagining the author and the journal in a contest, we asked whether an article was "good enough" or "right for us," whatever those terms meant. In the process of learning how to read articles, go over reviews, build arguments, and gain consensus, we learned another point of view. We learned to articulate our own assumptions and to engage with our authors in a dialogue.

Early in our history as an editorial group, in the process of reviewing a piece one associate editor said, "I don't care what century you are talking about, just tell me the mode of production." By this point we had already come to understand that every author and every reviewer came with a position. This episode forced us to confront the obvious: each one of us involved with *Signs* also came with a position that required articulation. The outcry that followed her statement involved us in a debate about different frames of reference—what they assumed, how they mattered, and what choice best served the argument of the author. We were not engaged in a contest of wills between authors and editors; we were engaging in a feminist process with an outcome that sought to benefit everyone involved. This episode became another on our things-we-have-learned list. In the following years we would say to one another: "You're not going to tell me that the century doesn't matter, are you?"

It was not just our intellectual positions that we had to identify for ourselves, but our racial and sexual positions and their attendant politics as well. As we worked together over the years, the differences in our racial backgrounds as well as our sexual identities came into play. In the early years, the African American women and lesbians on the board struggled with having to educate the full board to perspectives they felt board members and staff should already possess. Over time, as their perspectives were honored and trust developed among us, all of the associate editors and the staff came to grapple more directly with the complex and nuanced ways in which race and sexuality constructed our understanding and played into our decision making.

Another convention of the academy is that the academy breaks down into two sets of people: the faculty, who are experts in the subject matter, and a support staff, who are trained to implement details. Wrong again. Academic publishing requires a variety of professional talents, among which editorial talent and training are critical. Nevertheless, the idea that editing entailed more than extensive vocabulary and good grammar was one that I found died hard.

Early in the process of hiring staff and formulating policies and procedures, editorial skills remained an unrecognized and consequently undervalued aspect of the journal's operation from the point of view of the scholars involved. When first considering the criteria for hiring a managing editor and an assistant, we often tended to say that exposure to feminist scholarship, politics, general intellectual acumen, and familiarity with the campus were more important than editorial training and experience.

While the scholars involved eventually came to appreciate the crucial ways in which editors combine intellectual talents with practical and technical abilities, the initially prevailing view held that there are thinkers and doers, those who decide and those who implement. This hierarchical point of view not only hindered us from using the substantial skills that editors bring to the process, it also hampered the collaborative stance necessary to make good scholarship excellent. Yet it was not a surprising bias, for academic culture gives little credence to the multiple skills that make a complex organization run. The idea that staff members actually improve the scholarship of faculty members is not a widely held one.

Most faculty members have never worked with a professional editor, someone skilled at recognizing the essential merits of a piece of research and at bringing those ideas into full strength through optimal organization, fully articulated meanings, and the consistent use of argument. Professional editors know more than the merits of manuscripts. They know the myriad details involved in the technical processes through which manuscripts proceed as they become published articles; professional editors are sensitive to how those requirements establish the context within which winning presentations can be made. Again and again I found the expertise resting in the two professional editorial staff members critical to our ability to make judgments, to decide what to publish and why.

Academic authors talk to themselves and their closest colleagues in enclosed ways. Out of such scholarship, the staff sought to pull meanings that would make sense to other audiences. While the humanities and the social sciences involved different issues, both required editorial expertise. Authors in the humanities tend to build from a particular text without consistently tying their argument to other pieces of that text or to use more than a single text in their analysis. Laying things out in elegant language is not the same as building an argument. We spent many days and hours querying authors. "Does this section simply restate your claim on page 5?" "Is this statement consistent with what you argue in the second section?" "Can you explain how you get this reading from this particular piece of text more fully?" By contrast, authors in the social sciences tend to present elaborate data but recoil from articulating the interpretations that would make those data comprehensible to a broad array of readers. Here, too, manuscripts would be loaded with queries about unpacking statements, connecting ideas, and drawing inferences.

Scholars tend to work in a solitary setting or at most on small committees. Some even say that there is a bias in academic culture that dictates that the larger the group, the less effective and influential it will be. The *Signs* board was a relatively large decision-making group, typically composed of fifteen scholars and three staff members. Finding the mechanisms to develop consensus while working with individual viewpoints required thoughtful negotiation and considerable political skill on the part of everyone. The commitment to feminist practice, coupled with a good dose of Quaker experience, helped us to develop an ability to function as a group in spite of our size and the lessons of our previous academic experiences. In fact, the board became one long postdoc in feminist scholarship for most of us, moving each one of us farther into feminist dialogue as a result of our conversations on the board.

The major purpose of editing a scholarly journal is to publish articles. Conventional wisdom would have it that we would be judged by the end product we produced rather than by the processes we nurtured, especially since those processes would often reach maturity in a piece that got published elsewhere. Over time I came to understand that here too we might be wrong again. Publishing the journal comprises only one part of a broader, overall mission in an evolving field.

As editor, staff, and associates, we believed one of our main responsibilities to feminist scholarship was to help the field grow by developing all work— even work we did not publish. We spent a great deal of time giving feedback to work that needed considerable help and that we probably would not publish. Of course, we did not give the same degree of attention to all the work we turned down. But it became important to us to help scholars make their work stronger, especially scholars just beginning their careers and those who were first venturing into feminist territory. Even when a piece did not appear in *Signs*, we felt we were helping create better material for the field in general. This perspective grew from our understanding of the collaborative nature of the work we were doing as well as from the professional skills we saw ourselves developing. Both, it seemed to us, should be shared.

Influencing Directions in a New Field

Another set of lessons clusters around how we understood our ability to influence the directions of the field in ways that would begin to redress crucial absences. In writing our proposal, we were quite clear about what we wanted to publish: material that focused on the intersection of race, class, and gender; work that linked feminist theory to collective action; and scholarship that emphasized the process of curriculum transformation. While we did not say so, we thought we knew how to do this. We would use personal networks to locate good research and encourage its submission. We assumed the material was there; our challenge was to find it. And we believed that including such formerly absent material in the pages of the journal would initiate a self-sustaining process in which additional material would be produced and submitted. We were wrong yet again.

Looking back at the proposal, I see an almost sophomoric quality to our claim that simply through our selection as the new editors, the material in the pages of the journal would become different. We learned all too quickly that the exercise of influence is far more complex and subtle than good intentions and straightforward declarations. We were not simply a set of individuals with the ability to make things happen as we wished. Eventually I came to envision us as temporary custodians of a much larger process that we needed to nurture. How we reached this understanding and then exercised our intentions illustrates, I believe, the ways in which editorial decisions can influence trends in scholarship.

The power relationship between authors and editors is a reciprocal one. Yet authors often see the power relationship as totally skewed in the journal's favor; editors can say no, articles do not appear, and academic positions are in jeopardy. Journal editors see the relation from another vantage point; they have a relatively limited amount of control over the kinds of material they receive. Those associated with the journal as staff, associate editors, and national advisers can and do prompt their colleagues to submit material. But in my experience the amount of material that comes in via this route is small, perhaps not more than 5 to 10 percent.

Because scholars are generally familiar with a journal's orientation, they place their material where they think it will fit. Potential authors are often unfamiliar with changes in the journal's emphases—until the fifth year of our editorship, we still received materials addressed to Stanford! The vast majority of what was submitted for review came via the individual decisions of hundreds of scholars who "knew" *Signs*. Our challenge became how to enlarge what they "knew" about us while simultaneously working with what we already had.

We did have two direct ways of encouraging material: issuing calls for papers and putting out theme issues and books. Through calls for papers we were able to name topics and declare our interest in developing certain trends. In our five years we issued five calls for papers; their outcome illustrates how a new field is developed. Two of these calls, one for papers in the area of race and gender and a second on women in the Middle Ages, coincided with subjects just beginning to emerge in feminist scholarship. After several years in which the calls reached a wide audience whose scholars wrote manuscripts for submission, we gathered enough material to produce both a special issue of the journal and later a book on each topic.

Another call for papers on the idea of the family in Western ideology had a quite different story. We received few papers that critically engaged the idea of the family. The articles we received focused on the mother, seeing the family from her point of view. Thus, we modified our emphasis by thinking in terms of the ideology of mothering, eventually compiling both a special issue and later a book on this theme.

A fourth call for papers fared even more poorly. We wanted to examine women at the time of extensive national celebrations for the bicentennial of the U.S. Constitution in 1986. We received only one or two articles directly on the topic. Working with some other submissions, we again modified the topic to produce a special issue on women and the American political process. Unlike the issue on mothering, however, there was not enough additional material in past issues or in the manuscript pipeline to produce a book.

Our final call for papers involved a special issue on African women. We first made the call in late 1986. The difficulties of getting information to scholars outside the continental United States as well as the extensive amount of review required to turn groundbreaking primary research into feminist analysis for an international audience transformed this call into a six-year project. Not until 1991, after the journal had already rotated to Minnesota, were these manuscripts finally ready for publication in a special issue.

Compiling theme issues and books is a second way in which journal editors can shape the development of a new field. This approach relies upon the ability to "read" trends and to arrange materials in ways that further those trends. The first book that we compiled came out of the large amount of material we had been publishing on women and science but had never pulled together and emphasized. Published in our first year, *Sex and Scientific Inquiry* both encouraged more submissions in this area and issued a clear statement to the scholarly community that we at *Signs* thought the issue of gender and science central to the feminist agenda.

Early on we also recognized a number of articles on women's education and women's studies. Placing them together, first in a special issue and later in a book, enabled us to call attention to the continuities and changes in these two traditions. Similarly, we monitored developments in feminist theory closely, reading both the manuscripts we accepted and those that did not make the publication cut. We published both thematic and special issues around emergent questions and eventually compiled a new reader in feminist theory, *Feminist Theory in Practice and Process*. Publishing theme issues and books in both feminist theory and women's education resulted in an increased number of manuscripts dealing with these questions.

Both the associate editors (who were selected from the local community of scholars) and the national editorial board played vital roles in both these endeavors to chart new areas of inquiry. Whenever those associated with the journal steered material in our direction, we were far more able to shape the journal's contents than we were when we had to wait for whatever came in over the transom. We also relied on this inside group of scholars to help us interpret developments, to improve contacts, and to shape the final project.

Such direct interventions in the development of feminist scholarship were clear enough, albeit more complicated and time-consuming than we first envisioned. Over time what became more important than these direct interventions were the indirect ways by which we learned to use editorial practices to foster feminist scholarship. More indirect ways included both commissioning material and enhancing material that we had already received.

Commissioning certain kinds of material proved quite effective. In the first issue we published a conference report on the meetings in Narobi to celebrate the conclusion of the United Nations Decade for Women. We saw events at Nairobi as an important development both in feminism as a social movement and for a feminist research agenda. When we did not receive an article on this topic, we decided to solicit a conference report from six individuals of diverse backgrounds that would both record the event itself in the journal's pages and indicate our interest in analyzing similar developments. We created a new format to cover an important interest rather than allow the absence of traditional material to dictate our profile. In subsequent issues we covered a number of topics with conference reports, always indicating that we hoped to see scholarly treatments of the subjects over time.

Commissioning book reviews followed a similar logic. We were able to review only one in ten of the books sent to us. Decisions were ultimately made by an associate editor, but only after a winnowing performed by staff and interested graduate students. Our first cut included all books that made major theoretical advances, that either established new research areas or revised old ones, and that addressed neglected issues. Out of this pool, we selected those books and reviews that would expand the material we were receiving in manuscripts and point toward what we wanted to see included more often. Those directions grew out of discussions in our bimonthly meetings as we talked about what we were receiving and what we wanted to solicit. Thus, we were able to include materials on women of color through book reviews when we were not receiving such material in manuscripts. We were able to emphasize the daily realities of women's lives through accounts in books when we were seeing less of this material than we wished in the articles submitted to us.

Shaping material through the editing process was a final and crucial way in which we as editors gave contours to the field. It is also the most difficult process to describe. Authors who were subjected to it could probably do a better job than I of explaining what it means to have a lovingly written page returned with hundreds of questions and be asked to address them all!

The following few paragraphs come from a talk I gave in 1988 to the Southern Women's Cultural History Symposium, sponsored by the National Endowment for the Humanities. I had been asked to discuss how *Signs* had been influenced by being rotated to the South. In my talk I used prejudices about the South as a particular example to illustrate how our general approach to editing involved making little decisions daily that ultimately influenced the shape and inclusivity of the journal as a whole.

What do we do with the material, once it is in our hands for publication? Here I think you will find that we are active, if not ruthless, in our pursuit of the goal of attending to regional differences. We edit with eyes that ask questions like these:

1. Does this piece proceed as if the South simply does not exit? Is it "southernless" when it should not be? A recent piece on women in education had us believing that there were no southern women, African American or white, who had ever gone to school. I believe the final product that emerged from our editing was strengthened by the questions we posed to the author and the expansions that she added.

2. Does the manuscript single out a well-known southern woman or put forward a timeworn stereotype, ignoring the implications of what has been said? Having become aware of the degree to which women are marginalized in received knowledge generally, we talk constantly in the office about the marginalization of southern women, African American and white, when they are mentioned only in throwaway lines. Thus, whenever we are working with materials on family and work, we try to pay attention to the regional variations we know exist.

3. Are southern women, African American and white, separated from men? from each other? treated as anomalies? Is their experience seen as so different that it needs to be noted? What form does this recognition take? We often find ourselves reversing the order of the arguments in papers, putting the tensions that have been relegated to footnotes at the center of the analysis. I think this happens most in papers on politics and social life where authors note that women, particularly African American women, do not act and think like social scientists say they should. The problem is not with the women; it is with the conceptual models—which must become central to the analysis rather than hidden at the bottom of the page.

When women are the central actors, we try to figure out when it is important to make regionalism a distinction and when it is not. Questions of difference and commonality are difficult; addressing them adequately is a constant challenge. We struggle with helping authors frame arguments that acknowledge similarity yet analyze difference. When an author is analyzing contrasts, we ask them not to leave out the core of shared agency or oppression. The need to ask this particular set of questions emerges most frequently in papers from literature and philosophy, which tend to pigeonhole works by women of color. Part of the editing process involves diagramming the pigeonholes for readers.

Whether soliciting new material or sensitizing material to new concerns, we learned the importance of balancing the innovations necessary if the field was to grow with more orthodox subject matter or methodology that could be connected to already existing scholarship, practices, and frameworks. We experienced a constant tension between going too far and not far enough, between striking out for some highly innovative position and staying close enough to ongoing concerns to be heard. We learned how difficult it was to get outside our own mindsets (whatever they might be) while simultaneously keeping in mind that we bore some responsibility for developing the standards of an evolving field and therefore had to maintain a middle ground.

Scholarly Publishing in Everyday Campus Life

When I was a young academic, Anne Firor Scott, a social historian who taught women's history at Duke for many years, told me that to be considered an expert, you must have a briefcase, an airline ticket, and a job at least one hundred miles away from home. She neither praised nor condemned this aspect of academic life, only reported having seen it happen again and again.

When I became the editor of *Signs*, I found renewed wisdom in her remark. For women's stories to become part of the public discourse, they must be recorded, interpreted, distributed, contested, referenced. To paraphrase Anne, women must be put into printed form, analyzed from multiple perspectives and sources, supplemented with extensive footnotes, and sent through the mails by someone else. Publishing *Signs* from offices on the Duke campus helped feminist scholarship gain legitimacy on campus quite quickly.

In the summer of 1984, when I told people that *Signs* was moving to the area, two reactions were widespread. Everyone thought I had said *Science*, for that was a journal they knew. After clarifying that I was talking about *Signs*, of which they had not heard, many remarked that the editorial board "wasn't quite right." Several colleagues said this to me directly, one commenting on the lack of spelling ability I had amply illustrated in memos over the years. That is to say, we were not white, tenured, fifty-year-old males, the kind of scholar who comes to mind when the word *editor* is used.

After this first stage of curiosity and the recognition that *we* were doing *a feminist journal*, a second set of responses surfaced: our colleagues realized there might be something in it for them. For a quite remarkable thing began to happen. Letters from prospective graduate students and prospective faculty often requested more information about how they might become involved with the journal should they come to Duke. The journal became a recruiting tool for departments, and we opened a small visitor's bureau in the *Signs* office.

External recognition reached a new peak in 1987, when a special issue of the journal was selected by the American Association of Publishers as the best single issue of a scholarly journal that year. A fancy plaque was hung in the office and feature stories in the state newspaper claimed that *Signs* was the best journal of the year—in comparison with all other journals, not just feminist journals. Like the expert with the briefcase from afar, the presence of the journal and the external recognition it received were critical factors in making the local academic community deal with feminist scholarship.

Faculty members not involved in feminist scholarship were often pulled in when we asked them to formally review submissions or informally advise us. Again and again we would pick up the phone and ask colleagues to work through a question with us, engaging them in thinking about research on women and its impact on their field. The reference desk of the library, from the beginning a wonderful resource for our endless questions, gained even more expertise in feminist scholarship from the sheer volume of our calls. That expertise translated into innovative student papers when students approached reference librarians for help in formulating paper topics.

Each year we employed several undergraduate students as assistants. They made photocopies, answered the phone, logged manuscripts, blinded submissions, tracked down tardy reviewers, and generally backed up the staff. Their favorite activity was opening the stacks of books and manuscripts that came in each day; using a holiday metaphor, they talked about what they were discovering as presents. The opportunity to know what was coming out and who was writing what gave an immediacy to their work in feminist theory and women's studies that they cherished.

Because the availability of work-study funds at the graduate level limited the number of graduate students we could employ, we created a series of graduate intern positions. Some worked on exchange subscriptions with other journals, others maintained our contacts with foreign editorial board members, while still others helped on special projects. Many found that involvement with *Signs* became a source of empowerment for them.

Thinking back about *Signs*, one graduate student said, "Working as a volunteer at *Signs* was an opportunity for me to be in touch with women's studies, which I was getting away from during my first year in graduate school. And having all the Latin American journals there was really wonderful for me because I had no access to that material otherwise." She continued, "In my program I was very aware of an anti–women's studies bias. Working with *Signs* gave me a position and connection to something that was seen as legitimate even by the 'theory heads' among my colleagues. It definitely strengthened my commitment to doing women's studies at a time and place in which I felt it was not really the thing to be doing. In some ways it seems as if *Signs* helped me remain aware that there are other aspects to feminism besides academic feminist theories and literary theory. I felt that *Signs* and Women's Studies were a place where I could go, that someone there would understand the political problems I was having in my department."

The experiences in the journal office reinforced students' commitment to do feminist work in their courses. But those experiences also brought frustration. Working in a feminist space meant that their basic assumptions about the value of their work was accepted. When they stepped outside the office, they faced another reality. They were asked to defend the study of women in a seminar. They were asked to put aside explanatory frameworks that they found critical and employ old ones in their research.

One of the graduate students who worked on the journal explained, "I didn't have a paper topic. I wandered around for weeks asking what I was going to write about in this class. Then Mary gave me Buchi Emecheta's book[1] and I had a topic. I even named my cat Buchi. I don't think that help or support would have come in another environment because my experiences in graduate school have been intensely alienating. We aren't given support for our ideas. You have to figure out for yourself that what you say matters, either being very self-confident or going to a psychiatrist every week. The *Signs* office was one of the few places where I felt I could say something without being laughed at."

Undergraduates report similar reactions: "As an undergraduate working at *Signs* for my work-study job, because I had no experience anywhere else, I just assumed that of course, you can publish this kind of academic work because it's really interesting. Only later did I find out this wasn't the norm for academics, although I think it should be."

The experience of traveling between two different worlds was by no means restricted to students. Associate editors claimed again and again that their involvement with the journal enabled them to deal as feminist scholars with departmental cultures that ranged from indifferent to hostile. As editor, I felt a daily tension between what I did at *Signs* and my role as director of Women's Studies. I experienced moments of epiphany when I saw the two worlds collide and converge. My most frequent memory is of sitting at my desk, reading through proofs for an upcoming issue. I would read an exciting argument, like Patricia Williams's account of her grandmother.[2] Twenty minutes later I would find myself in my classroom, engaged in a discussion with students about the power relationships encoded in ideas of race and gender; I would be able to refer to her analysis of contract law as a means to help them understand community dynamics. Such convergence was enormously empowering to me as a teacher and administrator; I relished what I was learning and how I could apply it.

But collisions were also inevitable. The knowledge held by one group of scholars ensconced in one set of offices contrasted sharply with what other scholars did not know. Sometimes the differences appeared powerful enough to derail any efforts at infusing the campus with feminist scholarship. The most striking example came in a two-session seminar that we undertook with the administration.

By the 1986–87 academic year *Signs* had been an official campus presence for two years. All of us involved felt a certain sense of expertise. Issues had come out under our names, manuscripts were flooding in, students and colleagues sought our advice, and we were reading the materials with something of an experienced eye. We could recognize what was innovative about a piece, locate that piece in relation to other articles, and think about where it took the field. We were increasingly able to identify the ideas and trends that we thought should be furthered. This sense of expertise led to feelings of empowerment: we knew something about feminist scholarship and we were actively working to help it grow.

The 1986–87 academic year was also the third year that Women's Studies had been in full operation on the Duke campus. In this domain we were having a different experience. The administration had changed, and while it continued to fund the basic operation (a director, a secretary, and a pencils-and-paper budget), it did not grasp the potential for doing more, such as developing a graduate program, hiring faculty jointly with other departments, and initiating curriculum transformation efforts. A long-range program plan as well as more specific proposals were met by a wait-and-see attitude. From the point of view of the Women's Studies Advisory Board, *nothing* was happening when *everything* should have been, given the enormous energy generated by the presence of *Signs*.

The contrast between the empowerment I experienced editing *Signs* and the frustration I encountered directing Women's Studies led me to make a somewhat rash proposal to the dean. During one of our regular meetings, as I was explaining why we needed a series of joint appointments and he was looking rather vague, I simply stopped talking. "Look," I said, "suppose I just back off and stop asking about appointments. Suppose you and some of your colleagues sit down with some of us in Women's Studies and we actually talk about what we are doing and why we are so excited about it. Let's put on hold all administrative and policy questions and experience the intellectual excitement of feminist scholarship as we know it from *Signs*. Firsthand exposure might help you react to what we are proposing." It is difficult for a dean of arts and sciences to refuse a request to learn something new, so he agreed.

With a great deal of pressure exerted in the name of *Signs* ("After all, we have the leading feminist journal here on campus; we really ought to be familiar with its scholarship"), it was finally agreed that the dean of Arts and Sciences, the dean of the Graduate School, and the provost would meet with a group of Women's Studies faculty to talk during the summer and again in the fall. We would talk about ideas in feminist scholarship. We would not address policy issues.

I turned to the faculty on the advisory board, some of whom were on the *Signs* board and all of whom were active reviewers for the journal, to plot a strategy. We decided to select two topics outside the scholarly expertise of any one of us. We thought this would illustrate the powerful pull of interdisciplinary perspectives as well as demonstrate what we shared as feminist scholars, even when the subject was not "in our field." We decided to ask the deans to do a bit of reading in preparation for the seminar. We not so innocently choose six articles in six different books so that the participants would have to leaf through the whole book to read the article. We nearly broke the Women's Studies budget buying eighteen books. The books, along with a two-page introduction, were delivered to the appropriate offices weeks ahead of time.

We chose two topics—the rise and nature of the nation-state and the nature of occupational segregation. Here are two paragraphs taken from the introductions we wrote that suggest our approach:

> [The readings] build on Kelly's[3] insight that the state—the political institution that has been positively valued as a rationalizing, civilizing, modernizing force by several generations of historians—is not a neutral set of institutions that expresses or embodies the public interest irrespective of gender. Rather, because the state co-evolved with a particular system of gender relations, it embodies those relations of dominance, and it is founded on a segregation of public and private spheres in which only men's experience constitutes the legitimate public domain. Of importance to historians, therefore, is not merely the effects of the state on women, but also the way in which the state draws its character from the place of women in it.

> How to locate and measure gender inequality in the workplace is a central problem in the quantitative social sciences. What are the bases of persistent wage/salary inequality between men and women workers?

Twenty years of research in this area has expanded the explanatory model for this inequality from the exclusive reliance on human capital variables (e.g., measure of the education, skill and work attachment of *individual* workers) to the examination of the independent effects of workplace variables (e.g., occupational segregation, labor market segmentation, and discrimination derived from the *structure of the workplace*).

Then the real work began. Six of us from Women's Studies participated. (We had decided that we needed more people from Women's Studies to equalize the power relationships between us as female faculty and a male administrative group.) Each of us read the assignments as if preparing for preliminary exams. We met several times to review the arguments in each piece, practice tying themes together, expressing ideas, and imagining what these three deans would do with the same material. When the day for the seminar came, we were as nervous as I ever remember seeing any of us. I led off by recapping how we had gotten to this position, then opened up the discussion as one would for a graduate seminar. While the atmosphere in the seminar room was cordial enough—all nine of us knew one another in many different capacities, and we were munching on sandwiches and chips—there was silence. Finally one of the Women's Studies faculty spoke, naming a theme and commenting on its interest. The six from Women's Studies worked with the articles for some time, continually inviting by word and body language the participation of the deans.

Then it began to dawn on us. They did not understand the material. They could not "do anything" with it. Being generous and assuming they had read it, we realized that they did not know how to approach material that was foreign to their experiences and outside their frames of reference. Quickly, we fell back to a more basic level of discussion. We referred back to the introductory notes, careful to repeat the primary relationships. At the end of the first session, one of the deans remarked that reading this material reminded him of his experiences abroad, when he had had to learn to think like "the Romans." "Was approaching feminist scholarship similar?" he asked. We reacted with a mixture of bewilderment and appreciation. He was clearly connecting to the ideas, but at such an elementary level we did not know exactly what to do. So we ran with his remark, encouraging him to think of other parallels. The first session ended with the three deans saying how interesting the discussion had been, although they had hardly spoken. They agreed to the second.

The second session began with a bit more ease, less of an introduction, and an increased readiness to engage the ideas due to the material's policy implications. Eventually the conversation began to drift toward affirmative action issues at Duke. One of the deans realized we had strayed from discussing the ideas to their specific applications and called his colleagues back to our agreed-upon agenda. That detour and his comment made the discussion even more effective because we were able to point out both the theoretical and the practical ramifications of feminist scholarship.

At the conclusion of the second session, the dean of Arts and Sciences said that he and his colleagues had been impressed with their experiences in the seminar and now felt ready to move ahead with policy decisions. The experiment appeared to have worked at several levels. In subsequent months I was able to undertake specific policy initiatives in the program. It worked at another level for those of us in Women's Studies; we began to talk more often about how deeply involved in the new scholarship on women we were, how profoundly this scholarship had shifted our research and teaching paradigms, and how the process of integrating others into our work involved many, many steps.

Throughout the remainder of the semester we tried to build on our conversations with the administration and foster their understanding of feminist scholarship. Slowly the relationships between the journal, individual teaching and research, and administrative support became closely intertwined. After the dean of the Graduate School made funds available for the graduate seminar in Women's Studies, at semester's end I decided to send him excerpts from the students' journals. All of the excerpts (which I kept anonymous) spoke to the way their work in Women's Studies had improved their disciplinary work. This is his response:

> Thanks for sharing the students' final entry in journals kept for IDC 211. I read them all. As a result, I hope I moved just a bit further toward enlightenment. You know, the problem for many males who want to understand is that we have found it difficult to find feminists willing to take the time—and expend the patience—to help us understand.
>
> Reading through these journal entries got me further toward understanding in a single half-hour than I was able to progress the previous 362 days of 1987.
>
> May I one day share these entries with my children (not just my daughters)?

Signs, I would argue, made it possible to foster the academic discussion we as feminist scholars sought rather than be forced into a political discussion that those outside the new scholarship on women tend to embrace.

CHAPTER 1 4

Educating

beyond the Walls

The Politics of

Influence and

Fundraising for

Women's Studies

The Duke Women's Studies Program raised a million-dollar endowment from individual donors between 1986 and 1991.[1] I am often asked to describe what we did and how we did it. I am never asked *why* we engaged in an endowment campaign. While it is true that institutions raise money primarily to guarantee the funds they need to carry on their activities, Women's Studies raised funds for multiple reasons; as I will argue, the other reasons became as important as securing operating funds.

Understanding the philosophy of influence and fundraising became key to our eventual success. Money is given and received through an interpersonal network. Without that network, fundraising cannot occur. Donors give money to support their values. An institution is influenced by receiving monies. Donors manifest their concerns in other ways as well, and the institution receives their ideas about what it should emphasize along with their money in the fundraising process.

Women are latecomers to the process of understanding the politics of educational fundraising.[2] The Women's Studies Program at Duke linked education to philanthropy in ways that brought thousands of alumnae into a feminist conversation with the university, enabling their stories to be heard.

The Women's Studies Program at Duke was established in 1983, almost a decade after other programs at comparable schools. The reasons for this delay are many and need not be detailed here, except to say that Duke already had some of the programs and policies that other institutions sought to establish through women's studies programs. Duke had a number of courses on women as well as a reasonable number of women on the faculty. It had a reentry program for older women in the alumnae-established Continuing Education Program. Most significant, Duke could point to a history of educating women that reached into the late nineteenth century. Thus Duke thought about incorporating women into the educational institution as something already accomplished; this attitude forestalled student and faculty pressure on the institution to "do something about women" until the second wave of feminism was well underway.

A Bit of Duke History

The fundraising story of the Duke Women's Studies Program begins in the institution's history of educating women. Although the record is murky, it appears that some white women unofficially attended classes from the time of the institution's founding in 1839, so the school never had a formal ban on women. It is well established that the first women graduated from what was then Trinity College in 1878. Throughout the end of the nineteenth century and until World War I, white women entered Duke in increasing numbers. While they never received the services and facilities that the men did, they enrolled, excelled academically, and graduated. For a while it appeared as if the Board of Trustees might consider making Duke a fully coeducational institution on the model of Cornell, the University of Chicago, and Stanford (all then emerging as research universities with collegiate components).

With the arrival of a new president in 1914, a different course was chosen; President William Preston Few began to talk of a separate college for women. Plans moved ahead to build a new campus with the endowment from James B. Duke and to convert the old campus into a college for women. J. B. Duke signed the indenture in 1924, and a coordinate college for women, named the Woman's College, opened in 1930 alongside the college for undergraduate men, which assumed the school's old name of Trinity College. Together with the newly established professional schools, they became Duke University.

The Woman's College operated from 1930 through 1972. During those four decades, women were housed on a separate campus. Led by a remarkable administration of outstanding academic women and a nationally prominent set of female scholars, the college soon attracted outstanding female students widely held to have better high school grades and more academic promise than their male counterparts. They had their own student government and student services. Their campus had its own library. The women lived in residential colleges with resident adult advisers, programming, and facilities. Sex-specific social regulations were enforced, a situation that originally appears largely unchallenged.

Budgetary control rested outside the college, however; chronic debates over money meant that the Woman's College never achieved a separate faculty. Nonetheless, in the first decade a number of departments hired women to teach the first-year courses for women on their own campus. Thereafter women traveled the 1.4 miles through Duke Forest to the men's campus, where they joined the men's upper-level classes. Graduates of the Woman's College took enormous pride in their accomplishments; they thought of themselves as women for the "new age" (the title of a popular course on women taught from 1930 to 1954 by the dean for instruction).

By the 1960s, however, the different social restrictions that applied to women and men became a source of student dissatisfaction. Women active in the civil rights movement agitated for integration at Duke, which began in 1963. During that decade, the administration of the college, as well as its alumnae, faculty, and students, debated the future of women's education. A number of symposia were held to prepare students for the future as it was then understood—a future in which equality with men in coeducational colleges and universities would be the norm. Many alumnae argued for the advantages of single-sex education. But without either the data now available or a feminist explanatory framework, their perspectives gave way to the combined forces of student demands and administrative convenience. By 1968, the decision was made to merge the two undergraduate colleges into one coeducational institution that would use the male nomenclature, Trinity. Over the next four years that merger was completed. The last class of the Woman's College graduated in 1972.

During the next decade, women hired by the college stayed in place, students were happy with their new access to the men's campus, and alumnae resigned themselves to the change. Although data were not recorded by sex (so that today we have no reliable indicators), the consensus is that many alumnae restrained their support of the university thereafter. By the end of the 1970s, it became obvious to many faculty as well as students that the climate for women on campus was by no means one long success story. The memory of the Woman's College was dim. Female faculty hiring was not a priority. Whereas Duke's integration had been spearheaded by YWCA members, the faculty of the 1980s was less than 1 percent African American female. With one exception, the administration contained no women. A woman was not elected as student president until 1989. Attention to women's issues, academic or social, was at an all-time low. At that point, the effort to organize a women's studies program developed under the leadership of the first female dean of the now-coed undergraduate college.

The Beginning of Women's Studies

Women's studies began at Duke much as it had begun elsewhere: in response to campus pressure, a student-faculty committee was appointed by the dean. The committee investigated peer institutions and reported favorably. The effort was encouraged by the fact that a Center for Research on Women, jointly conducted with the University of North Carolina at Chapel Hill, had already been set up and received external funding; its presence made the absence of a women's studies program all the more glaring. Along with female colleagues, I had taught a prototype of the introductory Women's Studies course in the mid-1970s in addition to my regular classes. An internal search committee appointed me the first director of Women's Studies.

I assumed the position with my own particular history. Having been the director of Continuing Education for eleven years, I was familiar with the institution, both its strengths and its idiosyncrasies. On leave when asked to take the position, I had the luxury of several months in which to consider different approaches. During that time two insights emerged that have made a crucial difference to the development of Women's Studies at Duke.

The first insight sought to fit the initiative in Women's Studies into the university's perception of its mission. While the Continuing Education Program had grown into an impressive and large-scale endeavor, adult education was never reflected in the larger institution's official sense of itself. People flocked by the hundreds to the programs we offered; revenues exceeded expenses. Yet no form of lifelong learning ever found a place alongside the residential college and the research university as part of how the institution defined itself. In its review of the Continuing Education Program, an external evaluation team from peer institutions called attention to this oddity in strong terms; still there was no shift in attitude. I approached Women's Studies realizing it was critical that the institution incorporate feminist scholarship into its view of itself if Women's Studies were to escape the continual difficulties I had seen in Continuing Education.

The second insight hinged upon funding patterns in higher education. Throughout the 1970s, foundations and government agencies had played a central role in initiating women's studies programs. By the early 1980s, however, these sources were dwindling; colleges and universities were asked to incorporate the fostering of feminist scholarship into their own operating budgets. I realized that Women's Studies at Duke could not count on external funding. Yet operating funds could not cover lecture series, student projects, and additional courses. An innovative, interdisciplinary endeavor directed toward women's issues had little chance of becoming well funded in the male power hierarchies of a conservative university without someone other than faculty and students to advocate support for women's education.

These two insights came together into a strategy that was both substantive and practical. I conceptualized Women's Studies as the reemergence of the Woman's College in a new era. Historically, the college had guaranteed that women entered higher education. As a new field of inquiry, women's studies sought to guarantee that studying women mattered. Developmentally linking Women's Studies to women's education both built on Duke's particular institutional history while simultaneously extending that history into the future. Such an interpretation meant that Women's Studies could be seen as a continuation rather than a departure in the institution's story. Continuations, elaborations, and improvements are more politically feasible than departures, and we were on our way to being seen as integral to the university's view of itself. The fact that I entered Women's Studies with administrative experience was a plus for the program. There were to be many times when I knew that I was wrestling with bureaucracy rather than misogyny, although the two have a tendency to be found in the same places.

Gaining Institutional Support

As director of Continuing Education, I learned again and again that educational programs were launched in other sectors of the university because someone in the university had an idea that matched the idea of someone outside the university who was in a position to fund the idea. I also realized that even ideas matched with money could not be incorporated into the university's sense of itself unless those who define the institution's mission have been told by their peers (as opposed to their subordinates) that this is a good idea. Trained as I was in political science, all the old lessons about the multiple steps in influencing people's decisions flowed back to me. I understood that university officials rely on support from those above them before they respond to demands from those below them. I had to figure out how to build a group of influential allies for Women's Studies whose voices the university officers would hear.

At first creating such an influential group appeared impossible. Gaining access to those beyond the campus was a tightly guarded privilege lodged in the Development Office of the university. Private institutions like Duke University raise funds almost exclusively through their development offices. No one in that area had any apparent interest in Women's Studies, nor were they under any pressure from donors to develop such an interest. I did not myself know any donors or alumnae who might make the case for Women's Studies, a program just one year old.

Yet what about the 27,000 women who had graduated from Trinity, the Woman's College, and Duke University? Did not these alumnae form a potential source of support? I suspected that women were unaccustomed to institutional giving. Giving money is synonymous with directly using power, a practical and psychological move still unfamiliar to most women. Often women have simply not been in networks where asking for contributions is a quid pro quo of social interaction. Yet if they could come to see Women's Studies as an extension of what they had valued in their own education, particularly during the forty years of the Woman's College, we could raise both funds and friends. I realized that few alumnae knew anything about women's studies. But I was convinced this would change if they could engage with the emergent scholarship on women and experience the links between their own lives, the lives of other women, and the frameworks that women studies offered. If some of their children who were our students could embrace the new scholarship on women, if some of their sisters and college friends who had become professors could do so, then surely, I reasoned, at least some alumnae would respond in similar ways, since they shared the same liberal arts background. Funds were the short-term objective, friends the long-term goal.

I made an appointment with the vice-president for development and explained my ideas. He assured me that women did not give money. I argued that women had never even been asked—much less asked to give for their own interests. He said women were asked as men were asked for all university objectives. I decided not to push the issue of whether university objectives served men and women in the same manner. Despite the fact that we were coming from very different places, in my determination he saw a slight possibility that he, as a good fundraiser, was willing to entertain. He offered a challenge: he would consider supporting the fundraising effort if I could convince a prominent alumna to head up the effort.

Using networks of faculty women as well as women in administrative posts, I searched out the possibilities. Faculty women had established a professional caucus in 1975, the Women's Network; this group had opened dialogues on women's issues with some trustees as well as with women administrators at the staff level. Together we identified one trustee who we thought might be supportive. The vice-president of development agreed to arrange a meeting between the two of us.

One hot July day I sat for over an hour waiting for the trustee, Judy Woodruff, the Washington correspondent for "The MacNeil/Lehrer News Hour," to come out of a trustee committee meeting. Talking to a major media figure would have been stressful under any circumstances, but doing so with an unknown agenda, in compressed time, at the end of a long workday, seemed doomed to failure. Like the good investigative reporter she is, Woodruff listened to my presentation, asked a series of specific questions, and ended the conversation by saying she would consider it. A week later she agreed; I notified the vice-president of our success. He assigned the project a small budget as well as a modest amount of staff help (5 percent of one development officer's time). Now the challenge was to figure out what I had convinced Judy Woodruff to do. Aside from hearsay about the occasional wealthy woman who had endowed chairs in universities, I had no idea how to build a constituency that would give both dollars and voice to the feminist enterprise on the Duke campus.

Mobilizing Women for Women's Studies

A round of conversations began between the development officer assigned by the vice-president and those of us in the Women's Studies community. Although the development officer undertook this assignment with no background, she became increasingly involved and enthusiastic as she learned more about the program and the responses it was receiving on campus. Through her, we talked to the women trustees about other women who might be interested in getting involved with Women's Studies. She combed the records for women who had already been significant donors to Duke. We asked the Office of Alumni Affairs to name individuals who might have time and resources to commit. We met with local alumnae and asked them about possible contacts. Faculty whose former students were now in professional leadership positions added their names to the list.

These conversations made evident a revealing pattern of female invisibility in a coeducational but traditional university. The same names came up over and over again—usually alumnae in the public domain whom Duke claimed as "successes." The list never got beyond a dozen names. Sometimes the person with whom we were talking could not "think of any women." The donor records were almost shocking. Although more than one-third of the university's graduates were female, there were few major donors among them; a large number of alumnae had never contributed to the Annual Fund or to other capital campaigns. There were certainly no instances of women giving for women-centered activities. Records on male-female giving patterns did not exist.

We decided to bring some alumnae together, tell them about the new scholarship on women, expose them to Women's Studies faculty and students, and ask them to help us chart the necessary directions in fundraising. We sought women from different areas of the country, professionals as well as civic leaders and homemakers, women with personal money as well as women with experience in fundraising for organizations. Above all, we sought women who would develop an intellectual commitment to the study of women and who would have the resources to help us build the program. In spite of the meager lists and our seemingly inflated hopes, we compiled a list of some twenty names. Through the Development Office, faculty friendships, and the help of a core group of alumnae, we invited these women to join what we named the Council on Women's Studies, using Judy Woodruff's chairwomanship as a draw.

In February 1986 nineteen women traveled to campus for a two-day program billed as "Learning about Women's Studies." The women traveled at their own expense; we hosted them while on campus. Woodruff began the session by describing some goals for the council. She emphasized the importance of increasing the visibility of Women's Studies both on campus as well as among friends and alumnae by enlarging the audience for the new scholarship on women. She said the Women's Studies Program sought the advice of alumnae for the benefit of current students preparing to launch their own careers. And she asked the council to join her in identifying sources of financial support for the program. The council's objectives articulated, we spent the remainder of the two days in academic activities.

The alumnae heard an art history lecture entitled "Old Mistresses," arguing for the inclusion of women in discussions of painters, sponsors, subjects, and creators of art. They met with faculty and students from a residential course on professional opportunities and personal options, learning about the course's links with Catalyst, a national research effort on women's career planning. A well-known professor with whom many had studied gave a lecture entitled "Why I Teach Women's History." They toured a specially arranged exhibit in the main library that showed a decline in the proportion of women on the faculty since the merger of the Woman's College.

They also heard the president of the university speak about the difference Women's Studies makes to students. The program had been working hard to convince the president to support this initiative. He had learned that students and faculty were reacting positively to the new program, he was impressed with alumnae response, and he had asked for materials on other programs that demonstrated to him that we were taking leadership in linking Women's Studies to an alumnae audience.

As this brief chronology suggests, we emphasized an educational program that would introduce participants to the new scholarship on women by linking Women's Studies both to the historic efforts of women to get an education and to women's current push for personal achievement. The session closed with a business meeting in which council members were asked to "raise their sights" and think about others who would like to know about these initiatives and would consider supporting the program. Although the business meeting included presentations by those in the Development Office, the weekend stressed building networks among the council members and familiarizing them with Women's Studies. They were not yet asked to do very much themselves. Their enthusiasm was palpable, and they agreed to attend semiannual meetings.

In the fall of 1986 a similar program was held with faculty lectures, a historical retrospective on women at Duke, and meetings with graduate students about feminist research. The Development Office continued to introduce information about the need for financial support; they announced that Women's Studies had become an official part of Duke's ongoing Capital Campaign for the Arts and Sciences. The participants' reactions were even stronger this time: they wanted more people to know about Women's Studies and asked for an expanded meeting to which guests would be invited. As program staff, we walked a delicate line between explaining how much we were already doing and asking for more financial help to offer the lectures, courses, and projects that would make Women's Studies flourish. A general campaign plan for discretionary funds to support all facets of the program was presented, and the first year ended with some $75,000 in gifts from thirty-three individuals.

Over the next four years, this successful pattern was repeated, with a new dimension added each year. The Development Office allocated limited funds to host these weekends ($5,000 a year for the first two years, $2,500 for the following two years), and participants continued to cover their own expenses. University officials continued to make appearances at the social events. Council members continued to learn. Students and faculty continued to tell how transformative their Women's Studies experiences were. The program and the Development Office continued to think about how to mobilize this alumnae body, a group without prior friendships, with little substantive familiarity but great emotional connection to the project, and with a limited history of giving.

In the second year, 1987, we sent a direct mailing to all 27,000 alumnae, announcing a weekend symposium entitled "Educating Women for Leadership." We followed the earlier pattern of combining the council business meeting with faculty lectures, student conversations, small group discussions, and talks by university representatives. One hundred and twenty-five alumnae came, most of them unknown to us until they returned their registration forms.

While conducting these public programs, we were simultaneously setting up an infrastructure on campus. The Development Office had earlier assigned us a new staff member, far more knowledgeable and energetic than her predecessor, who had moved from the area. Plans were laid to publish a regular newsletter on Women's Studies as well as create a Friends of Women's Studies organization to provide operating funds for alumnae activities. The Friends included hundreds of women who were supportive of the program, while the council continued as a smaller group of thirty women serving in a leadership role. In an attempt to intellectually engage those alumnae whom we could not see personally, the first invitation for membership in the Friends organization was mailed with a survey to all alumnae about their experiences as women students at Duke and a copy of the syllabus for the introductory Women's Studies course.

By the end of the second year we had several specific endowments from individuals, a plan for two challenge grants to fund speakers and research, and a total of $150,000 pledged. The council members' energy soared, and they were ready to gather friends and funds; this was the most exciting development since graduation, they claimed. The university really was their alma mater, fostering mother.

At the 1987 symposium, reality intruded upon these positive developments in the form of greetings brought by a university official who "was sorry he could not stay for what promised to be an interesting session." His welcome consisted of a challenge to the program to show that it was worthwhile. He assured the alumnae of the university's interest in their responses, but made it clear that the administration would decide the program's future. The more generous of the alumnae regarded his remarks as uninformed and asked what they could do to help "educate" him. The more adamant were furious at his patronizing tone and his failure to see what they saw. They wanted him to know that his attitude was off base and that he had made them angry.

Whatever their individual reactions—and they were widely discussed during the weekend—the participants all agreed that despite the many benefits Women's Studies was bringing to students and faculty, there was a larger academic culture that remained ignorant. They were also unanimous in their frustration, a frustration many had already experienced in their own work and professional settings, that "things concerning women" were not "really important." This combination of positive personal experiences and negative social climate powerfully reinforced all that the alumnae had been learning about feminist scholarship over the past two years. Their support and sympathy increased with their understanding of the resisting culture in which Women's Studies existed.

The year 1988 brought additional growth. Gifts were up to just over $500,000, brought in by a series of individual contributions ranging from $10,000 to $50,000. Alumnae were joining the Friends of Women's Studies organization in large numbers, averaging 250 to 300 a year. New members joined the council, as Women's Studies staff visited ex-student groups in various cities, spoke at class reunions on campus, and made contact in campus publications. The new members who came to Women's Studies on their own initiative generally began with a deeper and longer commitment to feminist activities. The changed level of discussions at the meetings was extraordinary, as these women talked of the ways in which their introduction to Women's Studies had furthered their own understanding of women's lives and relationships in every setting.

The university climate outside Women's Studies, however, did not appear improved. A second male administrator, chosen by the administration to bring greetings at the symposium's opening session, was offensive to all. He appeared in sports clothes in a room full of council members and guests in professional attire. He told two slightly off-color jokes about women as his opener. This time council members protested directly. The new chair wrote him a letter (with copies to others), stating that he had offended friends and donors. Given her prominence in the world of educational finance, the ripples were immediate and extensive. Letters were exchanged and a series of conversations held, all with the purpose of explaining to this university officer and his peers how to act with professional women as well as why Women's Studies is an important intellectual endeavor.

Every time the council has visited campus, this duality has presented itself: enthusiasm for what Women's Studies can do alongside despair at the resistance women continue to face in their daily lives. There is a stark contrast in levels of understanding between those who have become engaged in the systematic investigation of women's lives and those who have not. Such contrasts are highlighted on council weekends when alumnae with more extensive knowledge and high enthusiasm meet with officials who are distant from the endeavor.

In 1989, the sesquicentennial year of the university's founding, the program staff and council seized on the chance to hold a major celebration. At the centennial in 1939 the Woman's College had sponsored a major event; we linked the 150th to that event. For the second time a mailing went to all alumnae, inviting them to a three-day symposium entitled "The Changing Patterns of Our Lives: Women's Education and Women's Studies." Alumnae enrollment topped 200; many students and faculty joined in the plenary sessions. Endowment funds were used for major speakers, both local and national; fifty workshops were held throughout the weekend. The campus was literally overrun with enthusiastic alumnae sharing their reactions with students and faculty.

In part because this weekend symposium joined the larger university effort and in part because, over time and with money, recognition for feminist scholarship was growing, the university's climate appeared more positive to alumnae. Official greetings were on target; representatives stayed through the sessions. The impact of numbers, voices, and not coincidentally money was clearly being felt. The alumnae were becoming quite conscious of their role in making this happen; in both formal sessions and informal conversations, they took pleasure in saying what they thought ought to happen with regard to Women's Studies.

That new directions were being charted in Women's Studies was particularly clear vis-à-vis African American alumnae. Duke had 750 African American alumnae. Their connections to Duke had never been specifically fostered until several African American alumnae on the council began to bring them into dialogue. The contact initiated through Women's Studies resulted in funds for a course on African American women as well as a foundation grant to bring alumnae into the course.

In 1990, 1991, and 1992 yet another pattern evolved in the council's activities. Subgroups of council members hosted a fall meeting in cities where alumnae are concentrated—Atlanta, Washington, and New York. All alumnae in the region were invited in the hope that many who could not consider a trip to campus could spend a day hearing Women's Studies faculty explain feminist scholarship. The "road show" appears to be an effective way of bringing growing numbers of alumnae and friends into dialogue around issues they find central.

The spring meetings are held on campus, are larger in scope, and are designed to intensify members' connection with the program. While their general contours remain the same, the character of these meetings has shifted over time as more and more women become involved. This brief overview does not do justice to the richness of the learning experiences that have taken place on all sides in this cooperative venture.

Building Coalitions for Women's Studies

Looking back over the five-year effort and anticipating what the future holds now that the endowment campaign is over, I am drawn to three groups of people involved in the process: the alumnae themselves; the campus outside Women's Studies, particularly the Development Office; and the faculty and students who constitute the program itself. Each group has its own story, yet each story intermingles with and shapes the story of the others. The coalitions that have been built, both among the various actors in each group and between groups, have become important influences for all.

Alumnae

Mobilizing alumnae for Women's Studies by building a coalition between them, the Development Office, and the program itself is perhaps the most noteworthy outcome of these five years. Historically fundraisers for coeducational institutions have paid scant attention to women. With the exception of the efforts of women's colleges to solidify alumnae support and the generosity of a few wealthy women who have endowed professorships, strategies for appealing to women as a group are in their infancy on most campuses. Nor do we know how to address differences between younger career women and older women who have not accumulated their own resources outside family structures.

In conversations about university fundraising, I often hear women blamed for not giving. I suspect that the reasons women have given relatively few large monetary gifts do not lie with women themselves. My experience suggests that many women have not given in part because of what they are asked to support. Until the Campaign for Women's Studies, female graduates of Duke University had never been asked to fund a project that directly addressed their experiences as women. They had been asked for all the usual things a university needs—buildings, scholarships, teaching funds, operating expenses. They had been asked to support the status quo. In our experience, many women thought the status quo needed changing.

The following excerpt comes from a talk given by council chairwoman Ann Curry as she reflected upon her $10,000 gift. She is speaking to other alumnae at the conclusion of the endowment campaign, explaining what motivated her to give a major contribution for the first time since her graduation in 1965:

In Women's Studies we all found a program that spoke to our needs, our feelings, our hopes for the future. And it did so, as I told a group of Duke administrators, for me, for the first time since my 1965 graduation, in a voice I could hear.

I think, however, that we gave not only to change the future, but to appease the past. Two major Women's Studies funds honor the grandmother and mother, respectively, of their donors. My own story . . . is similar. My gift honors my grandmother, born 100 years ago in rural South Carolina. A woman of enormous intellect and fortitude, she was a leader of our church, matriarch of our family, and shaper of my own ambitions. She wielded what I have come to call private power, behind-the-scenes advice given in calls to our home by our minister, who checked with my grandmother before taking any action. Yet she was never allowed to be part of the governing board of her church or even to pray aloud. Her own educational hopes had been thwarted when her father told her no one could spare the time for a buggy trip to the nearest high school and, as the oldest girl, she was needed at home to help out anyway. I knew all my life how much my grandmother had wanted that education. I also knew, and continue to know, how much of that deferred hope she pinned on me.

This past year I "delivered" for my grandmother, creating an endowment in her name that will become part of the teaching endowment. As I see it, the fund will help ensure that the special needs and accomplishments of women are always considered. And, while I have created a legacy for those to come, I have also paid back a debt, my grandmother's legacy to me.

What follows is part of a letter that accompanied another alumna's endowment gift:

As I explained during our September conversation, I feel profoundly out of step with Duke. I am disturbed by the values which I see in practice in the university—not the advertised values, rather the values that are lived out day to day. I see more arrogance than I am comfortable with. I see the talents of students and junior faculty wasted through lack of attention, lack of mentoring, on the part of faculty. I am concerned about a sort of anti-intellectualism on the part of the students, which, it seems to me, is a product of being ignored by the faculty, not treated as partners in the scholarly enterprise. It bothers me that, while a great deal of public relations lip service is paid to undergraduate education, the faculty are not rewarded, indeed are punished, if they are great teachers but less than superstar research talents. I am distressed by the attention given to power and status and the deaf ear frequently turned toward complaints by people with little power to bargain with. I am disturbed by the "them versus us mentality" I have observed among too many faculty (and the occasional dean) when talking about students. It bothers me that this attitude is passed on, by example, to graduate students—the future faculty.

I would like to believe there will be significant change in the institution as a whole, but I do not share [your] optimism, I'm afraid. There is too much reward for maintaining the status quo and too little incentive for the sort of changes I would like to see. In short, the powers that be seem to hold values different from mine. I think I'm basically out of step with the institution.

My gift, then, is not motivated by faith in Duke, rather by faith in [the Women's Studies Program]. I feel immensely encouraged and much more hopeful whenever I hear or see evidence of what Women's Studies is doing. When I attend one of the Women's Studies weekend programs for alumnae, I always feel as if I have found my home. I have great confidence in [your] ability to make a difference in the lives of young men and women participating in Women's Studies at Duke, and, through those young people, to make a difference in the larger community. The scholarship itself is of the utmost importance if we are to understand our present and act intelligently about the future; in addition, the respect for students and faculty which I see evidenced in the Women's Studies Program is what I value in an educational institution. I am personally inspired by [your] work and am pleased to be able to make a contribution toward that effort.

For both of these women, giving was a way to exercise some degree of influence over the future they wanted other women to experience. It was a way to make a dent in things as they are and to shape a vision for things as they ought to be.

These donors, like the several hundred others who joined them, did not know they could influence their alma mater until the Women's Studies Program asked them to do so and promised to help them make their voices heard. I maintain they would not have seen themselves as interested in exercising such influence if they had not become engaged in the educational process from a feminist perspective. Raising funds from women for feminist educational projects requires that alumnae themselves come to see what was missing in their own education, learn how the new scholarship on women fills in gaps that they had not previously named, and believe that younger women and men will begin their adult lives better equipped than they were. Like feminist scholars, alumnae learn to observe, to give voice, and to act.

Evidence for this suggestion—that how alumnae are asked is as important as what they are asked to fund—comes from changes over the five-year period in what women wanted to fund and in how much money they designated to do it. The first two large gifts ($10,000 each) came from women in their seventies who wanted women to have an education. For them, access to education remained an issue. As alumnae came to know more about Women's Studies scholarship, they were determined that others know too. The most obvious route to this destination was to sponsor campus events of general public interest that would involve new people. Thus, in the second year of the campaign, we received a $50,000 gift, a $25,000 gift, and a $30,000 challenge that later reached over $100,000 for three different lecture series. As alumnae became more familiar with feminist scholarship and saw the success of the lectures they had sponsored, they wanted to draw individual students into the process. Thus, in the third wave of giving, we received two endowed scholarships for students and faculty working on women and gender as well as award funds to recognize superior efforts in this area.

In the last two years of the campaign, giving took yet another direction. Familiar now with Women's Studies and assured of student involvement, alumnae recognized that they needed to influence the core of the institution, specifically its teaching and research mission. Following an initial gift of $30,000, the teaching endowment grew to just short of half a million dollars in two years. Money for teaching courses in Women's Studies came in $25 checks from recent graduates, in multiyear pledges of $1,000 from those who had attended weekend symposia, and in larger amounts from those with more extensive means. As alumnae began to network, they came to see themselves as part of a coalition for change that was advocating attention to women on campus in new and stronger voices.

It is important to stress that these giving phases did not result from a deliberate plan on the part of Women's Studies or the Development Office. They reflect the learning curve of the alumnae themselves. Because all of the endowments added essential resources to the program, each was welcomed in turn. And all along the way, many people gave to a director's discretionary fund, which was used to seed various initiatives, from the campus newsletter to office equipment and books.

It is also critical to note that such giving defies fundraising fundamentals. The conventional strategy is to secure a few large gifts—ideally half of the goal—before the campaign is announced, building a pyramid structure thereafter. Women's Studies began without a single large donor. The $1 million raised in the campaign came from some 1,500 people, none of whom gave as much as $100,000, the usual entry amount for any campaign.

The Development Office

Most academic units do not undertake endowment campaigns separate from those of the general university. A unit that does entertain such an idea often assumes that the Development Office would not lend its assistance because it has not done so in the past. One major accomplishment of the Duke initiative was to demonstrate that cooperation between academic programs and professional fundraising can lead to mutual success and new possibilities. The relationships built into one specific endeavor can carry over into other endeavors as relationships continue and deepen.

Fundraising for higher education is an extensive professional field; the Women's Studies Program at Duke could not have attracted endowment gifts without the cooperation of our Development Office. In retrospect, it is clear that our development staff made two significant contributions. First, they had the expertise to develop a campaign strategy, they had alumnae data from which to work, they had the contacts that led to other contacts, and they simply knew the day-to-day workings of fundraising. The initial difficulty of convincing the men in charge of development was never completely overcome; while some came on board, others simply did not include Women's Studies on their agenda when approaching donors. Their reluctance, however, was more than overcome by the enthusiastic support of most of the women on the Development Office staff. They quickly grasped the project's potential and went far beyond their assigned responsibilities to make the campaign work. Like the alumnae they contacted, these women connected personally with Women's Studies and became powerful advocates for the endeavor.

A second contribution was the growing recognition that Women's Studies received along with monetary gifts. The backing of the Development Office translated into feature stories in campus publications, invitations to participate in other university events, advocacy on campus for the initiative, and eventually national recognition for the project from a professional group, the Council for the Advancement and Support of Education. Some alumnae who worked on the Women's Studies campaign were brought into other advisory capacities in the university, exercising a feminist perspective on those boards and projects as well. Bringing more people into the Women's Studies circle, especially people with different university positions and external contacts, meant that the program became well known in places we would never have ventured otherwise. Through these contacts with nonacademic units on campus, Women's Studies was able to engage these units in conversations that contributed directly to giving women's concerns a higher priority on the institution's official agenda.

The Women's Studies Community

In addition to the alumnae and the Development Office, the third group of actors in this fundraising process was, of course, the faculty, students, and staff of the program itself. I see at least three ways in which those of us in Women's Studies were shaped by this five-year experience.

First, and perhaps most obviously, we were forced to develop a way of explaining feminist scholarship that was accessible to the nonspecialist. Faculty and students alike were challenged to translate the nuances of scholarly discourse into explanations and approaches that made sense to people who did not share similar backgrounds. That meant speaking without jargon, drawing on more than one discipline or single theoretical framework to explore and solve problems. That meant linking discussions of meanings with discussions of practical possibilities. That meant learning to think about those issues that came out of their experiences rather than putting forward only issues that scholars themselves had named as important. Talking with alumnae spurred us to explore the links between what people knew about a subject and how they felt about that subject.

At first, talking to development staff and alumnae audiences was demanding intellectual work. On the one hand, translating complex ideas into accessible presentations was difficult. On the other, while caring deeply about the issues being discussed, most alumnae had been trained not to use personal experience in building knowledge. Helping them do so meant helping them unlearn old paradigms and assume new ones, never an easy task. Encounters between alumna and scholar—whether in a group or individual setting—would often be summarized by the student or faculty member involved in some version of the following statement: "They were really interesting women. I enjoyed talking to them and I really learned a lot. And they asked such good questions! Do you think I got across to them?" The translation work paid off in improved abilities in the classroom and on paper as those of us involved in Women's Studies went about our other tasks as scholars.

A second direct benefit of working with the alumnae associated with Women's Studies was the feeling of empowerment that flowed from these encounters. Being a feminist scholar in contemporary academia is by no means easy; colleagues can reject, ignore, and isolate one's work. The appreciation these professional women expressed for what we as academics were doing went a long way toward validating the feminist enterprise. They were fascinated with what we were learning and demanded to know more. They represented an audience of people who are socially defined as powerful and who said to all of us, "Good work! Keep it up!" Many, many times, as weekend symposia were held and as news of gifts came in, faculty and students associated with the program talked about the new perspective they were gaining on their work. No longer solely dependent on the reactions of teachers, chairpeople, advisers, and colleagues, they now enjoyed an additional audience that was lavish in its praise, and it sustained them.

Third, our involvement with this alumnae fundraising project had a healthy effect on the internal dynamics of the program. Many women's studies programs, like the academic departments they resemble, become highly factionalized. Certain ways of approaching ideas and projects are held to be the only correct ones. While such politics are a part of group life, these struggles can sometimes intensify to the point of destructiveness.

The fundraising campaign brought us together in a common project where participation and its benefits outweighed more individualistic goals. This is not to say that differences of opinion do not exist among those affiliated with the program, nor that every faculty member or student was uniformly supportive of each initiative or that they participated in the same way. But many who were wary of the enterprise acknowledged its long-term benefits; others came to endorse the priority of securing a resource base of both constituents and dollars. We developed a mosaic rather than a hierarchical or factional model of operating that allowed relationships among the actors in the program and those outside it to develop for mutual benefit.

The Women's Studies Program is now at a turning point in its relationships with alumnae and friends. We anticipate conducting more intensive gatherings where there will be an opportunity for in-depth work in feminist scholarship. We envision continuing to mix faculty, students, and alumnae in these endeavors, convinced that sustained involvement will deepen the benefits we have already witnessed. And we think that alumnae voices are increasingly heard. An episode from the 1991 commencement suggests that the climate has changed as a feminist coalition is building.

After several years of nominating and lobbying, the Honorary Degree Committee chose Eleanor Cutri Smeal, a graduate of the class of 1961, as one of the five individuals to receive an honorary doctorate of laws. I made the nomination with the help of many others and wrote the citation for the president to read during commencement. I arranged for her to speak to the Women's Studies students at their recognition ceremony during the graduation weekend and planned a small dinner party for her the preceding evening. I thought my responsibilities complete until I received a call the week before graduation from the university marshal, an older scientist. It seems I had to think of a one-line description of the honoree for the graduation program.

Well, I began, I think she is above all a civic leader, a person who works from the premise that we all, male and female, ought to have a say in politics. Fine, he said, Civic Leader. Then, I added, I see her as an educator, a person who advocates that people think and learn as new situations arise. Good, he replied, Educator. We stalled here. Well, he said, we have to say something about women. Well, I replied, most people would say she is a feminist educator. Oh, that's excellent, he responded, Feminist Educator. You could hear him writing it down over the phone. Another pause.

Do you have to say three things, I asked, knowing the rules of classical rhetoric but hoping he did not. Yes, came the reply. Well, I said, again stalling for time and thinking about how what Eleanor Smeal represents could be put into a one-line description in a formal printed program. Well, I repeated, a lot of people look to her for her opinions on issues. Great, he said, that's it, Molder of Opinion. That's just great, Jean, thank you so much. And he hung up. The final program, the product of many additional hands, read: "Public servant; women's advocate; distinguished alumna."

The 1985 graduation podium could not have accommodated an alumna whose life work was women's issues. The campus climate changes evidenced in this one small event and the much larger effort that went into mobilizing women for Women's Studies cannot be measured easily. But they are connected in ways that we cannot untangle. We all benefit from the entanglement: the cheers Eleanor Smeal received were the loudest of the day.

Things You Can Never Prove in Court, Things the Human Psyche Never Misses

Coauthored with

Vivian Robinson

Putting feminism into action is a desire shared by many students who take women's studies classes.[1] The new ideas they obtain in the classroom turn on lights in their heads. And having had this experience, these students are anxious both to enlighten others and to try out these newfound ideas in other settings. But doing so is troublesome, as one student wrote in her application to join a women's studies project in the fall of 1991:

> The name WARP caught my eye. It reminded me of my father's attitudes toward all my Women's Studies classes, that somehow my perspective is skewed because I'm learning about women's history and gender relations. I see it as just the opposite; what has come before us is the warped image of women that needs to be adjusted. . . . [After my first Women's Studies course] I became aware of a whole range of emotions and experiences which were shared by other people and which gave definition to my personal history. I was so involved in the feminist mode of thinking that I applied that viewpoint to just about everything I could lay my hands on. . . . Outside the understanding I have achieved of myself and of my value as a woman, there is a whole world that doesn't yet share my opinion. How do we go about destroying the myths surrounding women without alienating those whom we are trying to reach? How do I take the knowledge and confidence I gain from Women's Studies and apply it to the world outside of the university?

This student and many others engage the feminist enterprise only to discover that it is by no means simple to connect what they know in one space

239

with the situation or behavior they would like to change in another. They express exasperation about how little some people understand. They wonder why it proves so difficult to get others to see the things they have learned to see. Students want to connect knowledge from women's studies with a wide range of issues in their lives, as evidenced in these student comments:

This project interests me because I often have problems relating the concepts that I learn in class to my everyday life. At times I feel like a hypocrite; I often question many of my own actions. Is there any way to change myself (and remain happy), or am I destined to be a victim of my own culture and upbringing?

I hope that working in this project will . . . get me thinking about translating my thoughts and actions on a personal level, a vital first step in the process of change in women's lives, starting with my own, and eventually moving into the public sphere where I feel action would do the most good.

I need to learn how to make aware those people who play important roles in my life that I have a certain agenda in mind for this life, and that by being part of my life they must be part of what I seek. And when they obstruct me in what I want to achieve, I need to be able to express this without alienating them either.

I also found a sense of frustration and continuing amazement at the conservativeness of this campus. It really surprises me less and less each year, and it bothers me that it surprises me less and less. The response to that is not that I become part of it, but that I feel a real detachment between what I am thinking at the moment and what I express. A lot of times I let things go on around me because I feel that this is too much, I can't even touch this, and you have to choose your battles. If I choose every one that I see, then I will be doing nothing else. It is a feeling of powerlessness.

The project described here, called the Women's Action Research Project (WARP), was conceived in the summer of 1991 as an attempt to connect student needs with the long-term goals of two campus administrative units, the Women's Studies Program and the Women's Center. Women's Studies is an academic unit that works primarily through teaching, sponsoring public lectures, and fostering the research and teaching activities of faculty and graduate students. The Women's Center is structurally located in Student Affairs; the center addresses issues of student health, safety, and personal development.

Some observers would say that Women's Studies emphasizes theory while the Women's Center works with practice. Yet on a day-to-day basis, these two units at Duke evidence more cooperative overlap than separation. The staff of each unit works from the premise that the two offices stand in partnership, neither operating effectively without the other.

When the staff from both offices met in the summer of 1991 to assess progress and to map out future possibilities, the three of us (Jean O'Barr, director of Women's Studies; Vivian Robinson, a 1989 graduate and the program coordinator in Women's Studies; and Martha Simmons, a graduate student in Women's Studies and director of the Women's Center) found ourselves in agreement about a gap: the lack of a forum outside the classroom where young women could discuss the meanings of what they were learning and explore how to connect this knowledge with other aspects of their lives.

At first we envisioned setting up a discussion group with a specific topic, such as women and leadership. The more we debated topics, however, the clearer it became that any single subject would be more limiting to students than empowering. In addition, we gradually came to see that our own questions as administrators were epistemological in nature; we wanted to see what would happen when students identify ideas from their own experiences and education, and then speculate about how to activate those ideas. More than that, none of us knew enough to simply instruct these students; we needed to research their process and document its outcomes along with them. What we proposed to do sounded like action research, an approach familiar to us from women's advocacy groups in the community.

How could two diverse academic units not only cross conventional lines of communication in the academy but implement an initiative derived from community organizing? We found inspiration in a career options workshop being conducted by the University of Michigan's Center for the Education of Women. The Michigan project was linking two separate practices in research universities. On the one hand, the Michigan center was using a student affairs approach by sponsoring a project to provide undergraduates with information in a space that allowed them to tailor that information to their diverse needs. On the other hand, the staff was using the workshop as a research site by interviewing, recording, and analyzing each individual's decision-making processes as well as the group's dynamics in the hope of learning more about how young women view career possibilities. By linking concrete results with investigative research, the center was simultaneously delivering and creating knowledge.

The Michigan model both fit our desire to explore a cooperative project between two academic units and also addressed students' requests as we had been hearing them. The student group we envisioned would draw women who were currently "actors" (those movers and shakers on the campus who wanted to think more reflectively about what they did) as well as women who were engaged in feminist scholarship but would not have described themselves as actors when it came to the university politics of gender. A project that accomplished multiple goals simultaneously appealed to us, for we saw so much that needed to be done on campus.

While we as planners knew we were not looking for novices who had never pondered these questions before, we also had no clear idea of exactly who might apply. Thus our advertisements were filled with text, in an effort to put the responsibility on students to read, reflect, and decide whether to join such an endeavor.

Nine women responded, all involved in Women's Studies. Two of the women were sophomores and seven, seniors. Two of the women were African American, the remainder were of European descent. No two students had the same major. Most of these women talked to one of the three staff members before writing a letter of application. In their applications, all nine women were quite clear that WARP was an opportunity they had been seeking.

The preliminary materials spelled out obligations (reading, participating, writing) and benefits (exchange of perspectives, skill development, faculty-staff interaction). Earlier in the summer, the three of us had decided to plan a general outline with readings in order to get the group moving. Yet we did not want to completely fashion the agendas and topics that the group would cover. The format we designed was open-ended, one that would enable us to observe and follow where the group was going, what questions were most pressing, and what future formats seemed most useful.

The first three fall sessions were structured according to this open-ended format. Participants would read material chosen by the three staff members and then write an essay that grew out of our discussion. These essays were to be distributed ahead of time, so that all group members could read each other's thoughts before the session began. Each session would be taped and then transcribed by work-study students in the Women's Studies office.

The three of us who were staff also decided to write essays, having deliberately chosen to be members of WARP who read, wrote, and discussed rather than instructed. This choice was the result of long discussions. We recognized differences in the power that each of us held as planners. We also knew we could neither simply dismiss our power as facilitators nor pretend that this power (however varied) was identical to the diverse powers that students wield. In our essays we planned to deal directly with differences in our ages, experiences, and status. By naming our specific powers alongside our vulnerabilities, staff members sought to balance the occasional interventions we would be making as facilitators responsible for moving the group forward with our own growth as we learned alongside the students.

Mirrors and Windows: The Fall Semester

Early in September 1991 bright orange posters peppered the women's dormitories, the library, and the student union. They asked undergraduate women who were curious about developing their organizational skills and their analytic abilities to join with like-minded women in forming a semester-long discussion group. The poster read:

> The purpose of the project is to learn about the process by which the knowledge we have about women in culture and society translates into effective action, as well as how action and activism around women's issues relates to feminist thought. . . . The acronym WARP refers to the first set of strings put on a loom. Seen by weavers as the foundation for their work, we envision WARP as the beginning of a new approach to how undergraduate women view themselves and are viewed by others as they bring together their classroom and campus lives.

Participants began WARP by holding up a mirror. What did each of us know and what could we learn together as a group of diverse women about the experience of being female in contemporary middle- and upper-class America? The opening reading was Susan Glaspell's "A Jury of Her Peers."[2] Written in the early twentieth century, Glaspell's short story tells the tale of two women who visit the house of a third woman after her husband has been killed, surmise that she murdered him, and then conspire together to hide the evidence. Themes were readily identified: the behind-the-scenes form that women's action often takes; the devaluation of women's experiences and knowledge; the strength created when women share knowledge; the isolation of women who are not in a community of other women; and the difficulties that obstruct achieving that community.

The images of women identified in these themes took us directly into recounting personal experiences of what it meant to "be a girl." The students' comments ranged from being denied pitching lessons because no girl—however good her arm—could ever play pro ball to having been subjected to scholarship interviews with elderly men who fretted that good money might be wasted on women who would drop out of college as soon as they met some man.

For the following session, we wrote papers about our experience of "being a girl." Participants shared sometimes funny, sometimes poignant, but always insightful stories that ranged from growing up with a mother who was too busy helping relatives from Liberia get on their feet in the United States to spend time with her daughter to being shamed by a boyfriend's mother who made assumptions about the student's sexuality. Additional themes emerged: the crucial role played by relationships with older women (mothers or others) as young girls struggled to accept or reject "being a girl"; the importance of connecting with other girls in solidarity; the feeling of isolation when connections with other girls and women were not there; the difficulty of bridging the generation gap between girls and women who did not remember what being a girl was like.

As we discussed the papers, we returned over and over again to the various ways in which our experiences as girls and women had been devalued. Discussion slowly shifted from *mirror* images that look inward onto past personal experiences to *window* images that look out onto the cultures that have also shaped us. Mary's experiences of being singled out as an exceptional student became our transition into the third session:

> My parents would always brag about my intelligence to their friends. I think I made them proud because my success meant that they were successful in beating the odds, that their supposedly "retarded" child was instead some sort of genius. But what bothered me was that they would make these comments in front of my brothers and sisters. I would think to myself, "Don't they realize they are isolating me within my own house?" From an early age, I felt like they, my siblings, were watching me too. On the one hand my parents' scrutiny kept the attention off of them; but on the other hand, I think, not maliciously, that they didn't want to see me do well because I had all the attention. Because of this, I never felt that my family, the people who were supposed to be the closest to me, really knew me. I never felt as though I had any backup, so I never did anything I thought would require it.

The third session (the last meeting that was planned in advance) focused on exploring feelings of being "exceptional." As women we felt that we constituted the exception to university norms. Not only did we still expect and value this "exceptional" status, but we used this status to measure relationships with other women. As Martha observed, this identity as an "exceptional" woman influenced the ways group members experienced being a feminist: "This is so interesting, because as the series of papers has developed, one of the things that has continued to come up is the notion of ourselves as exceptional women. We have in some ways gotten a lot of positive feedback for being exceptional women. Now, I am hearing that, as we all make this transition to exceptional in terms of being a feminist, we are finding ourselves in a whole other dimension here, [one] that is really lonely."

For the fourth and final fall session, the group together decided to think about competition and cooperation among women. In keeping with the shift in our conversations from examining internal obstacles and external barriers to negotiating both, the group also decided to think about what they envi-sioned doing during the spring. As the final writing assignment of the fall, each group member was to write an idea for an "action" project that could provide a first step in trying out the ideas we had been forming in our conversations throughout the fall.

The ideas were highly varied, ranging from producing a film on eating disorders to printing a feminist newsletter for the campus. But all the pro-posals contained many uncertainties. Elaine's essay put the dilemma bluntly: "Now comes the hard part. Step off the soap box, stop beating my breast in righteous indignation, and start changing things. Yet what I love about WARP, and Women's Studies in general, is that I can take apart my life's experiences and reconstruct the way I see myself." Vivian's essay captured a core concern for many:

> I have to confess a fear. It is that when groups take on a project, something accomplishable (if that's a word), the members get caught up in the goal, the finishing of the project, and lose the process they had with each other initially. Yet by the same turn, groups without an external project that they can define themselves with (or against) tend to lose energy, to get too caught up in their own circles, to wither away into pockets of resentment. My fear is choosing one or the other path, without being conscious of pitfalls in those choices. What I'm excited about is the immense possibility I feel that this group could create its own path, a path which has rest stops for reflection and conversations, but a path which doesn't get bogged down there but instead gets up and keeps moving.

At this point, the group was experiencing tugs in several directions. Mem-bers felt buoyed by what we had learned through our mirrors and windows exercises; we were only beginning to realize how valuable these WARP discus-sions had become to our sense of well-being. Everyone felt some degree of commitment to doing something that would share the benefits of the group with others, while simultaneously feeling frustration about how to decide what to do. We decided to put aside specific proposals in favor of using the upcom-ing holiday break as a time to do a little research on ourselves. We agreed that while at home for the holidays, each member would decide what constituted an action based on their own circumstances and then consciously "commit" that action. When writing up our experiences, we were to examine the process through which our ideas informed the action we chose to take. We would then follow our customary practice of sharing our papers when we reconvened in the spring, and, based on what we learned by comparing our experiences, decide on our spring agenda at that time. This decision, and the individual experiences of the group members over the holidays, proved to be critical in shaping the directions the group would take the following semester.

Talking Over the Holiday Break

WARP participants' holiday encounters turned out to be pivotal. Here is how Amy reflected on her three weeks at home in Arizona, as she grappled with the basics of expressing herself through words:

> I am thinking of the many times I have corrected my mother and her boyfriend when they used exclusive language. "Mankind." Scott infernally laughed at me every time I would say something. I don't think that he's sexist per se. But he is one of those people who wants someone to understand what he is saying rather than how he is saying it.
>
> You know, Scott (for now my archetypal male), you will never understand why it means so much to me to hear inclusive language until you have sat in on a science class with a sexist male teacher, and watched as every male felt affirmed in his dreams of winning a Nobel Prize and the females couldn't have appeared less interested. All due to the subtle psychological process of feeling so pervasively excluded by language cues.
>
> Things you can never prove in court. Things the human psyche never misses.
>
> . . . Back to my mom. We were driving in the car when she brought up the sexist language incident.
>
> "You know, Amy, I spoke to him later on that night."
>
> I looked at her blankly. "Mom?"
>
> "I told him that he'd never understand unless all he'd heard his entire life was 'she this' and 'she that.' Language as it is set up excludes women from the very start. It's like we are an anomaly that 'mankind' will never understand."
>
> I smiled. "I do hear what he's saying. But I really do feel like vocabulary is so often mentality."

While Laura's struggles also centered on language, she was primarily concerned with being typecast as a speaker:

At home one night, while drying the dishes after dinner, I thought about changing the world, or at least about changing my family. I wondered how I could do it. . . . I realized that I felt uncomfortable taking action in my family—in speaking (I envisioned ensuing arguments) on behalf of my beliefs—especially to my brother or father. It seemed harder than speaking out at Duke, or among friends, perhaps because in my family I play a certain role—I am the feminist one and everybody believes that they can anticipate my response to everything anyway so they don't really listen. Even to me it sometimes seems "automaton-ish." My brother plays another kind of role—he is the sexist one. . . . He's very loud, and carries on conversations all by himself, with himself, all the time, or makes obnoxious noises just to get attention and I tend to be very quiet and not say much of anything, even when things are burning inside. I let a lot slide by, because I know he's just doing it to provoke, like when we were decorating the tree and he made a big deal of how girls couldn't string lights, how that was a man's job, but girls could do the tinsel. I wish I could think of a way to really communicate with my brother, but I fear we are both caught up in these old patterns—I ignore him and hang up the tinsel, or I try to say something and he doesn't listen anyway and I still hang up the tinsel.

For Elaine, talk about language caused a divide that was deeply painful. She describes a visit to her old piano teacher:

We sit across from each other at her kitchen table, between us cups of tea and a plate of eclairs. What can I say about Mrs. ——? The first time I met her she frightened me half to death—this gnarled, wrinkly old woman with a strange guttural accent, not too much bigger than me, intimidating me with her resemblance to the Wicked Witch of the West. I was seven years old and dying to play the piano; she was seventy-seven and willing to take on another pupil. Little did I realize that lessons included more than scales and Bach; I would learn how to become an independent person, critical thinker, and creative artist. Fourteen years later, I find it hard to describe her to others because her voice mingles with my own in my head.

. . . And then the shock of hearing those strange words. . . . "I don't like feminists." Why? . . . I stared at her in complete disbelief. What could she be saying, this woman whom I want to be like when I reach the age of ninety? I asked her to stop; I didn't want to continue the conversation and shatter any more ideals, but I did continue because I couldn't help myself.

I had to know, my entire self-esteem yelped in fear. Normally she can make me see her point of view and accept its validity, even if I choose not to follow her advice. This time, I knew I felt too strongly on this issue to even discuss it with someone. And yet, to me, being a feminist means being able to act on my capabilities the way Mrs. —— has for her whole life. . . .

I asked myself whether it was possible to be a feminist and not think you are, and then I realized that Mrs. —— could not be a part of the women's movement because of her age, and her unique background and education. . . . Mrs. —— represents another case of the special woman who cannot identify with all women because she doesn't see herself in the same boat as a cleaning woman earning below the minimum wage.

As Elaine places her teacher's life against her own, she begins to see how a term has many meanings and how she might reconcile labels and lives. She concludes: "For some reason, it is much easier to question my own principles rather than my belief in her. How can I change from an individual perspective to one encompassing a wider range of people? This one conversation has been the most troubling shake-up on feminism that I have had in a long time. I don't know what synthesis of ideas will emerge from my doubt, but I am ready to lay myself open to the possibilities."

Leslie's story deals directly with the politics of talk:

My family and I were guests for dinner at another family's house over winter vacation. We were in the dining room, with cloth napkins and everyone on their "best behavior," when someone brought up the William Kennedy Smith trial. When my father said he "would have trouble feeling sympathy for a woman like that," I felt as if I were a student attempting to decipher a Zen koan. What did he mean by a woman "like that"? When he explained, "All I know is that she can't be totally blameless—out partying at three in the morning, that kind of thing. If a woman is in bed with a man, late at night with her clothes off, it would seem to me that she has already given her consent."

That experience, and this essay, is not really about change, unless it is about my own change. Listening to my father speak, and then listening to the silence of the eight others around me as I began to organize my anger (where does one begin to challenge those kinds of statements?), I experienced an epiphany.

I used to think that I was surrounded by people who see the world as I do. I didn't know that I could be close to someone who subscribes to a view so drastically different from my own, and from everything that I believe in. That this person has also contributed to my gene pool was a major factor contributing to my shock. . . .

I always knew that people whom I disagreed with affected me politically, as a voting citizen, as a student, etc. But the effects those strangers have on me are simultaneously placed on so many others—other citizens, other students. It wasn't personal. At the dinner table that night, I realized that there are also people who see the world differently than me who have everything to do with my personal life: my identity as Leslie-the-daughter, the sister, the friend.

This vacation, the bottom of a pail broke through. And I experienced the momentous event of reality.

The WARP meeting following the vacation break was held over dinner. Unlike the usual 8:30 A.M. sessions, the group did not get right to work. We caught up on personal news, discussed holiday TV commercials, and generally held back from discussing the essays. Then Jean observed:

> What strikes me as we get reacquainted is that all the talk [here tonight] is about talk and all the papers were about talk. Everybody's paper was about talk in an unfamiliar context or an uncomfortable one. Some people found they made a little progress with talk, while other people felt they weren't able to talk. I don't think the papers were ever as unified. . . . The first action everyone took was talk, and even that was difficult. . . . We are talking about how we are not practiced in certain types of talk. . . . I read in everybody's [paper], too, the enormous amount of work it is to know self and then try to speak to fathers or brothers.

With that intervention, the discussion took off, each person's experiences building on the others':

> LAURA: I feel like we need more practice doing things. I am looking at talking as doing something, and I could see myself trying to talk in the situations that I am in.
>
> JEAN: From the readings, it is just real clear that talking is the most profound action. It may be easier to stand anonymously in a march or write a letter where you don't have to confront things personally. I think that there is a cultural belief that talking isn't action, and I am saying that it is. We should think about why we think it isn't action.
>
> SALLY: I think we need some backing for it. I just had a conversation the other night with my roommate's boyfriend. . . . He said, "So you are one of those radical feminists"—and I had just met him. I was upset and said, "Don't corner me, or define me on this, because I don't want to be

defined by what you are thinking or see around you. You don't know me, you haven't talked to me." And I realized that I was freaking out about it for a day. I had to call up my mom because I was so hysterical. . . . Then I kept thinking, why am I so upset about this and, I need to know more.

MARTHA: It occurs to me that we are talking about talking in relationships, which is the key part of this.

VIVIAN: That is even harder, even more work than talking to complete strangers and being able to back up our statistics.

By naming how difficult we found talking about our feminist ideas, group members gained permission to know what they had known all along: they were changing in ways that did not necessarily meet with approval from significant others. When the change manifested itself through talking, the problem was not with the words or ideas used or with our ability to express them, but with the impact those words and ideas had on previous relationships with significant others. A much more subtle process than the exchange of information was going on: participants wanted to be validated through the experience of talking. As the group began explicitly considering both the experience of communicating and communication itself as one legitimate form of political action, we returned to Leslie's story and asked her what happened after the dinner party. Here is how Leslie described the aftermath:

I did get a response from my father. . . . I was so overwhelmed that I said, "I cannot continue this conversation, I have to leave the table," and I did. We spoke a few days later, finally. I feel it was my heightened passionate response that forced him to rethink it [his position], and it did change. I feel positively that yes, it [my action] made an impact. My dad said, "I didn't mean what I said; I think you misunderstood." I think that was his way of saying you were right. On the one hand, after it happened, I thought that maybe I should not have responded so vehemently. . . . [On the other hand] he would not have been forced, really forced, to rethink his thought process about what he had really said unless I had reacted that way. . . . I would be more likely, myself, to rethink something I had said that caused someone that much grief. For so long, I thought I should have handled the situation differently. Now, I think no, it was because my reaction . . . was so strong that made him say, "This is serious to my daughter and it is something that is causing a big rift between us, so I have to deal with it."

The January discussion forced us to confront the obvious: each of us had chosen some form of talk as the most profound action we could undertake, and each one of us did so within the domain of previous relationships. Until this January session, our conception of what an action group ought to do had often repeated conventional dichotomies (self vs. others, private vs. public, campus vs. the real world) without questioning them. Through the process of discussion, our idea of what constituted action shifted from a fuzzy, abstract idea of something done "out there and to others" to a concrete realization that our everyday encounters, in ongoing relationships, in ordinary words, were what mattered most to us. We became aware of the fact that we had not acknowledged the political nature of personal interactions and the powerful hold those interactions had on us.

As individual stories were elaborated, we realized that we collectively were doing something else for each other: in giving feedback to each other, we were practicing on each other, brainstorming ideas for "the next time this happened." WARP had suddenly become the safe space people had been seeking, a place where we could experiment with what we already knew.

As we located action in our interpersonal communities rather than in the abstract world at large, we moved from a notion of collective action to one of influence. This shift made it all the more important to share a practice space with others, both to work out our reactions to what we had done and to anticipate what we would do the next time around. The value of the space created by WARP came as a surprise. Why had no one ever suggested to any of us that newfound insights, like new skills at the keyboard or on the playing field, require extensive practice? This first session after break became a defining moment for the group as we realized that we had learned enough to modify our understanding, believe in our new perspectives, and be willing to undertake the hard work of experiencing and refining influence through talk over the long haul.

Practice Space: The Spring Semester

During the spring semester our format changed and we met more—seven times in all. Each session was led by participants who wrote a reflective piece that they combined with selected readings. Some participants presented alone, others in pairs. Several offered a specific project (such as a preview of a presentation on gender dynamics for an organization in which they worked), while others suggested a theme or problem for brainstorming.

This section examines two dynamics that took place that spring. One is the change in individual participants, and the other is the change in how the group understood the connection between the personal and the political and how that connection can be altered. We chose to focus on these dynamics because they illustrate two of the many ways in which practice with talk has an impact. At the individual level, each participant learned how to identify and articulate a tension point in her life and to begin to experiment with different approaches to addressing the tension. For the group as a whole, WARP provided a place to analyze the politicized nature of their worlds, to think through the messages they receive from those worlds, and to understand that the political content of those messages is typically denied. Unlike the other spaces undergraduate women inhabit on campus, WARP provided a space where women were at the center of analysis, where feminist frameworks would be employed, and where participants did not have to fight to get their issues on the conversational agenda.

One particular student exemplified the role that talking plays in learning and shaping ideas through practice. Upon first meeting her, Susan seems a fairly quiet young woman, timid in expressing her ideas unless directly solicited and even then not particularly forceful in delivery. A very good thinker, she feels more comfortable, as she puts it, in "the theoretical, 'thought' side of the spectrum."

Throughout the first semester, Susan struggled with feeling unable to communicate her thoughts to others; she spoke only once in the first two sessions. During that time, she constantly reflected upon her silence: "As far as I can remember, I have always been hesitant about my knowledge and perceptions. . . . In fourth grade, I knew that the teacher really liked me, but she stopped calling on me and I wanted to participate. I think that she thought I wanted to show off. Because this was the only area where I felt confident. By seventh grade, I did not participate. I would not raise my hand, although I knew the answer." Eventually, these ideas became ideas she held about herself—so deeply ingrained that it no longer mattered whether others held these ideas: "My ninth-grade English teacher and my Spanish teacher (both women) were constantly encouraging me and supporting me and trying to get me to participate because they were convinced I had something worth saying while I was convinced that I did not."

By the end of WARP's first semester, Susan began to tell the group about connections she was making between the way her experience of silence was changing as a result of participating in the WARP group and problems she was encountering elsewhere, particularly in her classes. Her paper for the final fall session compares democratic movements in Eastern Europe (the subject of one of her classes) with the change process she was experiencing in the group:

> Democratic change does not occur overnight but is the result of long years of organizing and self-activity. It involves democratic space and

movement building. Democratic space can be physical, or verbal, or just emotional, but ultimately provides a place for people to air their grievances about society in an atmosphere that is safe and conducive. Sort of like our WARP sessions . . . we air the issues that matter to us, and find out if other people have similar experiences and problems. I have found an empowering atmosphere in WARP because I find that I can identify with what almost anyone says, because it rings true to my experience, although our backgrounds are so different. . . . These are the first steps toward building the movement, in that we are creating a community for ourselves based on the need to share our experiences, have them validated, and provide a space to explore possible solutions to the problems we face in society.

In this same session, Susan shared with the group the steps she was taking toward challenging some of what she found problematic in her history class:

I was thinking about the difference between how things are there [in the history class] and here in WARP. Here we have a dialogue, a conversation, we share. In that class, we don't. In the last session, everyone got angry. I was very angry too. I actually exploded and started screaming. It took me until this week to realize why I was so angry. . . . We had the chance to talk with the author of the book we read because he is a Duke professor. And then we broke up into small groups to talk about the actors in the social movement—the workers, the party officials, etc. I asked about women. I was excited to be able to ask about women. I tried to get others to talk about women as actors in the movement, but since they weren't major figures in the book, the other students said they weren't important to analyze.

The argument over who knows what dominated the class because I was maintaining that one had to ask questions about women even if the author hadn't done so and others were saying that the author was an expert and that we had to accept his interpretations! It was so frustrating! Yet after the class, several people told me they liked my questions even though in class I felt completely isolated by my position. No one else seemed to support or hold it.

Moved to tears, Susan continued talking about how class situations often silenced her. As she related other incidents, WARP members validated her experience by recounting experiences of their own and began a problem-solving conversation about strategies for coping with difficult classes. After this session Susan became more vocal in WARP; she became something of a rabble-rouser in class; and she started exploring more deeply her self-perceptions and her abilities, both privately and in WARP.

Susan's investigations into her experience of being silenced culminated in the spring session that she co-led. Having decided to explore the issue of leadership rather than confining her discussion to broad theoretical terms, Susan chose to investigate leadership primarily in terms of her own leadership abilities or the lack thereof. In her paper she names many qualities that she believes a "leader" should have, and then proceeds to reject many of those qualities as they relate to her—a process that leads to self-doubt but a process that also feels right to her. Susan dialogues with herself, taking both sides of her position and essentially deconstructing the model of "leader" dominant in contemporary culture: "Leadership in our society is associated with power and control. . . . My biggest conflict is that I feel the traditional leader does things that I want to avoid, like telling others what to do and imposing his or her own vision of things on others. I would prefer to be someone who creates connections between people and groups, and helps people understand each other. Maybe I don't want to be a leader after all and once I come to terms with that, I will be a much happier person."

As the group began to elaborate ideas of leadership, Susan consistently applied her theoretical concerns to her own campus activities:

SUSAN: [In my coed fraternity] our motto is friendship, leadership, and service; and that's everywhere I go. It's like why aren't you a leader, why aren't you anything. . . . Applications—every application I write asks what leadership positions I've had, and I'm like, hmm, well, nothing. I've only been in 500 organizations that I didn't really get involved in; or I spent all my time doing my thesis and not being a leader, you know? I feel I'm not doing what the culture values, and so in a way, I guess I'm saying that I feel like I should be doing it and I know that it's what the culture values and I'm not even rejecting that. I'm saying, why can't I be that way.

AMY: Don't you think, after that whole essay, you came to the conclusion that you were just redefining leadership for yourself, that you were a leader in your own terms?

SUSAN: What I realized after I wrote it . . . is that leadership involves other people, so if I'm only changing myself, that's not really leadership, that's only me. Leadership means getting other people to go along with you, that's the way I see it, or getting people to agree with you to do things. I don't know. . . .

Group members questioned Susan's contention in her essay that "leaders possess some kind of intangible quality that makes people listen to them and follow them and respect them." Several proposed that often the people who "lead" a group are not the ones who accomplish things. Judy recounted a conversation with an eighty-six-year-old woman whom she had interviewed for a class assignment:

> She was saying [that] the people she respected most throughout her entire life are the people who have set examples by their lives rather than by what they tell people to do in their lives. So, anyway, what I was about to say is that a lot of times watching you [Susan] change, I think, can and will alter the people around you. And it's certainly shaped some of us, I'm sure. . . . But, I mean, it's neat to see how, just by the way you can change you can really [change people]—in ways people can never even ever tell you that you've touched them, but there are probably certain things that you've done by watching yourself change and spending time thinking and growing.

Judy's story led the group to distinguish between influence and leadership—what the group valued versus the scorn with which contemporary culture treats alternative definitions of leadership:

> LESLIE: One of the things in [the article that Susan brought in for discussion] that was really illuminating to me was the distinction between a star and a leader, and how so often media or other people pick up on star quality, and that's somehow who gets turned into a leader . . . [not the people] who are actually doing the work and exerting the most influence. . . .
>
> SUSAN: I was frustrated with the fact that I don't even seek leadership like that, I really avoided it until recently. And when I got a taste of it, it was hard to deal with. So what you're saying is the reason I avoided it is not because I'm just weak or passive, but because I just don't agree with what it is doing. . . .
>
> LAURA: It doesn't seem like you have time to be a "leader" and to pursue all your interesting, introspective [analyses], deciding how things work. It seems you value the other more. . . .
>
> SALLY: Maybe you need someone to tell you it's okay, that's great.
>
> ANNE: Absolutely—I'm a behind-the-scenes leader for a group; it's really tough. I really want to say, "Hey, look at what I've done, look!"— everyone else does, you know, "She leads the meetings, she does whatever," it's really frustrating. . . .
>
> JEAN: In fact, you said [in your essay], Susan, which I thought was fascinating, "It sounds like I should be a diplomat and not a leader," and I

circled that. A diplomat is a leader—that's amazing leadership. We need much more of that than we have.

Susan already knew what she did not yet believe: she needed to practice voicing what she did believe. Like an athlete warming up her muscles or practicing for an upcoming game, Susan used the WARP space as a practice field to try out new strategies and different maneuvers, pushing her limits in this safe space before using her skills in a game whose stakes were higher. Through this practice of working with her limits, Susan learned to stretch her limits—until they no longer held her back.

Just as there were stories of individual growth, there were instances in which the group reworked certain themes to the point of greater ease if not resolution. One such theme—the body, women's bodies, and the relationship between women and their bodies—came up repeatedly. As Elaine wrote in her final paper for the fall, "How are we perceived, who is defining us, why is image so important in women's experiences? How do our bodies relate to our varying roles in society? The human body defines social boundaries. It reflects the fundamental relationship all humans have to one another—although as the most private and individual aspect of ourselves, the body is also common to all people. Everyone has one. And yet women's bodies take on special significance."

Many group members located their first encounter with this theme at the time of puberty; hand-in-hand with their developing bodies grew feelings of separation and discomfort:

> SUSAN: I have often wondered how the physical changes during puberty relate to the girls' psychological crisis that Gilligan talks about, because I feel that a lot changed for me after that point, especially the onset of menstruation, a topic which I am uncomfortable bringing up in public, even just with other women. Somehow my relationship to my body changed, and this body became something that I could hardly escape or control. . . .

> AMY: I remember hating the fact that I was a girl. I didn't want to feel bad about crying. I didn't want the most noticeable thing about me to be whether or not I had breasts yet.

Many spoke about the gap between cultural standards for ideal feminine appearance and their own ideas about themselves:

> AMY: I both want to be beautiful but at the same time when I do put myself in a tight skirt and guys respond sexually I feel like punching them.

It feels good when I think that I look good but it feels bad when guys never appreciate my beauty that is a part of me. They see it as a thing that is outside of me, something that is theirs to have.

MARY: I cut my hair and people reacted strongly. They would say, "Oh, my God, she went to Howard . . . now you are this radical African American feminist. . . ." Other people would say, "Now that you are taking Women's Studies, you don't have to wear nail polish or lipstick," or "You are supposed to do this or that. . . ." They make you wonder: is this what they are trying to get me to buy into and is it only a matter of time before I stop wearing lipstick and stop doing things that I think are a part of me?

Interwoven with concerns about physical appearance were fears about vulnerability of women's bodies, fears that contradict ideas about their own autonomy:

LESLIE: This morning I walked into the gym, a few paces behind a male peer. I stared at the back of his T-shirt, a caricature of a goofy blonde in a pink bikini, spread-eagle. In between her legs were two beer cans. In equally goofy print was sprawled the following ever-so-clever slogan: "A beer in the hand is better than two in the bush." Ha, ha. Sort of like "Ten reasons a beer is better than a woman." Offensive on so many levels that it leaves a woman speechless. And actionless.

ANNE: When I was a sophomore, one of my closest friends was raped. . . . She expressed to me that she felt as if her rapist had taken something from her that she could never recover. I too felt as if something was missing from my life. I realize now that what he took, at least from me, was a sense of the sanctity of my body and my control over it; what he took from her was a sense of security in herself and her judgment. The fact that this man could do something like this to a person I completely respected and knew had good judgment and morals made me feel very vulnerable and weak.

Several group members connected their concerns with physical safety and appearance to their difficulty in negotiating emotions, insofar as emotions are strongly associated with women's bodies in a culture where emotional expression is devalued, if not completely denied. Anne observed:

Where does emotion come in? Is it just a waste of energy for me to be incredibly angry and upset when I think of how limited my life is by the threat of violence? [My friends] seem to think so; you can change the world without being angry and wasting your energy on that, they say.

Well, when can you be angry? When is it not a waste of time? Where can you find people who are just as angry and willing to act on feeling and not just the cold rationality of, "That's just the way it is." . . . Am I wasting my time being angry, or is the fact that I even question my right to be angry just another form of societal conditioning that women experience?

Elaine described her feelings this way:

The fact that I am writing this paper indicates just how far the walls have crumbled. In a way, two walls have started to fall: the outside one, which invalidated the way I thought to others, and the inner, deeply rooted one, which separated my emotions from my intelligence. I can no longer maintain the pseudo-objective distance from myself and what I am learning, although it has been the basis of structured learning for centuries. It has taken conscious effort to put "I" back into my writing after being told for years and years that "one doesn't do that." How does a lack of identification with what I write make the words any more weighty or true?

Named throughout the fall, these questions about sexuality, physical appearance, and emotions came together in a discussion led by Mary and Amy. Through the process of discussing their materials, the group began to pull together a complex of ideas with which participants had struggled all year, if not all our lives.

The significance of talk, its location (where talk occurs), and the way participants talk with one another were further clarified during this session. While the participants' words can be transferred from transcripts and essays, the emotion and inflection that accompanied the actual speaking of the words, along with body language, escapes translation. In attempting to speak about women's bodies, the participants' feelings carry as much meaning as their words. In this context, what is left unsaid is as important as what is actually voiced. Recognizing this, the group's response to Amy's readings signals important dynamics at work. Amy introduced her material this way:

Women are not allowed to be fully expressive. I am not allowed to be fully expressive, in a sexual or affectionate way, because it is going to be read in a way that will be detrimental to me. That is sexual violence. Women cannot be who they are because you always have to think of yourself in context to men. You always have to think of yourself as violatable in every situation. . . . It is ingrained in me: how I am vulnerable, how can I counter being vulnerable? If he attacked me, what would I do? Any guy that I have ever been alone with, I have had that thought.

The conversation took a somber note as one or two group members started to talk about their own feelings of vulnerability. With just a few comments offered, the subject was changed, significantly, to whether one could switch out of a female identity. In Laura's words, "But you can't code switch out of being a woman." Amy responded, "I am irked because there is an inclination to want to switch out of being the expressive female I want to be."

As we reread the transcript and remembered the session, it seemed clear that trying to talk about how sexual violence impacts women's lives was too much—too big, too threatening, too confusing. We as a group did not have a language in which to speak about our concerns and our fears or how we felt about them. Nor did we name our lack. By moving on to another subject, the group dynamic illustrated just how challenging it was to talk about subjects that were deeply felt, yet simultaneously how crucial such exchange is for deeper understanding and, ultimately, change.

The discussion on female identify continued with several group members' observations on the connections between being female and being emotionally expressive and the way it often interfered with communicating ideas:

> JUDY: You can't be emotional and talk about what you want to talk about in class. The statistics professor cannot relate when I say that test scores cannot clearly reflect grades—"That is the only standard measurement," they say. It is frustrating because the class thinks I am emotional. . . . It's when I feel I have an articulate way to express my views that I'll go for it, when I think it will be accepted by a couple of people in the class.

> LAURA: This reminds me that I also don't try to do anything unless I have a well-articulated way to back it up. . . . I don't feel comfortable saying, "I think there's something wrong with that. I can't quite figure out what it is. Just let me talk for a few minutes and I will figure it out." . . . If you are trying to impress a hostile group of people with your argument, [going on feelings] won't work. It's on their terms, we have to have a rational, well-thought-out argument to lay on the table. You don't let anyone see the process of it. You don't use your intuition.

We began to make more explicit connections between talking and emotion as well as our lack of practice in expressing our emotions through speaking. But it took Mary's presentation to bring our bodies back into the conversation and to begin to link the three corners of the triangle: bodies, emotions, and talk. Mary's essay and readings focused on the relationships between caring for one's body and caring for one's self. One of her selections, an article entitled "Heavy Burden," included this passage:

If the body is a metaphor on some level, and if we often express physically what we can't or won't express in other ways, then it is no wonder that an estimated 35 percent of Black women between the ages of 22 and 44, and half of us between 44 and 55, weigh more than the charts say we should. When you consider how many Black women are raising children alone and how gleefully social commentators lay every problem Black children have at the feet of their drained and exhausted mothers; when you think about the disproportionate number of us who are poor and have no idea about what having enough means, you begin to get a sense of the emotional weight we carry.[3]

Mary linked this article to her own life and the tensions she felt between caring for herself and taking care of everyone and everything else. Ignoring her own body and herself had become an issue:

How do you go out into the world without losing all of those changes you made for yourself? . . . The first time I read this article it really spoke to me because, with all of my courses in Women's Studies, I've never really spoken about body image and the impact that it has had on me. . . . For the first time I felt comfortable, like I was in control of myself and any changes I wanted to make in myself were not driven by these outside factors. . . . I think that everyone feels this way, but I don't know how you actually stop the clock from running and say, I can't go on this way, making all these meetings and doing all these papers, and chugging away without doing this for myself first. You feel that there are so many things that you could be doing for yourself. I found myself constantly de-prioritizing myself. . . . I constantly live in order to prevent failure, rather than provide for success.

As she continued, Mary shared how she had been doing more things for herself, taking time out to relax, to exercise, and to think more about her feelings about her body. In talking about her own process, Mary explicitly linked bodily well-being with emotional well-being. This link is significant if only for its implications for the fragility of women's emotional health when it is dependent upon a standard of bodily appearance that is, for most women, unachievable. Mary continued, making the final link to talk:

It has always been very strange for me that, in all of my friendships and relationships with people, when it came to body image, it's like fat is a bad word [that] is never said. "So, you are Mary, you are not a body," which is how it should be in a relationship. . . . When it does become an issue, then they say, "Oh, Mary, what are you talking about?" You have to stop them and say, "Look, I know that you see me as a person and I appreciate that, but also realize certain limitations." . . . I have never been able to talk about how these things have made me feel. They [friends] see the outward manifestations of what I go through, but they don't see the thoughts at all because for me it's very painful to get those thoughts out there when they make other people uncomfortable or make them have to deal with or think about something they don't necessarily want to.

In sharing her experiences, Mary identified talk as the connecting link between the body and emotion by describing the difficulty of talking about her feelings about her body. If the only acceptable way for women to talk is without emotion, and if thoughts about our bodies are deeply tied to emotions, then how are women supposed to begin talking about their bodies? And without talking about our bodies, how can women begin to explore and challenge the standards we set for our bodies and ourselves? In telling how her friends' discomfort with talking about how being heavy affected her life, Mary called attention to the remarkable lack of practice that we, as women, have in talking honestly with each other about how our bodies affect our feelings about ourselves and about each other. The discussion continued as other group members began to pull these ideas together, adding their own perspectives, and, most important, their thoughts about their bodies:

AMY: My roommate came home from jogging one day, panting and out of breath. I said, "I love the feeling of sweat, when your heart is pounding." She turned to me and said, "I am just trying to get in shape for bikini season." I was not even thinking about bikini season. I feel like such an inept woman.

ELAINE: My time is completely ruined when I swim or run less than what I am told is a productive workout, even when all I really want to do is swim or run for pleasure.

LAURA: In my kayaking class there are many fewer women than men, and a man said that women don't like to take classes which require them to wear a bathing suit. When I asked a friend what she thought, she said that I didn't have anything to worry about, but she was uncomfortable with her weight gain since Christmas. This is someone I would describe as almost skinny. I told her that I thought she was practically underweight and it was really weird. I wasn't fishing for a compliment.

VIVIAN: We could do at least two sessions talking just about body image.

This session synthesized numerous questions that had come up during the year about women and their bodies. Yet the course of the session made it clear that the group was tackling issues far too complex to be resolved in a ninety-minute session over coffee and bagels. For the most part, members thrived on the complexity, on taking the questions apart and opening them up for a deeper level of questioning. Yet from time to time we would find that the questions did not feel like adequate answers—not when we so deeply wanted resolutions.

Because the spring sessions took their issues from the lives of the participants, they were prone to evoke more dissatisfaction than those in the fall. Rather than bringing new interpretations to past occurrences, participants were opening new windows in the spring. They were asking questions that looked toward their futures. More was at stake, precisely because less was known. What WARP offered and created were not tools or skills to meet these questions. Rather, WARP gave members—both as individuals and as part of a collective entity—space in which to practice using the abilities they already had; safe space in which to learn to trust the knowledge they already carried; and space in which they could prepare to think and to act with an assurance capacious enough to embrace ambiguity and complexity.

Rethinking Teaching and Learning

The "We-They" Dichotomy

The last five years have led me to begin thinking more systematically about how we teach, how students learn, and how these two processes might relate. I once thought teaching "caused" learning. They, the students, responded if I, the teacher, knew a lot and presented it well; all I needed was for students to provide attention and respect. In this way of understanding the educational process, teachers and students play different and separate parts. I never thought to ponder the relationship between teachers and students any further.

At least not until my older daughter entered college in 1986; she spurred me to look at teaching and learning differently. These personal explorations coincided with the maturing of women's studies and the renewal of national debates about education. Longing for a place to explore the issues I was turning over in my mind, I set up a faculty workshop on gender and curriculum transformation. For me the workshop launched an ongoing odyssey into thinking about the cultures of teaching and learning. This essay maps out the spaces I have created, within the university where I work as well as within myself, to engage these questions. I know teaching has become more challenging and intriguing to me. I think learning is becoming more meaningful for my students. And I am sure that rethinking the relationship between teaching and learning is a particularly promising way to address a dichotomy that I now see as highly problematic, the "we-they" mentality.

Recognizing the Need for a Place

I began teaching the summer after my first year of graduate school at one of the regional centers of Purdue University. From that first 1965 survey in international relations to my current courses in women's studies and political science, I talked with colleagues and swapped impressions of students. I listened to students report on good classes, picking up techniques from their descriptions. I kept up with the literature, redesigning courses to take advantage of new information and ways of presenting it. I wrote elaborate syllabi, anxious for students to know the class expectations. I allowed ample time for discussion, even in lecture classes, knowing that processing information is an effective way to retain it. Over the years, I included personal experiences as concrete illustrations for theoretical points. I did all of these things from the point of view of the teacher who wanted to do a good, professional job. I assumed I knew them, "the students." It never occurred to me to conceptualize students as other than recipients of what I taught.

Then our older daughter entered Duke as a first-year student. At first, I did not imagine that her matriculation would affect me much. I did, however, think that my understanding of the university and its students might help her negotiate college. Over the years students had often told me that I was one of the faculty who understood them and to whom they turned for counsel on matters both personal and academic. What my daughter taught me long before she finished her first class was that students inhabited their own campus world, a world that differed significantly from mine. Shocked, I listened as she described what she did and saw and learned, in the very same places that I worked and taught. And I realized the boundaries of my perspectives.

During that first year, I was alarmed for her safety as I dropped her off at her dark dormitory parking lot. She pointed out lots of people she knew, coming and going; according to her, people were just starting to come out around midnight. I had never been on campus past midnight on a weekday night. The quad was more crowded than at noon and that fact shocked me. What were they doing? How could so much university life be going on without the faculty? When I expressed frustration because her sociology class on juvenile delinquency never mentioned women, she said that was just the way sociology was and I should get over it. From her first-year perspective, women's absence did not matter. I listened to her rank her classes, assessing those in which she would make an effort because she liked them and those classes which she would fit in if she had time. What motivated her to work on a course? As she described a teacher's lecture and then analyzed its contents, I tried to grasp why some topics stuck with her while she deemed others irrelevant.

Was my daughter typical? Listening to her friends with fascination and frustration, I came to understand that deciding whether my daughter was typical or atypical of college students was not an important question. What was important to realize was that after twenty years of teaching and literally thousands of conversations with undergraduate, graduate, and returning students, I knew relatively little about student life outside the classroom—at least beyond stereotypes. I certainly had not given much thought to how the campus experiences of other than older, returning students might influence what happened inside the classroom. I had not questioned whether what I was offering in the classroom by way of data and explanatory frameworks provided the tools for students to negotiate campus life. For all the talk of multiculturalism and teaching to diversity, just how a student's identity might interface with his or her learning in a particular class never surfaced as a question to explore. My Quaker background told me that living and learning were connected, but I had never tried to figure out the connections, much less apply them to what I was doing.

Thinking about these connections made me anxious. Should I just stop thinking about them, seeing myself as an overinvolved parent who was also a professor? I didn't think so. Was I approaching a taboo embedded in my training, my situation, and my position—a taboo I had never explored or confronted, indeed barely recognized? It seemed I was. Should I follow my experience as a parent, thinking about students as developing human beings and considering what might influence them? Or should I simply remain the professor who knows a lot and tells students what they should know?

Talking to colleagues increased my anxiety. Many dismissed my queries with flip remarks. Admissions rhetoric aside, institutions like this are not interested in teaching. Students are all alike—grade-grubbing careerists. Some denied the validity of the question; they claimed to know as teachers how to get students to pay attention in class, on a test, with an assignment; others said that while most students goof off, you occasionally get a really good one who makes it all worthwhile. Faculty consensus held that thinking about teaching gets you nowhere professionally and, in any case, that the few exceptional students are rewarding enough to foreclose any further thinking. One of my independent study students conducted interviews with the faculty who had taught her during her four years and asked them about the student-teacher relationship. While the answers varied with age, sex, and involvement in Women's Studies, the overwhelming response was that they had not given the relationship much thought.

At the same time I was experiencing these two Dukes and worrying about the differences between them, I was following the evolution of curriculum transformation projects nationally as well as experimenting on campus with other project approaches, as described in Chapter 10. The establishment of feminist scholarship and the growth of programs in the 1970s brought an emphasis in the 1980s to the conditions under which the new scholarship made its way into the university's curriculum. While projects stressed content, they always dealt with pedagogy, stressing the importance of alternatives to hierarchical teaching styles in order to include all learners. Funded by both foundations and university administrations, curriculum transformation projects introduced the new research to faculty, hoping to encourage the development of new courses and the revision of ongoing ones as well as experimentation with pedagogies.

The more reports I read and discussions I had, the more I reflected on what students said about gender in the classroom and the more certain I became that curriculum transformation involves much more than just teachers delivering new content in warmer classroom climates. The students in the introductory Women's Studies course taught me that they are keenly aware of the positions of men and women in contemporary society, both from their own experiences and from what they were (and were not) told in classes. They turned to me and my colleagues for explanations of why things were that way, how these arrangements came to be, and what they could do about them. As the essays in Part 3 indicated, I began investigating students' ideas. These investigations, combined with the teacher-centered discourse of the literature on curriculum transformation and frequent conversations with my daughter, pushed me to question further whether the ways in which teachers were accustomed to conveying ideas about gender in the classroom might well differ substantially from how students might best hear them.

How does what I do as a teacher relate to my administrative projects on curriculum transformation? How do students understand classroom gender dynamics? How does their understanding differ from mine? How do they play into teaching and learning more generally? What could I do as a teacher to connect a body of literature to their experiences? What could I do as an administrator to initiate conversations about how gender and curriculum transformation were intertwined?

These questions about gender and curriculum transformation led me to think about teaching and learning more generally. While I believed myself sympathetic to students' points of view, I had never systematically analyzed their perspectives beyond the needs of an individual student or of a given class. Placing student ideas next to faculty classroom practices in order to build connections between the two was a new step for me. What did the university look like to students? How did they characterize their learning experiences there? How could faculty members investigate these questions? How might teaching and learning change in light of such investigations?

Yet another independent-study student pushed me along. For her project she was recording her every move—"one day in the life of a college student." I read hundreds of pages; she was one of the university's merit scholars with high grades; and there was hardly ever any thinking devoted to her classes. She went to class but never reflected on what happened there. Instead, her thoughts focused on everything else in her life—family, friends, the future, world issues, her job, what she ate, arts and cultural events she attended, and so on. No matter how hard I pressed, she assured me that thinking about issues came only from some classes, usually Women's Studies classes, and that this semester, as she fulfilled her major in philosophy requirements, she wasn't wasting her time thinking about class when there was so much else to think about.

In the midst of these personal reflections, the national debates about the problems of the U.S. educational system heated up. As I listened to the many sides, I was struck again with its teacher-centered rhetoric. Scholars and pundits on every side pronounced that they knew what should be done—because they were scholarly experts in the field, because this way of doing things had worked for them personally, and because there was a traditional way to proceed that had stood the test of time. In all of the discussions, no one ever talked about students or inquired into their points of view. In these debates students functioned as a site for the assertion of power, just as women, people of color, and other marginalized groups have traditionally functioned in other public debates. If the current system of power was to continue, students needed to be muted. Yet I knew from my daughter's frequent comments delivered over folding laundry, walking the dog, and eating dinner that she and her fellow students enthusiastically discussed these very issues. As I record in earlier chapters, students greeted with interest my initial forays into investigating their ideas.

Having begun to hear student voices, I longed for a place where I could explore the questions and interconnections their words brought to light. I wanted a place for thinking rather than producing a report or designing a project. I had been in too many committee meetings where faculty made quick pronouncements about what "they," the students, did and thought, without any data and without mediating their personal experiences with reflection. The predominance of these stereotypes made it clear that faculty needed to think about these issues before attempting to formulate links between feminist scholarship, curriculum transformation, and teachers' concepts of students both in and out of the classroom.

As I pursued these ideas, a few other colleagues, along with the Women's Studies staff, became intrigued. Suppose, we asked ourselves, we invite others interested in Women's Studies to gather and look at the process of curriculum transformation on women and gender from a student-centered perspective?

What do we know already among ourselves? What do we need to learn? How would we go about such a project? And what difference would our doing so make to us as teachers and to our students? Excited, we decided to use our curriculum transformation resources to create such a space for faculty dialogue, offering a $500 honorarium for participation in a collaborative workshop rather than expending those funds on a single, conventional, individual award.

Creating a Space for Faculty Dialogue

Together with faculty colleague Wendy Luttrell, who specializes in the ethnography of education and gender, we planned a workshop that would model participatory learning and student-centered teaching. In September 1990, Women's Studies invited faculty in the undergraduate college of the university to join a workshop on gender and curriculum transformation.

Ten faculty members responded; two were male, eight female; they came from eight separate departments and programs in the humanities and social sciences; one of the men and one of the women had had no previous affiliation with the program. All ten enthusiastically welcomed the opportunity to explore gender, curriculum transformation, and teaching and learning with colleagues. The group began meeting monthly in October. While other responsibilities have caused some dropouts, eight of us have been meeting for three years and plan to continue as long as the process engages us. The eight are all women, a fact we have pondered many times.

The workshop set out to explore a model of teaching and learning that contrasts with traditional, hierarchical approaches that view teachers as singular, authoritative experts who transfer information to students. The workshop's model also differs from the therapeutic model so popular in the 1960s, which understood teaching and learning styles as extensions and explorations of the self. Nor does this model highlight techniques of presentation and discussion that teachers can imitate by watching "masters." Unlike critical pedagogy, the workshop deals with the mundane and practical issues of how bodies, minds, and emotions work in the process of learning rather than theorizing how social systems operate through teaching.

With the possible exception of critical pedagogy, all of these other models assume a dichotomy between self and others, we and they, teachers and students, in order to structure teaching and learning. In contrast, the workshop explores an alternate model that is student-centered, participatory, and collaborative. In order to do that, the workshop itself had to become more fully participatory and collaborative, a place in which faculty became "students."

Wendy and I designed the workshop to cross disciplinary and philosophical backgrounds, hoping thereby to enable faculty members to map out both the shared and the distinct view of teaching and learning that each participant brought to the workshop. Before every session, each participant wrote and distributed to the group an essay that addressed aspects of our own teaching and learning models, beliefs, values, and experiences. Workshop members wanted to begin by identifying and questioning the assumptions about students, classroom dynamics, and campus life embedded in each participant's routine practices and beliefs. We grappled with how to best characterize what we do in the classroom; we examined the ways our teaching and curriculum enhance or mask what students already know, particularly in terms of gender relations.

As the first year drew to a close, the model of collaborative learning with which the workshop was experimenting took on a life of its own. The group no longer relied on the direction provided by Wendy and me; rather, members of the group began to identify together those themes that emerged in our work and took responsibility for implementing monthly assignments and discussions. Throughout the second year, we collected interview material about what and how undergraduates understand their learning experiences. We continued to scrutinize our teaching practices, including experiments that some participants had initiated as a result of the workshop. In the third year, the group turned to the research literature on classroom gender dynamics and higher education to clarify and contextualize some of the issues that had emerged. We interviewed campus administrators charged with oversight of these issues and sought common ground. We made plans to write up our process and our findings. And we continue to revise our own pedagogical views and practices.

The insights of the workshop play in my head each day. Because the project is ongoing and we have yet to fully "go public," I have no sense of closure, of ultimate findings, of impact. Yet I do have a very strong sense that if connections are going to be made between what I am teaching and what students are learning, I have to know much more about the students themselves. While I do not need to become a campus-culture expert who provides a feminist critique for students, I do need to know that the campus is filled with encounters that shape how we will understand the material we are studying as well as the assumptions we make about it. I do not need to know the individual biography and current condition of every student; I do need to know that we each bring lives to campus that influence the connections we make. Rather than seeking a single template that will map out student lives and their learning style either for them or for me, I have begun taking steps toward building learning connections in the classroom.

Collaboration in the Classroom

Step One: Building Links

The first specific step I took as a result of being in the workshop was to explicitly and routinely link classroom material with student experiences outside the classroom. I thought I always did this in a general way. The workshop caused me to do so deliberately. My clearest example comes from the senior seminar in political science that I teach. The class is designed for majors to investigate an issue in political science that they have not studied at the introductory or intermediate levels. I title the seminar Contemporary American Feminism; we cover suffrage as a social movement, the rise of contemporary feminism, women and public policies, and theory on women and the state in varying degrees. But we begin in a very personal place.

In the second class, after the students have read a little about the history of women in politics, I ask each one to recount the first time that they remember making a link between women and politics. The range of responses is fascinating. Many women remember class elections in the fourth or fifth grade and debates among their peers about whether or not girls could be president. Students of both sexes recall parental conversations around national issues like the ERA, abortion, affirmative action episodes, inclusive language discussions in church, and so on. They remember trying to comprehend why their mothers and fathers took the sides they did and what it meant. Other students are quite forthright in their responses: they had never linked the subjects until they walked into this class, which they were taking to fulfill graduation requirements. Still others remember a friend or family member telling them to pay attention to something that was happening (Geraldine Ferraro's nomination as vice-president is frequently mentioned) and wondering what the big deal was.

As we go along, I add my own memories, memories grounded in the generation of their parents. Many ask their parents in their periodic calls home for additional perspectives on the issues being discussed in class. Comparing different generations as well as different experiences proves a rich source of information as the semester proceeds. Students who have strong early memories are astounded by the absence of those memories among others and vice versa. Differences in exposure to politics and to gender issues fascinate students: why is this what I know and you know something so different? they ask each other.

We do not leave the discussion at an exchange of personal circumstances; we read history, theory, policy analysis, and accounts of electoral behavior. As we read these analytic frameworks throughout the semester, we come back to these stories, using them to reflect on personal experiences. Through these stories we ask ourselves, what causes ideas to become popular? how do people take in an idea? and how do people's ideas make a difference in the actions they take? By locating themselves within the larger process of analyzing women in politics, the students in these seminars link the lessons they are learning with the questions they are asking about themselves, their worlds, and their perspectives. I would argue that we are not just bringing material from outside the classroom into it but that we are working the other side of the street—developing frameworks in the classroom that explain some aspects of gender and politics that we meet in the course of our daily activities.

Step Two: Encouraging Collaboration

As I look back on my two decades of teaching, I see that I always encouraged questions about the specifics of the material at hand. I was eager to say a bit more about the subject. Yet when the questions got too far outside the material I was presenting, rather than make connections, I drew boundaries, suggesting we get back to the topic at hand. Most significant, I answered most of the questions. Only rarely did I involve other class members in giving responses.

One semester, while I was in the workshop, I found myself unable to answer the questions being raised in the seminar. The conversations with my colleagues enabled me to approach this dilemma from another direction: why did I think I was solely responsible for all the information that was going to be made available to the students? because I was the expert, the teacher? What we were learning together was beyond my specific expertise. Unless I pulled all of us in, no one, including myself, was going to learn what we needed. With these reflections, I took a second step. In order to build connections, I must not merely acknowledge that teaching and learning are intertwined, I must intervene to further interweave those connections.

The specific situation was problematic. In the seminar of sixteen on contemporary American feminism, there were three African American women, all with a long history of involvement in the political struggles over race and gender, stretching back into their families. Kelly, the most knowledgeable, was doing a senior independent research project on her grandmother, a leader in the movement for women's education from the 1930s on. The class also had two highly vocal white conservative men: Stan was deeply involved in the student organization for the reelection campaign of Jesse Helms, the conservative senator from North Carolina; Matt headed up the Campus Crusade for Christ and had been selected as a missionary to the then Soviet Union after graduation. I am neither a third-generation college-educated African American woman with a history of political struggle, nor a conservative white man believing strongly in the abstract causes espoused by national organizations. As a student of such movements, I can do a great deal to contextualize both developments. But alone I could neither take the discussion and analysis to the level the students needed nor fully explore the questions they were posing about why people identified one way or another in politics.

In the first few class sessions, the differences among these two sets of students began to divide the class. I would respond to questions and comments but felt more and more out of my depth because I did not know how to push the discussion forward as the classroom dynamics pulled us into separate corners. Simply getting the principals to more fully articulate their positions and confront each other did not strike me as productive from what I had seen thus far. So I divided the class into working groups of four, giving them issues from the readings and our previous debates for deliberation. I was careful to see that each group contained a mixture of positions. For several class sessions we devoted some time to the four-person format and some time to our entire group. From time to time I rearranged the class into different groups of four; at other times I let the students sort themselves out. I traveled from group to group, adding my voice as I thought necessary.

Around mid-semester the class dynamics changed. No longer were the books I had chosen and I the only sources of information. Others in the class drew on what they knew to become experts as well. Students would address questions to one another, offering additional detail in return. They would refer to each other's ideas as well as information from their own experiences for the full group to process. The project of learning about women and politics had been transformed from an abstract exercise that I had created with my background and my books into a collaborative enterprise about what we all knew and what we had to figure out.

At semester's end, when we read selections from Angela Davis's work, Kelly ventured that Davis's rhetorical style was similar to President Reagan's, producing comparable effects. Stan was able to hear the possibility and engage with Kelly in a thoughtful way. In addition, Matt and another woman in the class were taking a second class together and teamed up for a project on women in that class. They sought my help developing a research methodology to compare feminist and right-wing women for their project. Without having developed a history of learning from one another, the class could not have entertained such topics, much less productively discussed them with each other, reaching new levels of critical analysis, in this class and in others, as the result of collaborative effort.

Step Three: Dealing Directly with Power

Collaborative learning means that each one of us makes some contribution to what is becoming known. In order for such collaboration to occur, I as a teacher must contextualize my own expertise, acknowledging where my knowledge comes from and how what I know resonates with broader themes in my life and work. Collaboration in the classroom cannot succeed without this third step, by which we cross the boundaries of teacher-student relationships as we have inherited them in contemporary higher education. Dealing with power and knowledge differences directly creates a space in which all together reflect on their dynamics.

Somewhere along the line I grasped that, given our histories of schooling, I would be responsible for giving them permission to link their lives with their learning, a fusion students have typically been told to avoid. Again and again, students would ask: will it be objective if I tell what I think? how can I use the first person in my essay when all my English teachers have told me not to? how do I know that what I am thinking is worth reporting? don't I have to have statistics to show this is true? Again and again, I would explain that the process of creating knowledge, of knowing, is the process of investigating facts, beliefs, and ideas by putting those findings into an explanatory framework that makes sense. Making sense required putting themselves in the equation and saying where they stood. I was busy advocating that *they* do this. One day I realized this had to be a reciprocal process. I had the same responsibility to link my own learning and living.

This realization came as a shock. All of my training dictated that I should remove myself completely from what I did for and with students. Revealing who I was and how I had come to be that way would bias the material I was presenting, material that should stand no matter who presented it. Yet this inherited position contradicted the position I was coming to take about how students learn most effectively. And when I started listening, I realized that students were constantly asking of me just what I was asking of them. When, they asked, did I get into feminist scholarship? What, they wanted to know, fascinated me so much? Didn't I ever burn out? What did my parents, my husband, my daughters think? Did my work cause arguments? How did people respond to what I did? How did I think this was going to turn out—was the world really ever going to take feminism seriously?

With their questions, students were asking me to name the power dynamics in the classroom so that we could negotiate them directly. By not naming this discrepancy as an issue of power dynamics, I was denying that each one of us is constantly negotiating power "under the table." On the one hand, by keeping personal questions about me out of classroom discussion, I claimed the power to define what was allowed in the classroom. On the other hand, indulging in personal material exclusively or extensively asserts that I have no more or less power in the classroom than the students. Either extreme positioned me and my power in the same way. By arrogating power or ignoring its presence rather than discussing and negotiating it, I was leaving the students alone to figure out the power differentials that are always at work in any classroom and within the larger educational system. What a contradictory and irresponsible way to handle power if I sought to create a space conducive to building learning connections!

As I thought about why students persistently asked me personal questions, I came to understand that they grasp ideas more fully if they are aware of the context in which these ideas evolve. Moreover, it is dangerous, indeed wrong, to remove ideas from their context. A female teacher, a feminist teacher, is sufficiently different from the assumed norm of "teacher" to provoke such questions. This learning came in a painful moment. Like all marriages of almost thirty years, at times and on certain issues agreement is the norm; at other times and on other issues, we argue passionately. The decibel level at the dinner table was particularly high one season; my husband and I differed on several issues and we hammered away at them with regularity.

In the midst of that time, in a discussion of professional norms and the academy, one of the male graduate students reported that graduate students discussed our marriage regularly. Their consensus was that we made having two professional careers seem easy. I was flabbergasted. Having just come from a discussion better described as an argument with my husband, I knew that the balance between personal and professional was by no means "easy." Yet talking about how I balanced these relationships seemed to fall outside the bounds of student-teacher relationships. However, by never mentioning them, I was contributing to what I now learned some of my students called "the O'Barr myth." My silence rendered me complicit with a set of practices about how we know, practices that I profoundly and explicitly disagreed with. But how do I talk about these mutual responsibilities? If students learn by asking how people live with ideas, in what ways can I convey to them how I live with mine? I have no single, ready-made answer here other than to acknowledge that seeing a class as a community of learners depends on my assuming and participating in the activity I was advocating. My thinking comes out of my living as well as my reading and talking. Working the context of my ideas into my discussion of them is necessary if I am going to teach students to do the same.

On Sewing

Like any convert, I wanted to talk with colleagues about my new insights. Within the workshop space, it was easy and I found my ideas developing continuously there. But in other spaces and places, the full force of the "we-they" dichotomy hit me. The "we-they" dichotomy, as I conceptualize it, refers to the practice among faculty members of generalizing about students. Whenever faculty members gather, socially or in professional capacities, the conversation often turns to characterizations of students. Pronouncements flow readily. Students are always one undifferentiated clump. They are not highly motivated, except for grades. They certainly cannot write. The constant refrain of they, they, they echoes through the conversation. When one of these statements is challenged, speakers often retreat, saying, "Well, last semester I had one exceptional student who . . ." By making a point of the exception, the rule is reinscribed. All students do such and such. The exceptional one, the one who stands out and does differently, is remembered only to emphasize the general characterization.

Two aspects of what I have come to call "*they* conversation" bother me profoundly. One is obvious: the "we-they" dichotomy undercuts any possibility of collaborative learning. Yet collaborative learning is particularly important if we are to convey to this generation of students the experiences of women of earlier generations, for the recorded material on the topic falls far short of the task. Second, the "we-they" dichotomy assumes each group is homogeneous. Nothing could be farther from the truth. Much recent scholarship, often coming from feminist scholars as well as from those with a commitment to multicultural education, has emphasized the diverse backgrounds students bring to the classroom and the multiple ways in which people learn once there. There are many ways to process information; every individual follows combinations appropriate to them. I struggled for a long time with how to talk with colleagues when their conversations slipped into the "they" mode. It was here that my mother-of-the-bride experiences furthered my feminist work.

When my older daughter, whose story began this essay, announced her plans to marry in 1992, I found myself in an identity crisis. The director of Women's Studies becomes mother of the bride? How, I asked myself, was I going to cope with the details of contemporary American wedding culture, a culture based on practices and beliefs very different from my own? As the months passed, I learned to take wedding rituals one at a time—where did I want to take my stand? where could I let things go? and where was the process fun?

The clothes part turned out to be fun. I had grown up in a household where my mother sewed. I had learned from her. I enjoyed fabric, thought about structure and design, often browsed in fabric stores when visiting other cities. When we chanced on a local store where the owner made dresses at half the cost of ready-to-wear, I was pleased, and not just by the dollars saved. I got hooked into the old discourse about sewing. The dressmaker, my daughter, and I joined together in many a detailed conversation about fabric, fit, design. When friends heard me recount these conversations, I got strained reactions. Custom-made dresses belong to elites and past centuries. They are not something that directors of women's studies order, much less enjoy talking about.

I pondered this. Sewing is clearly not a common activity or metaphor in today's academic circles. It is associated with women of the past, and its salience has declined for a variety of sociological, historical, and economic reasons. Women, as well as men, now wear mass-produced clothes, manufactured according to standard sizes and designs. But only rarely does a ready-made item fit well. When something doesn't fit, the absence of information derived from sewing further confounds the problem, for we do not usually know what is wrong or how to fix it. As a culture, we accept the standard as normative and blame ourselves for having arms that are too long or shoulders that are too sloping. We do not demand that women's clothes come with varying sleeve lengths (as men's do), nor do most of us know how to shorten the sleeves. We just roll them up with each wearing and carry on.

The lessons taught by thinking about our experiences with standardized clothing and the lack of fit apply to thinking about teaching and learning. When the "*they* conversation" is launched, I am apt to ask whether the speaker's mother sewed. And where did your father get his clothes? Have you ever thought about the amazing assumption that the vast variation in bodies can be accommodated by ready-to-wear? What kinds of trouble do you have with standard sizes? Have you even considered the analogue to students—that every one is an individual in mind as well as body, struggling to fit into a standard size? What can be done about it? When my colleagues take up the analogy, a lively conversation ensues about assumptions, experiences, and possibilities. I sometimes get far enough into the conversation to suggest that women's perspectives on the cultures of teaching and learning, like their historical association with everyday sewing, give them an additional vantage point with which to view a cultural practice. And we always agree, together, that when something fits, the wearer is not only more comfortable but more confident—and hopes to get another just like it. Which is what we want to say about the students' experiences in our classes.

CHAPTER 17

Women's Studies
as a Discipline

T he Women's Studies Program at Duke is undertaking two curriculum reviews during 1992–93, the first since the program was founded a decade ago. At the undergraduate level, we are asking whether we should have a major in women's studies and, if so, what it should look like. Here we are responding to student demands for "more" as well as confronting very practical questions about how to enhance the status and impact of Women's Studies within the broader university. At the graduate level, we are pondering a series of questions raised by graduate students: how explicit should I be about my interest in women and gender when I formulate my dissertation? should I put women's studies on my vitae? should I mention it in my cover letter when applying for a position? should I seek a position jointly or fully in women's studies? Here we are thinking about how to prepare future faculty with both a disciplinary degree and an interdisciplinary focus. We are also conscious of the fact that the topics graduate students choose for their research is one of the prime ways in which the faculty encounter and engage new fields of inquiry. In negotiations with the dean for a second joint appointment between the program and a department, explaining women's studies arises yet again. In these contexts and others, I find myself asking just what it means to say women's studies is a discipline.

At the same time that Duke is going through this self-examination, research on women's studies as a field is emerging. The distinct impact that women's studies has on its students is becoming a subject of investigation. The Association of American Colleges recently completed an extensive study of college majors, the first such investigation since the major was instituted as the organizing principle in higher education a century ago. Women's studies was selected as one of the twelve majors studied. A series of books and reports have followed from that endeavor, including *The Courage to Question: Women's Studies and Student Learning, Liberal Learning and the Women's Studies Major,* and *Students at the Center.* New works are being published—examples include *Engaging Feminism,* which we edited here at Duke, and *Calling: Essays on Teaching in the Mother Tongue,* a book that many claim is the best writing on being female in the academy we have.[1]

Disciplines

An important distinction can be made between an administrative unit and the subject matter and methodologies of a field, although the two are usually used interchangeably. Thus, when we say *anthro,* we mean both the people clustered in the Social Science Building and the study of society and culture, in certain places, with certain methodologies. And, of course, the minute I give these two definitions, one thinks of people outside the Social Science Building who would be said to "do anthro," and one questions the way I defined what the people in the building do. So, while an administrative unit and a field of study are not the same thing, we tend to think a department is necessary in order to have a discipline and vice versa—a discipline requires a certain kind of structure. And sometimes in the politics of the academy, that's true.

By custom, we agree in general on what constitutes a field of inquiry. It has a subject matter and a research tradition that is manifest in books and journals; it is practiced by a set of people who say they specialize in it; and courses are taught and degrees offered in it. But when we get to specific cases, there is less agreement. Some fields are historically or politically important enough to be given a place at the academic table. Others are not. So while women's studies has attributes of a discipline, its specific historical and political characteristics prevent easy classification as one, a point elaborated below.

The origins of a discipline influence both how it operates and how it is perceived by itself and by others. Some fields are breakaways from older fields—psychology from moral philosophy, for example. Others are new candidates for inclusion—English literature in the 1920s. Disciplines overlap with one another—linguistics and anthropology, for example—although their origins and overlaps are rarely as complex as those of women's studies. And some disciplines, like cultural studies or African studies, deliberately set out to challenge disciplinary structures, as does women's studies.

A final point: the creation and workings of disciplines within the academy are not themselves the subject of extensive research. Thus, women's studies is rarely put in a comparative context. I doubt anyone has ever said, "Well, just like the introduction of computer science in the late 1950s, women's studies . . ." We know very little about what issues are faced by all new disciplines and what issues are distinctive to a discipline focused on women and gender. Nor do we know much about the relationship between seeking disciplinary status and having that status imposed on a field, between what the scholars in a field think would be the ideal case and what the political context of the time demands. And, finally, we have little experience asking how—and if and with what consequences—an interdisciplinary field is transformed into a discipline.

History

The history of women's studies sheds some interesting light on its characteristics as a discipline. Let me make a distinction between its institutional history and its conceptual travels, as is usually done when undertaking such an exercise. In a sentence, I would argue that institutionally women's studies has moved from confused to organized while just the opposite has occurred conceptually.

In the late 1960s, when the social movement known as the women's liberation movement demanded change for women, academics—students and faculty alike—responded by generating information and teaching courses. The courses were taught in any number of locations, from Y's to Ivy League schools; with any number of formats, from large lecture series to small consciousness-raising groups; to diverse student audiences, from reentry women to first-year undergraduates; and on every conceivable topic.

The chaos of those first years was evident in the responses to these initiatives. Administrators could not figure out what was going on, but they were pretty sure it was bad, on any number of dimensions. Faculty struggled with what to cover since the traditional resources for generating and organizing knowledge—graduate school training, books, experts—were absent. And students wanted everything about women explained, immediately.

Gradually, as campus after campus went through this process, the content of interdisciplinary courses offered through women's studies became somewhat standard. Research appeared in usable forms. A professional association emerged. And disciplinary courses joined interdisciplinary offerings to constitute programs. Majors followed in many places, especially the public institutions and the formerly all-male schools. In the 1980s other parts of the women's studies enterprise emerged—feminist research centers and curriculum transformation projects. Sometimes women's centers had preceded academic programs, others times followed, each always emphasizing the need for the other.

The program format we know at Duke is similar to what is found on some 650 other campuses. Programs most frequently call themselves Women's Studies, a designation that calls attention to the imbalance in power between men and women, but they describe themselves as working on women, gender, and feminist theory. And this organizational structure appears to work: students major in, faculty research and publish, and institutions are changed by the presence of feminist scholarship. According to some, it works too well, and women's studies has experienced some cultural backlash.

Conceptually the field of women's studies is much less tidy. In fact, many would claim it is downright messy. Some would say the mess is well deserved, the result of not really being a field. And others would acknowledge the mess and see it as the very sign of intellectual ferment. To me, the conceptual shift from simple to complex in the history of women's studies says a good deal about the field, its place in the academy, and its future.[2]

In the late 1960s and early 1970s feminist scholars argued that the disciplines ignored women as subject matter and as practitioners. They said that the frameworks then in place made it impossible to investigate women. And they concluded that the knowledge being produced was partial and therefore distorted and inadequate. This first round of scholarship was reformist and directed at the disciplines. The task was to add material about women. It revolved around the distinction between sex and gender. It looked primarily at male-female differences, at the patriarchal systems creating those differences, and at both the agency and the oppression that women experienced as a result of those systems. Women were the subject matter, and their subordination and shared experiences were the basis of investigations. The outpouring of empirical work was nothing short of extraordinary.

The more work that appeared on women in the disciplines, the more the basic category Woman disappeared. Pushed by developments in certain branches of theory in the humanities, the emphasis shifted to questions of epistemology. Women's studies scholarship became incredibly richer because scholars recognized and investigated the pervasive differences among women, while wondering what unified the field. It became increasingly clear that women's experiences of their bodies varied widely, that the nature and degree of their subordination did as well, and that the way in which women are symbolically represented in culture was an even more complex issue. Struggling with how to understand the effect of language and the place of individual personal experiences, women's studies scholars worked the ground between those practicing high theory and those demanding concrete social changes. The current challenge, as I see it, is twofold: to increase our research into, and appreciation of, the heterogeneity of women's experiences while keeping our focus on the shared nature of those experiences; and to work out the complex symbolic relationships between the representations of women in texts of every kind and the realities of women's daily lives in such a way that the multiple, and often conflicting, interconnections can be understood and addressed.

Contemporary feminist scholarship is clearly tackling these very questions, as indicated by the formulation developed by the Radcliffe consortium.[3] Scholars focus on how socially constructed systems of meaning work themselves out as they adopt cross-cultural perspectives on power and difference in a post-colonial world. Studies of race, racism, ethnicity, and difference; issues of conflict and violence; problems of connections and community; explorations of sexualities; and the policy implications of all these investigations constitute a research and teaching agenda that makes women's studies distinct. The conceptual core has become incredibly more complex and nuanced than it was three decades ago, a development that I would argue was made possible by its institutionalization. Thus, rather than seeing these two trends at cross-purposes, I see them as interdependent.

From Here?

What do we mean when we claim women's studies is a discipline? Do we want to make the claim? What's involved in doing so? Looking at the definitions of a discipline and reviewing the history of women's studies as an institutional and conceptual development, the clear answer is yes, women's studies is a distinct field of inquiry. And when I say that, I want to say, "Yes, but . . ." Why do I want to add the *yes, but*? Because I can play out all the responses the claim of disciplinary status usually evokes:

- Women's studies is young. New disciplines always have to justify themselves to themselves and to others—an exercise both invigorating and threatening. Recently, at a roundtable on introducing feminist scholarship into Russian studies, a colleague, Jehanne Gheith, posed a thoughtful query about her area: are we being defined by not knowing how to define ourselves? Does that apply to us in women's studies?
- Women remain "others," marginal to the society and culture at large in many ways. The status of the study of women reflects that same marginality. Can and should women's studies ever be just like other disciplines when women remain "others" socially?
- Women's studies is practiced primarily by women. Is this another aspect of marginality? How would its status differ if men undertook feminist scholarship?
- Women's studies insists on something that no other discipline does: it insists on being simultaneously on its own and in a position to critique others; it insists on its subject matter while pushing to have others adopt that subject matter. It is characterized by a critical and supportive

community that displays tenacity on questions of support for women's studies as a separate endeavor and commitment on questions of feminist curricular transformation in other disciplines. Other disciplines do not assume this dual focus as frequently or as forcefully.

- Women's studies is self-reflective, dealing continuously with the problem of destroying the master's house with the master's tools—and teaching students to worry about this problem too. Does moving into the mainstream mean that it will cease being reflective and concentrate instead on its own competitive position vis-à-vis other disciplines?
- Some claim that the feminist community surrounding women's studies is a moral community, a group of faculty and students united by a cluster of beliefs and committed to a set of goals. Is it? Should it be? Does it recognize itself as such? How does changing its status relate to its view of itself as a like-minded community?
- Women's studies openly identifies the political aspects of its own position, of its subject, and of the frameworks it uses to investigate that subject. It intends to change the world, or at least the part within its sphere. In all these ways, it goes against the grain of the status quo, bringing up for discussion the very issues of politics and power that the academy has customarily hidden. This is true both of the subjects studied and of the practices employed. Would women's studies lose its critical edge if it had the prerequisites of a department to protect?
- Women's studies does not just cause trouble in the academy. It takes the same issues and crosses the ivy boundaries into the communities where it is located, insisting that the relationship between theory and practice is at the center of all its concerns. How much of women's studies is defined by its extramural links?
- Women's studies is clear in its commitment to educate the whole person, to bring together mind and body, reason and emotion as interactive systems. Some educational reformers claim this is a direction for all teaching and learning efforts. What does women's studies have to offer other discourses in the academy? At what price to itself?
- And to top it off, the new research suggests that women's studies has a profound impact on students. Students seem to learn new things in women's studies classrooms, to talk about them outside class, and to translate their new frameworks into daily activities. And while such outcomes are the rhetorical ideal of a liberal arts education, they are sufficiently rare to be suspect, ridiculed, or admired, depending on the position of the respondent.

I'm tempted to conclude that women's studies is too different from other disciplines to be one—just exactly what a discipline ought to be. Women's studies seeks disciplinary status under some conditions—when resources are being allocated, for example. And it rejects being restricted by traditional disciplinary definitions under other conditions—when new subjects and methodologies are not pursued, for example. Which is where some of our students are, those who propel much of this enterprise. This is Katie Kent, a fifth-year English graduate student, a women's studies major from Williams, writing in *Engaging Feminism* on the subject:

> While, as in feminist politics, the eventual goal of women's studies would logically be its own demise (and this is my own standpoint on the issue), it could only end as a distinct discipline when women succeed in ending their own oppression (with the help of others of course). So, there is a need for both an autonomous women's studies program, and simultaneously there is a need to integrate it into all the disciplines. But what about the women who are coming up in the ranks, the students who want to get Ph.D.'s in women's studies, the many universities which may be on the important verge of making the important leap from the title "women's studies program" to "women's studies department," something which implies a whole new field of legitimacy since a department by definition implies disciplinary boundaries and methodologies, not to mention institutional legitimacy and full-time paid faculty members? But how many courses in "women's studies" should a student take? Again we come back to the point or characteristic of women's studies that is both its strength and its source of controversy, namely that its power comes from its many interdisciplinary perspectives. The fact that these perspectives are often in conflict, I would argue, as I did above, makes it even more powerful as it places much responsibility on individual students and/or scholars to make their own decisions as to which methodologies and ideological tenets they believe are the ones most satisfactory for their goals, beliefs, and selves.[4]

My conclusion: women's studies should continue to be *both* a discipline and an interdisciplinary field, working the rich ground between academic success and complacency, between knowing what we know and wondering what we need to know, between claiming an education for ourselves and demanding to be part of the education of others.

Introduction

1. Ann Curry, after-luncheon remarks, reprinted in *Women's Studies Newsletter*, Spring 1989.

2. I use three conventions in identifying students and colleagues in this collection: a general reference for brief mention; a fictitious name for students discussed in some detail; real names for those with a formal connection to the program.

3. Sheila Tobias, ed., *Female Studies I* (Pittsburgh: Know, 1970); Florence Howe, *Female Studies II* (Pittsburgh: Know, 1970); Florence Howe and Carol Ahlum, eds., *Female Studies III* (Pittsburgh: Know, 1971); Elaine Showalter and Carol Ohmann, eds., *Female Studies IV* (Pittsburgh: Know, 1971); Rae Lee Siporin, ed., *Female Studies V* (Pittsburgh: Know, 1972); Nancy Hoffman, Cynthia Secor, and Adrian Tinsley, eds., *Female Studies VI: Closer to the Ground—Women's Classes, Criticisms, Programs 1972* (Old Westbury, N.Y.: Feminist Press, 1973); Deborah S. Rosenfelt, ed., *Female Studies VII: Going Strong—New Courses, Old Programs* (Old Westbury, N.Y.: Feminist Press, 1973); Sarah Slavin Schramm, ed., *Female Studies VIII: Do-It-Yourself Women's Studies* (Pittsburgh: Know, 1975); Sidonie Cassirer, ed., *Female Studies IX: Teaching about Women in the Foreign Languages—French, Spanish, German, and Russian* (Pittsburgh: Know, 1976); Deborah S. Rosenfelt, ed., *Female Studies X: Learning to Speak—Student Work* (Old Westbury, N.Y.: Feminist Press, 1976).

4. Caryn McTighe Musil, ed., *The Courage to Question: Women's Studies and Student Learning* (Washington, D.C.: Association of American Colleges and National Women's Studies Association, 1992).

Chapter 1

1. Gail Sheehy, *Passages: Predictable Crises of Adult Life* (New York: Bantam, 1976).

2. David Demko, "Toward the Development of a Conceptual Framework of Educational Programming for the Older Population" (Paper presented to the Adult and Continuing Education—Education Gerontology Workshop, Ann Arbor, Michigan, April 15–16, 1977).

3. Helen S. Astin, ed., *Some Action of Her Own: The Adult Woman and Higher Education* (Lexington, Mass.: Lexington Books, 1976). See in particular Elizabeth Cless, "The Birth of an Idea: An Account of the Genesis of Women's Continuing Education," pp. 3–22.

4. George Parkyn, "Towards a Conceptual Model of Life-Long Education," *Educational Studies and Documents* (New York: UNESCO, 1973), p. 19.

5. Paolo Freire, *Pedagogy of the Oppressed* (New York: Herder and Herder, 1971).

6. Harry R. Moody, "Education and the Life-Cycle: A Philosophy of Aging" (Paper presented at the First National Congress of Educational Gerontology, June 1976), p. 10.

7. Northrop Frye, "Clair de Lune Intellectuel," in *The Modern Century* (Toronto: Oxford University Press, 1967), pp. 87–123.

8. A. A. Liveright, "Learning Never Ends: A Plan for Continuing Education," in *Campus 1980*, edited by Alvin Eurich (New York: Delacorte Press, 1968), pp. 149–75. The quoted phrase is from Eurich's introduction, p. iv.

9. Dyckman W. Vermilye, ed., *Individualizing the System* (San Francisco: Jossey-Bass Publishers, 1976).

10. Burlington Lowery, "Those 'Emerging Women' as Undergraduates," *Washington Post*, September 15, 1976.

11. Nathan Teitel, "Learning at Night," *Saturday Review*, May 1973, pp. 1, 11–12.

Chapter 2

1. An excellent summary is found in "Reentry Women: Special Programs for Special Populations" (Washington, D.C.: Project on the Status and Education of Women, Association of American Colleges, 1981); and "Re-entry Women: Relevant Statistics" (Washington, D.C.: Project on the Status and Education of Women, Association of American Colleges, 1981). Both are available from the association at 1818 R Street NW, Washington, D.C. 20009.

2. Ruth B. Ekstrom and Marjory G. Marvel, "Educational Programs for Adult Women," in *Handbook for Achieving Sex Equity through Education*, edited by Susan S. Klein (Baltimore: Johns Hopkins University Press, 1985), pp. 431–54.

3. Gay Holliday, "Addressing the Concerns of Returning Women Students," in *Facilitating the Development of Women*, edited by Nancy J. Evans (San Francisco: Jossey-Bass, 1985), pp. 61–74.

4. Irene Thompson and Audrey Roberts, eds., *The Road Retaken: Women Reenter the Academy* (New York: Modern Language Association of America, 1985).

5. Arlene T. McLaren, *Ambition and Realization: Women in Adult Education* (Washington, D.C.: Peter Owen, 1985).

6. Florence Howe, *The Myth of Coeducation* (Bloomington: Indiana University Press, 1984), examines the way in which feminist scholarship was necessary to fully realize the education for civil rights workers and draws similar links.

Chapter 3

1. Kate Millett, *Sexual Politics* (New York: Avon Books, 1971).

2. Simone de Beauvoir, *The Second Sex* (New York: Knopf, 1953); Betty Friedan, *The Feminine Mystique* (New York: Norton, 1974).

3. Patricia Hill Collins, "The Meaning of Motherhood in Black Culture and Black Mother/Daughter Relationships," *Sage* 4, no. 2 (Fall 1987): 3–10. For other examples see Aida Hurtado, "Relating to Privilege: Seduction and Rejection in the Subordination of White Women and Women of Color," *Signs* 14, no. 4 (1989): 833–55.

4. See in particular Carol Gilligan, *In a Different Voice: Psychological Theory and Women's Development* (Cambridge: Harvard University Press, 1982); and Carol Gilligan, Janie Victoria Ward, and Jill McLean Taylor, eds., *Mapping the Moral Domain: A Contribution of Women's Thinking to Psychological Theory and Education* (Cambridge: Harvard University Press, 1988).

5. See Carol Meyers, *Discovering Eve: Ancient Israelite Women in Context* (New York: Oxford University Press, 1988).

6. Most helpful are two articles by Elsa Barkley Brown, "African-American Women's Quilting," and "Womanist Consciousness: Maggie Lena Walker and the Independent Order of St. Luke," in *Black Women in America: Social Science Perspectives*, edited by Micheline Malson et al. (Chicago: University of Chicago Press, 1990), pp. 9–18 and 173–96.

7. Caryn McTighe Musil, ed., *The Courage to Question: Women's Studies and Student Learning* (Washington, D.C.: Association of American Colleges and the National Women's Studies Association, 1992).

8. Kerith Cohen, "Why Am I So Angry?," in *Engaging Feminism: Students Speak Up and Speak Out*, edited by Jean O'Barr and Mary Wyer (Charlottesville: University Press of Virginia, 1992), pp. 19–20.

9. Heather H. Howard, "Abortion," in *Engaging Feminism*, p. 106.

10. Miriam Peskowitz, "What If We Stopped Recognizing Their Authority?," in *Engaging Feminism*, pp. 113–14.

11. Stephen T., "I Avoided Intimacy," in *Engaging Feminism*, pp. 35–36.

12. John D., "My Parents Separated," in *Engaging Feminism*, pp. 34–35.

13. Suzanne Franks Shedd, "The Idea That You're 'Special,' " in *Engaging Feminism*, pp. 67–68.

Chapter 4

1. This debate was sparked in part by Allan Bloom, *The Closing of the American Mind* (New York: Simon and Schuster, 1987). See also William Bennett, *The War over Culture in Education* (Washington, D.C.: Heritage Foundation, 1991), and *Our Children and Our Country: Improving America's Schools and Affirming the Common Culture* (New York: Simon and Schuster, 1988); and E. D. Hirsch, *Cultural Literacy: What Every American Needs to Know* (Boston: Houghton Mifflin, 1987).

2. Florence Howe, "Toward Women's Studies in the Eighties: Part 1," *Women's Studies Newsletter* 8, no. 4 (Fall 1979): 2.

3. Edward B. Fiske, "Lessons," *New York Times*, October 5, 1988.

Chapter 5

1. See Ann Oakley, *Sex, Gender and Society* (New York: Harper and Row, 1972).

2. Annette Kolodny, *The Land Before Her: Fantasy and Experience of the American Frontiers, 1630–1860* (Chapel Hill: University of North Carolina Press, 1984).

3. William L. Andrews, *Six Women's Slave Narratives* (New York: Oxford University Press, 1988); and Harriet Brent, "Incidents in the Life of a Slave Girl," in *The Classic Slave Narratives*, edited by Henry Louis Gates (New York: Penguin Books, 1987), pp. 333–513.

4. Jane P. Tompkins, *Sensational Designs: The Cultural Work of American Fiction, 1790–1860* (New York: Oxford University Press, 1985).

5. Carol Gilligan, *In a Different Voice: Psychological Theory and Women's Development* (Cambridge: Harvard University Press, 1982); and Carol Gilligan, Janie Victoria Ward, and Jill McLean Taylor, eds., *Mapping the Moral Domain: A Contribution of Women's Thinking to Psychological Theory and Education* (Cambridge: Havard University Press, 1988).

6. Rebecca West, *The Clarion*, November 14, 1913; cited in Cheris Kramarae and Paula A. Treichler, *A Feminist Dictionary* (London: Pandora Press, 1985), p. 160.

Chapter 6

1. Kate Millett, *Sexual Politics* (New York: Avon Books, 1971); Robin Morgan, *Sisterhood Is Powerful: An Anthology of Writings from the Women's Liberation Movement* (New York: Random House, 1970), and *Going Too Far: The Personal Chronicle of a Feminist* (New York: Random House, 1977).

2. Florence Howe, "Toward Women's Studies in the Eighties: Part 1," *Women's Studies Newsletter* 8, no. 4 (Fall 1979): 2.

3. Roberta M. Hall and Bernice R. Sandler, *The Classroom Climate: A Chilly One for Women?* (Washington, D.C.: Project on the Status and Education of Women, Association of American Colleges, 1982), and *Out of the Classroom: A Chilly Campus for Women* (Washington, D.C.: Project on the Status and Education of Women, Association of American Colleges, 1984).

Chapter 7

1. Robin Morgan, *Sisterhood Is Powerful: An Anthology of Writings from the Women's Liberation Movement* (New York: Random House, 1970); Vivian Gornick and Barbara R. Moran, *Women in Sexist Society: Studies in Power and Powerlessness* (New York: Basic Books, 1971).

2. Michelle Zimbalist Rosaldo and Louise Lamphere, eds., *Women, Culture, and Society* (Stanford: Stanford University Press, 1974).

3. Catherine Stimpson with Nina Kressner Cobb, *Women's Studies in the United States* (New York: Ford Foundation, 1986).

4. Florence Howe, *Seven Years Later: Women's Studies Programs in 1976* (Washington, D.C.: National Advisory Council on Women's Educational Programs, 1977).

Chapter 8

1. Carol S. Pearson, Donna L. Shavlik, and Judith G. Touchton, eds., *Educating the Majority: Women Challenge Tradition in Higher Education* (New York: Collier Macmillan, 1989).

2. Mary Hawkesworth, "Knowers, Knowing, Known: Feminist Theory and Claims of Truth," *Signs* 14, no. 3 (Spring 1989): 533–37; and Mary Hawkesworth, *Beyond Oppression: Feminist Theory and Political Strategy* (New York: Continuum, 1990).

Chapter 10

1. A special issue of *Women's Studies Quarterly* 17, nos. 1–2 (Spring/Summer 1990), entitled "Curricular and Institutional Change," exemplifies this approach. All twenty articles, totaling 225 pages, focus on the content of the materials to be used and are written exclusively from the faculty point of view. The question of student participation is not addressed. The following sources are indicative of earlier work that has been done: Susan Hardy Aiken, Karen Anderson, Myra Dinnerstein, Judy Nolte Lensink, and Patricia Mac-Corquodale, eds., *Changing Our Minds: Feminist Transformations of Knowledge* (Albany: State University of New York Press, 1988); Anne Chapman, ed., *Feminist Resources for Schools and Colleges: A Guide to Curricular Materials*, 3d ed. (New York: Feminist Press, 1986); Sandra Coyner, "The Ideas of Main-streaming: Women's Studies and the Disciplines," *Frontiers* 8, no. 3 (1986): 87–95; Linda Dittmar, "Inclusionary Practices: The Politics of

Syllabus Design," *Journal of Thought* 20, no. 3 (Fall 1985): 37–47; Margot C. Finn, "Incorporating Perspectives on Women into the Undergraduate Curriculum: A Ford Foundation Workshop," *Women's Studies Quarterly* 13, no. 2 (Summer 1985): 15–17; *Forum for Liberal Education* 4, no. 1 (October 1981); Susan Douglas Franzosa and Karen A. Mazza, *Integrating Women's Studies into the Curriculum: An Annotated Bibliography* (Westport, Conn.: Greenwood Press, 1984); JoAnn M. Fritsche, *Toward Excellence and Equity: The Scholarship on Women as a Catalyst for Change in the University* (Orono: University of Maine Press, 1985); *Journal of Thought* 20, no. 3 (Fall 1985); Kay F. Klinkenborg, "A Selected Bibliography for Integrating Women's Studies into the College Curriculum," *Feminist Teacher* 4, no. 1 (Spring 1989): 26–31; Constance Miller, "Standard Forms of Information Organization: Academic Libraries and Curriculum Transformation," *Women's Studies Quarterly* 13, no. 2 (Summer 1985): 23; Peggy McIntosh, "A Note on Terminology," *Women's Studies Quarterly* 11, no. 3 (Fall 1983): 29–30; Betty Schmitz, "Women's Studies and Projects to Transform the Curriculum: A Current Status Report," *Women's Studies Quarterly* 11, no. 3 (Fall 1983): 17–19; Betty Schmitz, "A Current Status Report on Curriculum Integration Projects," *Women's Studies Quarterly* 10, no. 3 (Fall 1982): 16–17; Betty Schmitz, *Integrating Women's Studies in the Curriculum: A Guide and Bibliography* (Old Westbury, N.Y.: Feminist Press, 1985); Bonnie Spanier, Alexander Bloom, and Darlene Boroviak, eds., *Toward a Balanced Curriculum: A Sourcebook for Initiating Gender Integration Projects Based on the Wheaton College Conference* (Cambridge, Mass.: Schenkman, 1984); Karen J. Warren, "Rewriting the Future: The Feminist Challenge to the Malestream Curriculum," *Feminist Teacher* 4, nos. 2–3 (Fall 1989): 46–52; "A Special Feature: Transforming the Traditional Curriculum," *Women's Studies Quarterly* 10, no. 1 (Spring 1982): 19–31.

The impact of women's studies and curriculum integration on students and faculty is discussed in the following sources: Ruth Crego Benson, "Women's Studies: Theory and Practice," *American Association of University Professors Bulletin* 58 (1972): 283–86; Robert J. Bezucha, "Feminist Pedagogy as a Subversive Activity," in *Gendered Subjects: The Dynamics of Feminist Teaching*, edited by Margo Culler and Catherine Portugues (Boston: Routledge, 1985), pp. 81–95; Christine Bose, John Steiger, and Philomina Victorine, "Evaluation: Perspectives of Students and Graduates," *Women's Studies Newsletter* 5, no. 4 (Fall 1977): 6–7; Lorelei R. Brush, Alice Ross Gold, and Marni Goldstein White, "The Paradox of Intention and Effect: A Women's Studies Course," *Signs* 3 (1978): 870–83; Renate Duelli-Klein, "Berkeley 'Freshwomen' Look at Women's Studies," *Women's Studies Quarterly* 9, no. 2 (Summer 1981): 24; Leslie A. Flemming, "New Visions, New Methods: The Mainstreaming Experience in Retrospect," in *Changing Our Minds*, pp. 39–58; Fritsche, *Toward Excellence and Equity*; Sarah Hoagland, "On the Reeducation of Sophie," in *Women's Studies: An Interdisciplinary Collection*, edited by Kathleen O'Connor Blumhagen and Walter D. Johnson (Westport, Conn.: Greenwood Press, 1978), pp. 13–20; Renate D. Klein, "The Dynamics of the Women's Studies Classroom: A Review Essay of the Teaching Practices of Women's Studies in Higher Education," *Women's Studies International Forum* 10, no. 2 (1987): 187–206; Genie O. Lenihan and Melanie Rawlins, "The Impact of a Women's Studies Program: Challenging and Nourishing the True Believers," *Journal of the National Association of Women Deans, Administrators, and Counselors* 50, no. 3 (Spring 1987): 3–10; Nancy M. Porter and Margaret T. Eileenchild, *The Effectiveness of Women's Studies Teaching* (Washington, D.C.: National Institute of Education, Department of Health, Education, and Welfare, February 1980); Cheri Register, "Brief A-mazing Movements: Dealing with Despair in the Women's Studies Classroom," *Women's Studies Newsletter* 7, no. 4 (Fall 1979): 7–10; and Jayne E. Stake and Margaret A. Gerner, "The Women's Studies Experience: Personal and Professional Gains for Women and Men," *Psychology of Women Quarterly* 11 (1987): 277–83.

2. Johnella E. Butler and John C. Walter, eds., *Transforming the Curriculum: Ethnic Studies and Women's Studies* (Albany: State University of New York Press, 1991); Susan Hardy Aiken, Karen Anderson, Myra Dinnerstein, Judy Lensink, and Patricia MacCorquodale, "Trying Transformations: Curriculum Integration and the Problem of Resistance," in *Reconstructing the Academy: Women's Education and Women's Studies*, edited by Elizabeth Minnich, Jean O'Barr, and Rachel Rosenfeld (Chicago: University of Chicago Press, 1988), pp. 104–24.

3. Janet E. Wright and Margaret A. Talburtt, *Including Women in the Curriculum: A Report to the Ford Foundation on the Current State of Knowledge about the Impact of Curriculum Integration Projects* (Ann Arbor: Formative Evaluation Research Associates, August 1987).

4. Peggy McIntosh, *Interactive Phases of Curricular Re-Vision: A Feminist Perspective*, Working Papers Series, no. 124 (Wellesley, Mass.: Wellesley College Center for Research on Women, 1983); summarized in Margaret L. Andersen, "Changing the Curriculum in Higher Education," in *Reconstructing the Academy*, pp. 49–50.

5. Bernice R. Sandler and Roberta M. Hall, *The Classroom Climate: A Chilly One for Women?* (Washington, D.C.: Project on the Status and Education of Women, Association of American Colleges, 1982); and *Out of the Classroom: A Chilly Campus for Women* (Washington, D.C.: Project on the Status and Education of Women, Association of American Colleges, 1984).

Chapter 11

1. While a great deal has been written on curriculum transformation from the perspective of teachers and administrators, we have found almost no examples of studies that approach such issues from the student perspective. The most recent collection of materials on curriculum transformation, Johnella E. Butler and John C. Walker, eds., *Transforming the Curriculum: Ethnic Studies and Women's Studies* (Albany: State University of New York Press, 1991), continues the tradition of seeing curriculum transformation exclusively through the eyes of those faculty members who are bringing new material into the classroom. While the effects of this material on students are assumed, they are not systematically investigated. A special issue of *Women's Studies Quarterly* 19, nos. 1–2 (Spring/Summer 1991), entitled "Women, Girls, and the Culture of Education," begins with a series of articles that explore listening to women and girls. However, they do not look specifically at women's studies classrooms, nor do they consider the content and process of women's studies as an intervention. Jean O'Barr and Mary Wyer, eds., *Engaging Feminism: Students Speak Up and Speak Out* (Charlottesville: University Press of Virginia, 1992), and Caryn Musil, ed., *The Courage to Question: Women's Studies and Student Learning* (Washington, D.C.: Association of American Colleges, 1992), illustrate two recent assessments of student learning in women's studies that challenge the earlier tradition and chart new directions.

2. Especially Carol Gilligan, "Joining the Resistance: Psychology, Politics, Girls and Women," *Michigan Quarterly Review* 29, no. 4 (Fall 1991): 501–36. Also see Carol Gilligan, "Women's Psychological Development: Implications for Psychotherapy," in *Women, Girls and Psychotherapy: Reframing Resistance*, edited by Carol Gilligan, Annie G. Rogers, and Deborah L. Tolman (New York: Harrington Park Press, 1991), pp. 156–73, as well as Carol Gilligan, *Making Connections: The Relational Worlds of Adolescent Girls at Emma Willard School* (Cambridge: Harvard University Press, 1990).

3. Brenda Denzler, a graduate student in the Religion Department at Duke, helped compile information and conduct interviews during the early stages of the project.

4. College levels refer to the year the students took WST 103; we interviewed them one year later, when three were juniors and one was a senior. For the past several years, there has

been a fairly consistent 60 percent of the enrollment reporting little or no previous experience with women's studies classes.

5. Gilligan, "Joining the Resistance," p. 512. Some of the similarities between Gilligan's findings and our own may be due to the fact that young girls at Emma Willard School were also living in a space where all their social institutions were controlled by the school.

6. Dorothy Holland, *Educated in Romance: Women, Achievement, and College Culture* (Chicago: University of Chicago Press, 1990), illustrates the dynamics of college as a time of significant and extensive cultural coding for women.

7. This task is complicated by a number of factors. As teachers, we are accustomed to an institutional perspective that focuses on the content being offered and the way we offer it. Thinking about the experience from the perspective of what it is like to learn certain material rather than what it is like to teach it requires a major shift, one for which there seem to be few models. In addition, there is the problem of documenting classroom experience. The number of tasks involved in running a course makes it difficult to have much time or energy left over for investigating—beyond the level of, "Are the students understanding the material?" "Are they engaged and interested?"—how students are experiencing the learning process. We negotiated these issues by working as a group, reading all the students' written assignments and evaluations, and conducting interviews with the students.

8. Karen is referring to Jean Kilbourne's 1978 film *Killing Us Softly*, an analysis of the images of women in advertising.

9. Adrienne Rich, *On Lies, Secrets, and Silence: Selected Prose 1966–1978* (New York: Norton, 1979); Virginia Woolf, *A Room of One's Own* (London: Hogarth Press, 1931).

Chapter 12

1. Ethel M. Kersey, *Women Philosophers: A Bio-Critical Source Book* (New York: Greenwood Press, 1989).

2. Susan Stuard, "The Dominions of Gender: Women's Fortunes in the High Middle Ages," in *Becoming Visible: Women in European History*, edited by Renate Bridenthal and Claudia Koonz (Boston: Houghton Mifflin, 1977), p. 166.

3. Joan Kelly, *Women, History and Theory: The Essays of Joan Kelly* (Chicago: University of Chicago Press, 1984). See especially the chapter entitled "Early Feminist Theory and the *Querelle des Femmes*."

4. Michelle LaRocque wrote these journal essays as a graduate student in the fall of 1988. She has expanded her analyses since these first writings, as she continues to work on these and similar questions in her own philosophical research.

5. Mary Wollstonecraft, *A Vindication of the Rights of Woman*, excerpted in *The Feminist Papers: From Adams to de Beauvoir*, edited by Alice Rossi (Boston: Northeastern University Press, 1973), pp. 40–85. Page numbers in the text refer to this excerpt.

6. Elizabeth Cady Stanton, Susan B. Anthony, and Matilda Joslyn Gage, "The Kansas Campaign of 1867," excerpted from *The History of Woman Suffrage* in *The Feminist Papers*, pp. 455–56.

7. Matilda Joslyn Gage, *Woman, Church and State: The Original Exposé of the Male Collaboration against the Female Sex* (1893; reprint, Watertown, Mass.: Persephone Press, 1980), pp. 238–39. See also Lynne Spender, "Matilda Joslyn Gage: Active Intellectual (1826–1898)," in *Feminist Theorists: Three Centuries of Key Women Thinkers*, edited by Dale Spender (New York: Pantheon Books, 1983), pp. 137–45.

8. Julia Anna Cooper, *A Voice from the South with an Introduction by Mary Helen Washington* (New York: Oxford University Press, 1988), pp. xliii–xliv.

9. Charlotte Perkins Gilman, *Women and Economics*; Jane Addams, *Utilization of Women in City Government*, both excerpted in *The Feminist Papers*, pp. 572–98 and 604–12 respectively.

10. Virginia Woolf, *A Room of One's Own* (London: Hogarth Press, 1931), p. 33.

11. Simone de Beauvoir, *The Second Sex*, translated by H. M. Parshley (New York: Knopf, 1953), p. xxvi.

12. bell hooks, *From Margin to Center* (Boston: South End Press, 1984), p. ix.

Chapter 13

1. Buchi Emecheta, *The Joys of Motherhood* (New York: George Brazillier, 1979).

2. Patricia Williams, "On Being the Object of Property," *Signs* 14, no. 1 (Autumn 1988): 5–24.

3. Joan Kelly, *Women, History and Theory: The Essays of Joan Kelly* (Chicago: University of Chicago Press, 1984).

Chapter 14

1. Women's Studies continues to solicit and receive funds. This chapter covers only the now-completed five-year period of the official Capital Campaign for the Arts and Sciences from 1986 through 1991.

2. The academic literature on fundraising for feminist causes in higher education is not well developed. It appears to fall into three clusters: newspaper and magazine accounts of specific projects, usually about alumnae giving for general purposes; reports from foundations and funding organizations on funding for women and girls and on women as donors generally; and the reports from individual campuses on specific women's studies initiatives.

Particularly useful newspaper and magazine accounts include Fox Butterfield, "As for That Myth about How Much Alumnae Give," *New York Times*, February 26, 1992; Keller Freeman, "For Women, a Time to Close Philanthropy's Gender Gap," *Chronicle of Philanthropy*, June 2, 1992; Debbie Goldberg, "Women Now Match Men's Gifts to Colleges," *Washington Post*, August 10, 1986, and "How the Other Half Gives," *CASE Currents*, March 1989, pp. 10, 12, 14–15; Anne Mathews, "Alma Maters Court Their Daughters," *New York Times Magazine*, April 7, 1991; Liz McMillen, "College Fund Raisers See Their Alumnae as Untapped Donors," *Chronicle of Higher Education*, April 1, 1992; Letty Pogrebin, "Contributing to the Cause," *New York Times*, April 22, 1991; Susan Tifft, "Asking for a Fortune," *Working Woman*, November 1992, pp. 66–70, 94; Kathleen Teltsch, "Network of Women Hopes to Change American Philanthropy," *New York Times*, May 14, 1986.

A number of organizations concerned with philanthropy have published reports on women and giving. Among these are a November 1988 report from the Woman's College Coalition; "Short-Changed: A Look at Funding for Chicago-Area Women's Organizations" (September 1985) by the Chicago Women in Philanthropy; "Women and Families in the 80's: A Role for Philanthropy" (Spring 1985) by Women and Foundations; "Getting It Done: From Commitment to Action on Funding for Women and Girls" (April 1992) by Women and Foundations; and the proceedings of a Wingspread Conference (October 1992) by the Center for Women and Philanthropy at the University of Wisconsin.

Some women's studies programs have conducted fundraising campaigns. Examples include Brandeis University, the Center for the Education of Women at the University of Michigan, Ohio State University, Princeton University, the University of North Carolina at Greensboro, the University of South Carolina System, and Wichita State University.

Chapter 15

1. We have given the student participants fictitious names to protect their privacy while retaining the names of the three faculty and staff initiators. Our commitment to creating a space for listening to students grew, in part, from the publication of *Engaging Feminism: Students Speak Up and Speak Out*, edited by Jean O'Barr and Mary Wyer (Charlottesville: University Press of Virginia, 1991), an anthology of writings by sixty students in Women's Studies at Duke. These essays, journal entries, exams, letters, and reports powerfully argue for the fact that students make connections between the various facets of their lives when they engage feminist scholarship and that these same students lack any institutionally legitimized space for conversations about these connections to occur.

2. Susan Glaspell, "A Jury of Her Peers," in *U.S. Stories: Regional Stories from the Forty-Eight States*, edited by Martha Foley and Abraham Rothenberg (New York: Hendricks House—Farrar Straus, 1949). We chose this story, originally published in 1918, as our first reading because it illustrates the fact that women have long had similar experiences, but only with the current wave of feminism have some of those practices been named and addressed. Moreover, we felt a short story would be more immediately engaging than a nonfiction piece, which might require a reader's familiarity with the subject. As a way to broaden our perspectives in preparation for the first reflective paper, we read Carol Gilligan, "Joining the Resistance: Psychology, Politics, Girls and Women," *Michigan Quarterly Review* 29, no. 4 (Fall 1991): 501–36, an essay that reports some of research with eleven-, twelve-, and thirteen-year-old girls.

For the third session, which was to examine socially constructed barriers against women, we read Adrienne Rich, "Towards a Woman-Centered University," in *On Lies, Secrets, and Silence: Selected Prose 1966–1978* (New York: Norton, 1979), pp. 126–56; and Berenice Fisher, "Wandering in the Wilderness: The Search for Women Role Models," *Signs* 13, no. 2 (Winter 1988): 211–32.

For the fourth and final session of the fall, we read several different pieces that examined competition and cooperation among groups of women. These included some published and unpublished material from female employees of *St. Petersburg Times* who had formed a coalition to lobby against discriminatory practices; from Louise Bernikow, "Conflict: Off with Her Head," in *Among Women* (New York: Harper, 1980), pp. 193–224; and Toni McNaron, "Little Women and Cinderella: Sisters and Competition," in *Competition: A Feminist Taboo?*, edited by Valerie Minder and Helen Longino (New York: Feminist Press at CUNY, 1987), pp. 121–30.

3. Rosemary L. Bray, "Heavy Burden," *Essence* 23, no. 9 (January 1992): 45, 52, 54, 90–91.

Chapter 17

1. *Liberal Learning and the Women's Studies Major* (Washington D.C.: Association of American Colleges, 1991); Gail B. Griffin, *Calling: Essays on Teaching in the Mother Tongue* (Pasadena: Trilogy Books, 1992); Caryn McTighe Musil, ed., *The Courage to Question: Women's Studies and Student Learning* (Washington, D.C.: Association of American Colleges, 1992); Caryn McTighe Musil, ed., *Students at the Center* (Washington D.C.: Association of American Colleges, 1992); Jean O'Barr and Mary Wyer, eds., *Engaging Feminism: Students Speak Up and Speak Out* (Charlottesville: University Press of Virginia, 1992).

2. I have been helped in this formulation by papers (undated and unsigned) sent to me from the University of Michigan's Women's Studies Program.

3. The Graduate Consortium in Women's Studies at Radcliffe College began using these

categories in the spring of 1993 in a graduate seminar called "Feminist Perspectives in Research: Interdisciplinary Practice in the Study of Gender." Faculty were drawn from Boston College, Brandeis University, Harvard University, Harvard Divinity School, Massachusetts Institute of Technology, Northeastern University, and Tufts University.

4. Katie Kent, "The Power of Interdisciplinary Perspectives," in *Engaging Feminism*, pp. 121–22.

Civil rights movement, and women's studies, 96

Classes, Introduction to Women's Studies, 99, 109–10, 115–16, 154; heterogeneity in, 106–7; graduate, 116–17; presuppositions about, 137; power in, 138, 159–60, 273–74; gender dynamics of, 148–51

"Click," 5, 20, 72, 94–95, 192; and change, 21

Collaboration, 268, 271–72

Collaborative learning, 263–76; and history, 275. *See also* Education; Learning

Colleges, community, 37

Colonialism, 147

Commonalities, 9, 104–18

Communal living, 190

Communication, 163, 167–68. *See also* Talk

Community, 33; and women's studies, 282 (*see also* Institution building)

Competition, 245

Connections, 2, 3

Consciousness raising, 47, 153, 279

Consensus, 206–7

Contextualization, 11; of knowledge, 272–74. *See also* Positionality

Continuing education, 10, 37–38; definition of, 27; and women's studies, 35–45

Continuity, women's studies as, 223

Cooper, Julia, 188

Cooperation, 245

Council for the Advancement of Support of Education, 235

Council on Women's Studies, 4, 226

Cross, Patricia, 26

Culture: dominant, 9, 124; as system, 43; maps of, 108, 109; campus, 114, 122, 130–31, 264, 269; and knowledge, 130

Curriculum, 98–99; problems in, 41; access to, 45; exclusivity of, 51; change in, 60, 64–65; and learning, 61–66; breadth in, 66; in women's studies, 87–88; hidden, 107; and pedagogy, 108; evaluation of, 115–16, 136; and gender analysis, 131; womanless, 139–40; integration of, 141–42, 146–47, 222

Curriculum transformation, 24, 88, 100, 133–52, 193–94; and pedagogy, 134–35, 265–66

Curry, Ann, 4, 231

De Pisan, Christine, 182–83

Development, personal, 37

Disciplines, academic, 278–79

Discrimination, career, 174

Discussion group, 241

Diversity, 104–18, 274–76; in the classroom, 106–7. *See also* Heterogeneity

Divorce, 37

Double standard, 21

Duke, Benjamin N., 2

Duke, James B., 2

Duke, Washington, 2, 4

Duke University, 95, 114; Women's Studies Program, 1–2, 59–67, 77, 222–23, 232–33, 235, 277–84; Nursing School, 3; Medical Center, 17; Continuing Education, 17, 18, 25–34, 95, 222; Institute for Learning in Retirement, 17, 33; Political Science Department, 95; Office of Alumni Affairs, 225; Development Office, 228, 234–35; Women's Center, 240

Dunlap, Louise, 4

Economics, 189; pedagogy in, 149; and housekeeping, 189–90

Editors and scholarship, 205–6

Education: process of, 9–10, 19, 23, 37; and space, 19; classical, 23; models of, 24, 28; nature of, 27; right to, 27; adult, 28; and leisure, 29; access to, 29, 45; cooperative, 30–31; goals of, 32, 39; limitedness of, 35; barriers to, 38; history of, 51; meaning of, 67; and progress, 80–81. *See also* Collaborative learning; Continuing education; Learning

Emecheta, Buchi, 214

Emotion, 56–57, 158, 187, 257–62, 268

Empowerment, 7, 173, 236; and gender-role violation, 126; and women's studies, 168

Environmentalism, 175–76

Epistemology, 11, 46, 63–64, 78, 92, 110, 241, 280; and change, 60–61; women's studies' challenge of, 179. *See also* Knowledge

Equal Pay Act of 1963, 48

Equal Rights Amendment (ERA), 49
ERA. *See* Equal Rights Amendment
Ethics, focus of, 148–49
Eurich, Alvin, 30
Exceptions, women as, 58, 140–41, 145, 211, 244–45, 248
Experience, 9, 32, 280; recording, 1, 74, 121; and theory, 8; generalization of, 23; life, 29; and learning, 34, 270–71, 273; and knowledge, 44, 126, 131; differences in, 78; documenting, 95; and scholarship, 99; of students, 107–10, 120, 241, 243–44; of alumnae, 236
Explanation, 8; gap in, 18; traditions of, 18; and women's studies, 153; and voice, 169

Faculty, change among, 64–65
Family Leave Act, 50
Fashion, 83, 134, 172
Feminism: second wave of, 7; social, 47, 51; definition of, 49; opposition to, 49–50; and women's studies, 50–58, 81, 96, 101; scholarly, 51, 78, 115; meaning of, 155; advocacy of, 193; practice of, 239–62
Feminist, 249–50; self-definition as, 121–22
Ford Motor Company, 22
Foremothers, institutional, 2–6
Frameworks, 43–44; interpretive, 7; explanatory, 117, 152; searching for, 132; and voice, 157; and silencing, 160; and experience, 270–71
Friedan, Betty, 48
Friends of Women's Studies, 228, 229
Funding, 198
Fundraising: politics of, 219–38; and visibility, 226

Gage, Matilda Joslyn, 184, 186–88
Gap, 8, 9, 18, 103, 132, 142, 183, 241
Gelpi, Barbara, 200, 201
Gender: differences in, 20, 82–83; assumptions about, 22; consciousness, 50; social construction of, 52, 72, 109, 123, 154, 156–57, 183; valorization of, 56, 57–58, 182; and communication, 74; in analysis, 78; teaching about, 120–21; understanding, 126–30; systems, 129; and pedagogy, 132; dynamics of, 148–51, 266

Gender roles, 143–45; violation of, 109–10, 115, 119–32, 162; socialization of, 123. *See also* Social roles
Geriatrics. *See* Aging
Gerontology. *See* Aging
Gheith, Jehanne, 281
Gilligan, Carol, 83, 154, 156, 173, 176, 177, 256
Gilman, Charlotte Perkins, 189–90
Glaspell, Susan, 243
Gornick, Vivian, 96
Green, Edith, 49

Harvard Project on the Psychology of Women and the Development of Girls, 156
Hawkesworth, Mary, 110
Hawthorne, Nathaniel, 82
Heilbrun, Carolyn, 93
Heterogeneity, 6–7, 50, 142–43, 147, 192, 274–76, 280; in the classroom, 106–7. *See also* Diversity
Heterosexuality, bias toward, 107. *See also* Homophobia
History, 42–43, 48, 52, 62, 97, 128–29; feminist, 48; nature of, 61; interpretation of, 61, 62–63; of social roles, 79–80; oral, 116, 169; pedagogy in, 147; of feminist thought, 178–94; and collaborative learning, 275; of women's studies, 279–81
Homophobia, 175. *See also* Heterosexuality, bias toward
hooks, bell, 192–93
Hopkins, Pauline, 188
Hostility, 192
Housekeeping and economics, 189–90
Howe, Florence, 90
Hypatia, 180–81

Ideas, 9
Identity, 158–59; female, and emotions, 259
Ideology, 47
Inclusion, 180; manner of, 151
Influence: politics of, 219–38; versus action, 251; and leadership, 255–56
Institution building, 1, 6, 11; and women's studies, 12; and space, 197; and scholarship, 281

Institutions: institutional foremothers,
2–6; policies of, 38; changing, 98
Interdisciplinarity, 61–62, 100, 117, 216,
283
International Congress of University Adult
Education, 30
Ironsides, Ellen, 104
Isolation, 20, 23, 117, 244

Journals, scholarly, 101; *Signs*, 200–218

Kelly, Joan, 182
Kennedy, John F., 48
Kent, Katie, 283
Keohane, Nannerl, 114
Knowing, 253; process of, 24. *See also* Epistemology
Knowledge, 51; increase of, 29; and experience, 44, 126, 131; politics of, 46–58; critique of, 52, 161–62; production of, 81,
88, 200–218; and power, 84, 151–52;
claiming, 95; correction of, 97; transformation of, 98, 101–2, 178–94; and pedagogy, 120; and culture, 130; relevance of,
142; gatekeepers of, 151–52; fragility of,
157; and conflict, 173; negotiating differences in, 215–18; extension of, 239–40;
and activism, 243; and silencing, 252–54;
possession of, 253; collaboration in, 271–
72; contextualization of, 272–74
Kolodny, Annette, 80

Lamphere, Louise, 96
Language classes, 145; pedagogy in, 159–60
Leadership, 254–56
Learning: adult, 18; process of, 28, 53–58,
138–39, 153–77, 241; and experience, 34;
interdisciplinary, 61–62; and curricu-
lum, 61–66; context of, 266–67. *See also*
Collaborative learning; Education
Lesbianism, 107
Liberal arts: definition of, 59–60; and
women's studies, 59–67, 72, 85–93, 282;
as process, 60–61; interdisciplinarity of,
61–62; nature of, 61–62
Life cycle, 26–27
Listening, 12, 19, 22; to critics, 23; to stu-
dents, 23; conditions for, 24; and the

social conversation, 103; and feminist
scholarship, 146
Literature, values of, 82
Liveright, A. A., 30–31
Lowery, Burlington, 32
Luttrell, Wendy, 268

McIntosh, Peggy, 139
Maddox, George, 17, 18
Maps, conceptual, 127
Marginalization, 96, 192–93, 281
Medicine, 173–74
Methodology, 136–37, 143, 154–55
Millett, Kate, 47, 87
Modern Language Association, 38, 101
Morality, 83
Moran, Barbara R., 96
Morgan, Robin, 87, 96
Motherhood, 164–65, 166, 170, 208

Naming, 7, 11, 90, 174; of absences, 2, 19;
failure in, 259
National Coalition for Research on
Women's Education and Development,
74
National Commission on Women, 75
National Endowment for the Humanities,
210
National Identification Program, 75
National Women's Studies Association,
101
Networking, 227, 231; and scholarship,
203–4
North Carolina Museum of Art, 83
North Carolina State University, 119
Northwestern University, 11

Objectification, 125, 156, 157, 171, 176
Office of Women in Higher Education,
74
Oppression: housekeeping and, 190; social
construction of, 191–92
Otherness, 192

Parlors, 1, 2–4
Patterns: identification of, 18; of development, 26–27; of marginalization, 81; in
learning, 110

Pedagogy, 137–38, 148–51, 198, 263–76; reevaluation of, 31–34; and curriculum, 108; and knowledge, 120; and gender, 132; and curriculum transformation, 134–35; in language classes, 145, 159–60; in the arts, 146–47

Percy Amendment, 95

Polarities, 182

Political practices, 186, 252, 282

Politics, 61, 86–87, 270–71; and socialization, 97

Portraits, 2–6

Positionality, 203–5. *See also* Contextualization

Power, 193; and knowledge, 84, 151–52; in the classroom, 138, 273–74; and socialization, 192–93; and relationship between authors and editors, 208; negotiating, 242–43; and leadership, 254; and students, 267

Practice of feminism, 239–62

Problem solving, 91–92

Process: reflection upon, 8; of learning, 28, 53–58, 138–39, 153–77, 241; of education, 37; in the liberal arts, 60–61; and consensus, 206–7; versus product, 207; of change, 252–53; hiding of, 259

Professionalism, 21

Progress: social, 75; and the university, 78; and education, 80; and women's studies, 92–93

Public-private debate, 83, 89–90, 153, 189–90, 216–17, 251–52

Publishing: and scholarship, 207; and campus life, 213–14

Querelles des femmes, 183

Questioning, 53

Radcliffe consortium, 281

Rap groups. *See* Consciousness raising

Reality, 48; gendered, 9; nature of, 90, 96

Reason, 184, 185, 259; moral, 83; and emotion, 187

Regionalism, 210–11

Relationships, 162–63, 165–67, 171, 172–73, 176–77; and talk, 250–51

Religion: and silencing, 169–70; and subordination, 187

Research: on women, 7; nature of, 19; on adult students, 38

Rich, Adrienne, 73, 175

Risman, Barbara, 119

Robinson, Vivian, 241

Roe v. Wade, 48

Role models, 105, 168

Roosevelt, Eleanor, 48

Rosaldo, Michelle Zimbalist, 96

Ross, Betsy, 89

Rutgers University, 200

Sacks, Jean, 200, 201

Safety, 257–59

Sanden, John Howard, 5

Sandler, Bernice, 92, 139

Santareli, Constance, 4

Scholarship: feminist, 2, 21, 43–44, 115, 133–34, 146, 279–81; systematic, 22; process of, 203–4; role of editors in, 205–6; and publishing, 207; influencing, 207–12; commissioning, 210; legitimizing, 212; disseminating, 235–36; and institution building, 281

Schumann, Clara Wieck, 145–46

Science, 83–84, 107, 160, 161, 209

Scott, Anne Firor, 212

Self, 258, 260–61, 268, 273

Semans, Mary Duke Biddle Trent, 4

Sewing, 274–76

Sexism, 54, 164

Sexuality, 55, 89

Shavlik, Donna, 74

Sheehy, Gail, 27

Sherrill, Robert, 201

Signs, 200–218

Silencing, 41, 156, 159–62, 164; refusal to submit to, 166, 177; and religion, 169–70; and knowledge, 252–54

Simmons, Martha, 241

Smeal, Eleanor Cutri, 237–38

Social construction, 281; of gender, 52, 72, 109, 123, 154, 156–57, 183; of oppression, 191–92

Social issues: and women's studies, 174–77; in the nineteenth century, 186

Socialization: and politics, 97; of students, 117–18; understanding, 126–30; and power, 192–93

Social roles: construction of, 72, 109, 123, 156–57, 183; history of, 79–80. *See also* Gender; Gender roles

Society, values of, 182

Society of Friends, 9, 12, 265

Southern Women's Cultural History Symposium, 210

Space, 1, 3, 117, 164, 241, 251; creating, 1–6, 10, 263, 273; and power, 2; transforming, 3; dynamics of, 4; importance of, 6; in women's studies programs, 7; and process, 7–8; and education, 19; public and private, 83; appropriation of, 124; and gender-role violation, 131; and voice, 156–57; and women's studies, 158, 214; and institution building, 197; for practice, 251–62

Stanford University, 200

Stanton, Elizabeth Cady, 184, 186

Statistics, 259; pedagogy in, 149; and change, 168

Stefanco, Carolyn, 73, 74

Stimpson, Catharine, 200

Stuard, Susan, 181–82

Students: adult, 10, 19, 21, 25–26, 27, 29, 30, 31, 32, 35–45, 222; voice of, 18; age of, 29, 36, 37; gender of, 36; strengths and weaknesses of, 39; definition of, 42; obstacles to reentry of, 42–43; heterogeneity of, 104–6; experiences of, 107–10, 120, 241, 243–44; isolation of, 117; socialization of, 117–18; culture of, 130–31; expectations of, 151; and curriculum transformation, 152; needs of, 155; and women's studies, 226; and power, 267

Study of curriculum transformation, 135

Suffrage, 186–87

Talk, 18, 163, 168, 258, 259–62, 274; as activism, 246–51. *See also* Communication

Taylor, Emily, 74

Theory, 97; and experience, 8; feminist, 209; versus change, 280

Title IX, 41, 49

Tompkins, Jane, 82

Tradition, 48

Transformation of knowledge, 97, 98, 101–2, 178–94. *See also* Curriculum transformation

United Nations Decade for Women, 95, 210

University, the: nature of, 26; changes in, 31–32; modification of, 75; and progress, 78

University of North Carolina at Chapel Hill, 25, 95, 114, 200–201, 202, 222

Values, 92

Violence, 22; domestic, 90–91; sexual, 161, 257, 258–59

Visibility, 2, 44, 78–79, 84, 85–86, 103; of women's studies, 102; and fundraising, 226; of Duke University Women's Studies, 235

Voice, 116; students', 18; and frameworks, 147; dismissal of, 150; and space, 156–57; and African Americans, 157; and silencing, 157; struggle with, 167; and activism, 167, 172; and explanation, 169; in the Oz books, 187–88; and alumnae, 233

Wage earners, 47

Waner, Susan, 82

War, 83

WARP. *See* Women's Action Research Project

Wells, Ida B., 188

Williams, Patricia, 214

Wollstonecraft, Mary, 184–86

Woman, idealized, 2

Woman's College, 1, 25, 220–21, 226, 229

Women Administrators in North Carolina Higher Education, 75

Women's Action Research Project, 198, 239–62

Women's Network, 224

Women's studies, 6, 7, 87–88; and institution building, 12; and continuing education, 35–45; history of, 50–58, 74, 94–103, 279–81; and liberal arts, 59–67, 72, 85–93, 282; mainstreaming, 64–65; explaining, 74; questions about, 77–84;

and feminism, 81, 96, 101; defined, 86–87; goals of, 88, 96–97, 100–101; men in, 91; and critical analysis, 91–92; and civil rights movement, 96; success of, 102; visibility of, 102; and pedagogy, 120–21; and curriculum transformation, 133; and space, 158; and empowerment, 168; and social issues, 174–77; and students, 226; as academic discipline, 278–83